Christmas 1991

To Darling Graeme

"Merry Christmas"

With Love,

Sue.
x.

THE OFFICIAL BOOK OF THE
RUGBY
WORLD CUP
1991

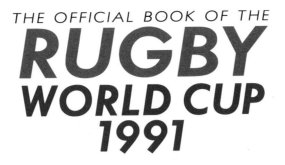

*Mick Skinner in full flow
for England against
Australia.*

Heinz
THE OFFICIAL BOOK OF THE
RUGBY
WORLD CUP
1991

EDITED BY IAN ROBERTSON

RUGBY
WORLD CUP

STANLEY PAUL

LONDON SYDNEY AUCKLAND JOHANNESBURG

The
PERFECT ENDING...

True Spirit · Genuine Character

CONTENTS

Acknowledgements

The publishers would like to thank Colin Elsey, Andy Cowie and Stewart MacFarlane of Colorsport for all the excellent photography in this book; also Stephen Jones for invaluable editorial assistance

Prince Edward opens the 1991 Rugby World Cup at Twickenham.

Stanley Paul & Co. Ltd
An imprint of Random Century Group
20 Vauxhall Bridge Road, London SW1V 2SA

Random Century New Zealand Limited
PO Box 40–086, Glenfield, Auckland

Century Hutchinson South Africa (Pty) Ltd
PO Box 337, Bergvlei 2012, South Africa

First published 1991

Printed and bound in Great Britain by Butler & Tanner Ltd,
London and Frome

A catalogue record for this book is available
from the British Library

ISBN 0 09 174881 X

FOREWORD

The great success of the 1991 Rugby World Cup brings rugby not to the beginning of the end but the end of the beginning. For over 100 years the pleasures of rugby for players and spectators were confined almost monastically by region and by class, and now to echo the words of W. B. Yeats, 'All is changed, changed utterly.' The change agent has been the Rugby World Cup and it is the nature of this change that is so exercising and so exciting. If the change is inclusive and imaginative, it will improve the laws and extend the horizons of the game. But if it is narrow, defensive and crassly commercial it will damage the soul of the game and endanger the Corinthian values which captured the imagination of the world in October 1991.

On balance, the 1991 tournament was a remarkable success. There were few, very few, regrettable incidents and a host of memorable moments. You cannot expect Barbarian-style champagne carefree rugby when a World Cup is at stake but some of the tries were of vintage quality. They came, as well, not just from the superstars of Australia and England and New Zealand but from unlikely quarters such as Italy, Japan, Zimbabwe, Western Samoa, the United States and Canada.

Heinz were pleased to be sponsors of the Rugby World Cup and we look forward to a continued association through the proposed World Cup Sevens and on to the 1995 tournament.

This book will help to preserve our memories of 1991. The distinguished authors and photographers have matched some of the brilliance we saw on the field and recorded for history a new dawn in one of the great sports of our times.

Dr A J F O'Reilly
Chairman, President and Chief Executive
H J Heinz Company

No matter whose name goes on the cup, ours will be on the plate tonight.

Tonight the Royal Lancaster Hotel hosts the closing dinner for the
Rugby World Cup 1991.

Alongside this afternoon's winners there'll be players and officials from all
16 countries who took part in the tournament.

And no matter whether they're from the other side of the world or just down the road,
we're confident they'll agree, for the big occasion there's no match
for our service anywhere.

For details of banqueting and conference facilities at the Royal Lancaster please call
the Sales Department on 071 262 6737 or write to:
Royal Lancaster Hotel,
Lancaster Terrace, London W2 2TY.

RUGBY
WORLD CUP

INTRODUCTION
ALL ASPIRATIONS FULFILLED
RAY WILLIAMS
RUGBY WORLD CUP
TOURNAMENT DIRECTOR

Everyone involved with the task of organising the Rugby World Cup 1991 – and what a massive and complicated task it was – was quietly confident that the tournament would be successful. The structure was in place, the millions of details had been attended to in years of effort. The scene and the backdrop were all set to await the arrival of the 16 competing nations in what was generally recognised as potentially the biggest sporting event in this country since the 1966 World Cup.

Yet possibly, no-one was quite prepared for the sheer scale of that success. The tournament was a phenomenon. It was spectacularly successful from almost every point of view. It was a commercial success despite the ravages of the recession and the war in the Gulf; the interest in the tournament was simply staggering for all those involved because suddenly, people who had never been attracted to the game were following the action keenly.

Furthermore, the TV audience all round the globe broke all records. Rugby World Cup chairman Russ Thomas was able to report at the end that over 70 countries took coverage from the tournament. The gospel was well and truly spread.

And of course, the players did us proud by serving up a tournament which was full of high standards, drama, emotion and colour. Every competing nation played a part. It was a tribute to the dedication of the teams and their coaches and medical men that the action on the field lived up to the occasion and showed the game of rugby union

in the best possible light. On a personal note, I was sad that Wales failed to qualify but the rise of the likes of Western Samoa and Canada added greatly to the stature of the event and showed that the old order has now disappeared for ever as the new countries strive to catch up.

Some aspects of the tournament are particularly worthy of comment. For a start, the number of replacements needed by the teams was almost unbelievably low. Only three were called in, two of those being Western Samoans. In 1987, some individual teams exceeded that number on their own and there was considerable activity as players were shunted back and forth.

This time, the overwhelming number of teams went through the tournament with exactly the same squad. I feel that this is a tribute to the advances in fitness and conditioning, to the dedication to fitness of the players and the efforts of the back-up people.

Another remarkable feature was the almost complete absence of incidents of foul play. There was some adverse publicity about the regrettable events at the Parc des Princes during and after the France–England quarter-final.

But these were genuinely isolated incidents. Given the high level of pressure and considering what was at stake, especially in the knock-out stages of the competition, it was a clean tournament and a credit both to the competing players and to the referees and linesmen. The final, the biggest match the game has ever seen in that receipts at Twickenham reached the £1m mark, was played hard and fast but in an excellent spirit.

Afterwards, I heard many people expressing the view that rugby would never be the same again. In many ways, this might be true, but I am certain that the spirit of the game remains intact. Already, I would imagine, rugby followers are keenly anticipating the events of four years' time when once again, the Webb Ellis Cup will be at stake and rugby union willl be at the centre of world attention.

The advertisement that appeared for the Royal Lancaster Hotel within the programme of the 1991 Rugby World Cup Final.

SELECTION

is crucial

Success on the Rugby pitch depends on making the right choice
at the right time.
Friends Provident has been helping people choose the right insurance
and investment policies for more than 150 years.

FRIENDS PROVIDENT

POOL 1

THE BIG FISH FIND SHARKS IN THE POOL

IAN ROBERTSON

From the moment the World Cup draw put New Zealand, England, Italy and the United States into the same pool, it was generally assumed that there would be one magnificent match of epic proportions (between New Zealand and England) followed by five matches of precious little consequence. The reality proved vastly different from the hypothesis.

As it transpired, the big shoot-out at Twickenham smacked of anti-climax as neither New Zealand nor England hit top form and both seemed overawed by the occasion. There is no doubt they had the best players in the pool but they fell a very long way short of producing the best match. The abiding memory is the heroic, almost superhuman effort of the unconsidered Italians in holding the mighty All Blacks to 10 points at Leicester. This captivating performance was the highlight of the six Pool One games, closely followed by the American displays against both New Zealand and England and the marvellous USA – Italy match at Otley.

Those who had anticipated the two unseeded sides losing by cricket scores watched dumbfounded and riveted by the thrilling exploits of the underdog. Needless to say, one admired the glittering skills of backs like Guscott, Carling and Underwood of England and Fox, Kirwan and Innes of New Zealand as well as savouring the bone-crunching battle of two superb packs.

But this pool had a lot more to offer. There were also great individuals in the Italian and American teams desperate for an opportunity to show the world that producing exciting rugby players is not the sole prerogative of the major International Board countries.

Before this World Cup you may never have heard of Paolo Vaccari, Fabio Gaetaniello, Gianbattista Croci and Marcello Cuttitta of Italy or Kevin Swords, Tony Ridnell, Rob Farley and Mark Pidcock of America. Well, you have now. These are top-class rugby players by any standards.

They have all graduated from the relative obscurity of playing the game in countries where the importance of rugby lies somewhere between anonymity and indifference. Despite this, these players and their teams have made their mark in the rarified atmosphere of the World Cup. In the 1987 World Cup, Italy lost to New Zealand by 70 points to 6. In 1991, the score was 31–21. These emerging nations have now emerged and the game is all the richer for it.

There could hardly have been a more dramatic opening match to the 1991 World Cup than the Grand Slam Champions of the Northern Hemisphere, England, against the current World Champions and reigning Champions of the Southern Hemisphere, New Zealand. Both camps had talked of little else for the preceding twelve months and the whole rugby world waited anxiously to discover if the All Blacks were at last vulnerable, and just conceivably, a team with their futures behind them. The build-up to the match was intense in the extreme.

England fielded the whole of their Grand Slam pack and looked fully capable of matching the might of New Zealand in what was inevitably going to be a war of attrition. Up to half-time the battle was absolutely even, with each side winning 50% of possession but, partly because they were able to raise the pace of their game and partly, I'm sure, through a more positive and even fanatical attitude of mind, the All Blacks dominated the second-half and deserved their victory.

They have earned their formidable reputation mainly through their ruthless, relentlessly oppressive driving forward play which gradually knocks the heart out of all but the very bravest and most determined opponents. The word 'pressure' is bandied about in most rugby analysis but with the All Blacks it is spelt in bold capital letters. They have added several dimensions to their application of pressure. Up front, they drive as a collective unit

Above: The killing try in the opening match. Michael Jones canters over almost unopposed after a set move from an All Black scrum cut England's defence to pieces.

Left: John Kirwan tries to keep Jeremy Guscott in check during a rare English break-out at Twickenham.

at every available opportunity, until they break the will of their opponents.

Think back to that memorable television picture of Bernhard Langer trying to sink the final five-foot putt on the 18th green to retain the Ryder Cup. Severiano Ballesteros said, the moment after Langer missed, that no player in the world should ever be put under such intolerable pressure as no player

could have coped. Imagine, as Langer lined up his putt, 15 All Blacks thundering across the green towards him and you begin to appreciate the pressure England experienced. New Zealand's rugby teams always impose that sort of pressure in big matches.

England's forwards were unable to win the high quality possession which they had enjoyed in the

Five Nations Championship and this pressure was transferred to the backs. Richard Hill, who has had two excellent seasons behind the dominant England pack, threw out three wayward passes into no-man's land, the first of which Andrew did well to scramble clear, but the second led indirectly to a penalty which Fox kicked for New Zealand. That was a shaky start.

Andrew at fly-half and Webb at full-back both played particularly well and England's defensive organisation, with a couple of notable exceptions, was as leak-proof as ever. Ackford and Dooley shared the line-out with the All Blacks; but the big difference was in the scrum count. The phenomenal driving play of the New Zealand pack meant that they were going forward at virtually every ruck and maul throughout the second-half, no matter which side had the ball. That resulted in them winning the put-in to the scrum on almost every occasion. England are not the first side taking on the All Blacks to learn that it is very difficult to play without the ball. New Zealand won 90 per cent of all scrums in the match.

The apex of their thrust in the open was their dynamic flanker, Michael Jones. He is all raw-boned power and pace, and is unequalled by any other contemporary loose forward. He tormented England to the point of distraction. New Zealand also had the satisfaction of out-scrummaging England. Even though they did not win a strike against the head, they always had the edge and the initiative.

Furthermore, they treated every piece of possession as a prized commodity of inestimable value wrapped in cotton wool and not to be wasted under any circumstances. Graeme Bachop at scrum-half linked well with his loose forwards and varied the target area nicely with some splendid attacking kicks – a few to the box, a couple wide, a few high and some rolling into touch. Fox kicked well at fly-half and he also varied his game well, to keep England guessing.

The three-quarters all ran hard and straight and Terry Wright was a threat at full-back, which meant England could never relax. The centres, Innes and McCahill were a potent mixture of bruising power and blistering speed, and even if they were well held, there was always John Kirwan, New Zealand's top try scorer lurking ominously on the wing.

But once again New Zealand proved, if proof were necessary, that even though the individuals are all very accomplished players, it is their remarkable collective strength that makes them so successful.

They play, run, support, tackle, cover and hunt as a team and that is what finally overpowered England.

Not that England could possibly have made a better start. Andrew kicked off to Fox. Fox kicked towards the touchline (8 seconds gone). Webb caught the ball near half-way and hoisted an up-and-under (11 seconds played). Michael Jones late tackled Webb and the referee awarded a penalty (15 seconds after the match started). Webb kicked the goal and England led 3–0.

Yet within 10 minutes, New Zealand led 6–3 after two penalties by Grant Fox. The first was awarded against England for collapsing a scrum, and the second when Moore went over the top at a ruck. Gary Whetton was penalised for a head high tackle on Chris Oti after a quarter of an hour and Webb levelled the match. Soon after, Fox put the All Blacks ahead when Winterbottom was penalised for throwing a punch – which actually landed on Dean Richard's backside well away from any New Zealander.

Webb levelled the scores with his third penalty after New Zealand collapsed a scrum and, almost on the stroke of half-time, Rob Andrew dropped his 13th goal for England and 14th in international rugby from a tapped penalty taken by Hill. It was 12–9 to England at half-time.

The only try of the match came early in the second half. From a scrum about 25 metres out, Bachop broke right and looped round Innes. Winterbottom and Richards tackled Innes but by then Bachop, challenged by Carling, passed on to Kirwan. He broke through Oti and when tackled by Webb, passed inside to Michael Jones, who scored. Fox converted and kicked another penalty to clinch victory.

Perhaps it was not a pretty or spectacular match but after heavy overnight rain the conditions were very difficult. New Zealand played a ruthlessly efficient game of percentage rugby, to leave England in the second half trying to play the game on the back foot, on the retreat without a ball. Rumours that this All Black team was over the hill and all washed up were greatly exaggerated on this evidence.

England captain Will Carling said afterwards that his side had lost control in the second spell and they had not done themselves justice. The basic truth is that they had simply not been allowed to by a very good all Blacks team. It was a tremendous disappointment given the long and intense England build-up.

The Italians and the Americans were both aware that there was a World Cup Final scheduled to be played at Twickenham on the first Saturday of November but they acknowledged quite openly it would not involve them. They knew that their own particular World Cup Final was to be played at Otley on the first Saturday in October. Italy won 30–9 in a vastly entertaining match.

There was no doubt that this was the most important game of the whole tournament for both these sides and they expressed disappointment that the match was being played at Otley and not Twickenham. In discussing this with them beforehand, I explained that the atmosphere of a capacity crowd at Otley would be far more inspirational than playing at Twickenham with the ground and grandstands largely empty.

To encourage them, I pointed out that Otley had been the scene of one of the greatest games of the Seventies when the North of England beat the mighty All Blacks in November 1979, with fanatical spectators hanging from branches of trees overlooking the ground.

I was delighted that by lunchtime on October 5, spectators once again were perched precariously in the trees to watch the first ever meeting at international level of the two sides.

The sheer intensity of every game in the World Cup exerts tremendous pressure on teams and if it is hard for the best sides in the world, it is that much harder for the emerging nations. Italy and America lacked nothing in terms of passion and enthusiasm, commitment and a fierce determination to win, but they lacked sufficient skill to execute their plans at the frantic and frenetic pace at which the match was played.

In such a situation, where parts of the match are reminiscent of an old Keystone Cops film with people shooting off in several different directions, at breakneck speed, it only requires a couple of very cool generals to take control of the game, conjure up the best tactical appreciation of what is needed and guide their team to victory. In their half-backs, Ivan Francescato and Diego Dominguez, the Italians had just such a pair of experts; the Americans lacked such players.

Scrum-half Francescato was the real star. With his long, flowing black hair he looked like a refugee from the hippy era but his innate footballing skills and lightning reactions meant he was the focal point of everyone's attention throughout the game. He whipped out an excellent service to fly-half

Ivan Francescato, the outstanding Italian scrum-half, prepares to feed his backs in Italy's victory over the USA in the compelling match at Otley.

Dominguez, made the most spectacular breaks in the match, one leading to a magnificent try which he scored himself, and he kicked superbly to keep his pack thundering forward and the Americans constantly under pressure.

Dominguez also kicked with rare accuracy to nurse his pack and he organised the whole Italian defensive effort so well that the American backs never threatened to break through and score. Francescato and Dominguez would be the first to admit that they could not have weaved their magic spell without the heroics which the pack produced, especially in the loose, and the potent combination of a powerful pack and outstanding half-backs sealed the Italian victory.

The influence of the French coach, Bertrand Fourcade, gave the Italians an extra dimension which the more straightforward and orthodox

Americans lacked. It was fascinating to see the Gallic style reflected in the Italian driving at the line-out, their introduction of the rolling maul, the use they made of back row moves and the way they supported in depth in the open to keep the ball in play and the American defence stretched.

The Americans shared the honours in set-piece play but their less flexible approach and general lack of variety made their attacking play a shade too predictable. They will surely learn from this experience and soon become a more formidable force on the world stage, because there is little question that they have the raw materials.

The fast pace caught out the Americans early on and when they had their third kick charged down in the first few minutes, after a delightfully weighted and perfectly placed up-and-under from Francescato, Gaetaniello broke clear and Barba scored. Each side kicked a penalty to leave Italy leading 9–3 at half-time.

Early in the second-half, Favaro won a line-out on the American ten-metre line and Francescato switched the angle of attack quite dramatically by doubling back down the blind side. He accelerated past Flay, went outside Daily and side-stepped off his right foot at a wicked angle inside the left wing, Whitaker, before proving that was no fluke by doing

exactly the same to beat the full-back, Nelson. All that remained for him to do was to outflank the remaining cover, Higgins and de Jong, to score one of the best individual tries of the entire World Cup.

Francescato made the next try when he stole the ball from the base of a scrum won by America, he drew Whitaker and delivered a perfectly-timed pass to enable Vaccari to score in the corner.

The Americans showed commendable spirit to keep running at the Italians and after taking four tapped penalties in the space of three minutes, the big lock, Kevin Swords, crashed through two tackles to score. The Americans deserved this try, which was the end result of 80 minutes honest endeavour. But the Italians deserved victory with their enterprising play and more sophisticated approach.

They scored a fourth try when Gaetaniello took a crash ball from Dominguez after a line-out near the opposition line. Dominguez converted and kicked a late penalty to give a final tally even Grant Fox would have found impossible to beat – 6 successful kicks out of 6. And, you may wonder, who fired out the glorious spin pass to Dominguez from the line-out for that last try? The same person who put up the teasing kick which led to the first try, the person who scored the second try and made the third – Ivan Francescato, the hero of Italy at Otley.

Despite the scoreline of the Gloucester clash between the USA and New Zealand, this was a day that the American players will not forget and the New Zealand All Blacks will not remember with affection. The American Eagles played some of the best rugby of their international careers and for the first time in a long time, the All Blacks actually looked vulnerable, even though they won 46–6. Suffice to say that after watching New Zealand play for the past 30 years this would rank as one of their worst-ever performances, despite a final try count of eight to none in their favour. Rather than simply castigate the All Blacks for their embarrassing chapter of errors it would be more fitting to pay tribute to the sterling efforts of the Americans in adversity.

They knew only too well that they were regarded as tadpoles swimming around in a shark's tank. Their defeat by Italy gave them precious little confidence and for a side which had qualified for the World Cup by finishing third out of three teams behind Argentina and Canada, there was a distinct possibility they could lose by a record score.

A conversation with the American team PR, Liz Goldenburg, on the day of the match quickly scotched all thoughts of a morbidly-pessimistic attitude from the Eagles. Kevin Swords took over the captaincy from the injured Brian Vizard and at the team meeting the night before the match, at the Golden Valley Hotel, he indulged in a heart-searching analysis with his players on exactly what lay ahead. In the great American sporting tradition, the players bared their souls and enthusiastically rallied to the clarion call of their new captain. Thus began the first few faltering steps towards the American Eagles 80 minutes of glory. The battleground for the psychological war was perfectly simple. The All Blacks would probably not be 101 per cent psyched up to play the game of their lives because a 50 or 60 or even a 70 point win was generally regarded as a formality and was being predicted by everyone. On the other hand, the Americans were relishing the prospect of sharing centre stage with the current World Champions and, knowing they had absolutely nothing to lose, were all ready to play the game of their lives. This was their supreme rugby test and they were totally committed to run and cover and tackle and ruck and maul, and to do it all over again and again, until they dropped.

They played with real fervour. They showed a fantastic energy and sense of urgency from the kick-off, right through to near the end when finally they had played themselves to a standstill and, almost out on their feet, they conceded three tries. Up to that point, they had been furiously and fiercely competitive and combative and shown just how glorious the role of underdog can be. Individually and collectively, they rose to the challenge and justified in the most emphatic manner imaginable that they deserved to be in the World Cup and playing against the New Zealand All Blacks.

Kevin Swords was immense both as a player and as a captain and the loose forwards, Tony Ridnell and Shawn Lipman, were tremendous. The half-backs, Mark Pidcock and Chris O'Brien and centre Mark Williams plagued the All Blacks all afternoon. Williams also managed to kick two penalties from two attempts.

The sheer fanaticism of the Americans shook the All Blacks and definitely broke their concentration, control and rhythm. Seldom can I recall any New Zealand side dropping so many good passes and giving so many bad passes. Even worse, they became so rattled that they often took the wrong option after winning rucks and mauls. New fly-half

Jon Preston may well develop into a top class player but he failed to come to terms with the pace of the match and allowed himself to be hustled and hounded into mistakes. Full credit to America for picking on a potential New Zealand weakness.

Uncharacteristically, even the forwards fell sharply from grace. They were out-jumped in the line-out and were also guilty of poor support play, making far too many mistakes and errors of judgement. Coach John Hart said that his side spent 80 minutes struggling to reach the heights of mediocrity. Fellow coach Alex Wylie was equally disappointed with their performance. The tactical and line-kicking were a long way short of the very demanding standards the All Blacks have always set themselves.

For all the American heroics, it has to be stressed the result was never an issue, although it took New Zealand 20 minutes to score their first try. Earl crossed from a five-metre scrum. The explosive Michael Jones then burst through to make a try for Terry Wright and good lead-up work by McCahill and Earl gave Wright a second try. Bachop played a hand in that try and two in the second-half by the wings, Timu and Tuigamala. Purvis charged over from a tapped penalty and late on, Innes scored after a break by Preston and Terry Wright got his third try. Preston kicked four conversions and two penalties.

A famous American football coach once said: 'Winning isn't the most important thing – it is the only thing.' By that criterion, the American Eagles failed against New Zealand at Kingsholm. By every other realistic criterion, they did themselves and their country proud.

Alan Whetton of New Zealand in control of the line-out with Tony Ridnell and Shawn Lipman (7) struggling for height.

(Inset) Gary Whetton, the All Black captain, has only a fingertip control on events as American defenders converge in the thrilling match at Gloucester.

The group continued in disappointing fashion at Twickenham, where England beat Italy by 36–6. Into every life a little rain must fall, but very few of the large crowd who made their way to Twickenham could possibly have anticipated what a wretchedly dull match this would turn out to be.

The pre-match chemistry was quite encouraging. England had come within one score of holding the All Blacks in the opening match of the World Cup and Italy had produced some very good passages of play to run out impressive winners against the United States. Both teams had exciting runners in

Will Carling side-steps a lone Italian defender during England's pool win over the Italians, a frustrating occasion for both teams.

the back divisions and there seemed every reason to hope for a good game of open rugby. The Italians surely had nothing to lose and it was assumed they would be happy to take the game to England.

After all, they had complained that Otley was not

a fitting and suitable stage for their game against America. Now here they were about to perform on the biggest and most famous stage in the most important rugby theatre in the world in front of countless millions of spectators. They craved for an opportunity to show people back in Italy how popular rugby was and by showing how good they were in matches against the big International Board countries, they hoped to promote the game of rugby throughout the length and breadth of their country.

The scene was set; the producers had played their part. Now it was up to the actors. The performance, regrettably, was a disaster. In 80 minutes of rugby, the Italians conceded 37 penalties, the great majority for either offside or going over the top of the rucks. This wilful disregard for the laws wrecked the game as a spectacle because no matter how hard England tried to play good rugby, the Italians deliberately gave away penalties rather than risk tries being scored; they left the English players, the referee and the spectators extremely frustrated.

It was a dreadful advert for rugby and there was tremendous sympathy for the referee, Brian Anderson, who had no option but to penalise the Italians over and over again for killing the ball. Indeed, so outrageous were the Italian tactics that the referee would have even been entitled to have sent off every single player who persistently infringed the same law. In that case, at least half of the Italian pack could have gone.

It has to be argued that if the referee was rigidly interpreting the laws at the rucks, concerning the killing of the ball he was surely duty bound also to stick rigidly to the letter of the law about sending off players who persistently infringed.

The sad truth is that the Italians went into this game determined to execute a damage limitation exercise. Their French coach, Bertrand Fourcade, presumably the director in charge of tactics, was unrepentant afterwards and actually claimed that a better referee would have helped the flow of the game. That evades the issue that his players gave away 37 penalties, which means they were guilty of conceding a penalty almost every two minutes of the match.

It is hardly surprising that the England manager, Geoff Cooke, said that he was very disappointed in the way the Italians played this match. 'It made life very difficult when every time we tried to develop the game the Italians infringed,' he added at the press conference.

The real tragedy is that Italy have several very good players and as they showed against America and New Zealand they are capable of performing at a very high level indeed. But, sadly, they lost by 30 points on this occasion after indulging in dull, negative, spoiling tactics. The score may not have been much worse if they had played the forthright, positive, attacking rugby which is certainly within their capability and they would have had the bonus of winning a lot of friends as well as helping to promote the game in Italy.

Nonetheless, for all their faults, it has to be pointed out that they defended courageously throughout, tackling and covering with wholehearted determination and they made England work hard for their four tries. They even scored a good try themselves midway through the second-half when centre Fabio Gaetaniello reacted quickly to a loose ball and their exciting wing, Marcello Cuttitta, scored. Dominguez converted.

However, England were in control for most of the rest of the game. They won almost three-quaters of all set-scrum and line-out possession and even more at the rucks and mauls. Jon Webb was in excellent goal-kicking form, landing four penalties out of five attempts, all before half-time, to help England build up a commanding lead of 24–0.

He also converted all four tries, most of which were scored near the corner. He had an outstanding game in attack and defence to re-establish himself as England's top full-back. He even scored the last try after Redman made ground from a tapped penalty before passing to Guscott on the short side. Guscott found Webb sprinting into a gap in support to burst through and score.

Earlier in the match, Underwood had scored from a break by Hill on the blind side and then Guscott helped himself to two splendid tries. Carling made the first with a searing break in midfield on the half-way line. He drew Luigi Troiani perfectly and Guscott had a free run to the line.

His second try was a marvellous individual gem. Webb started it with a glorious long, flat, spin pass from the right to Andrew who quickly fed Guscott with another long, accurate pass. Guscott weaved past two would-be tackles and then delightfully wrong-footed the last defender to glide in at the corner. This was the highlight of the match, although the game will also long be remembered as the day Jon Webb set a new record for an English player in international rugby with 24 points. The total came from one try, four conversions and four penalties. He, at least, was probably grateful to the Italians for giving away so many penalties.

A few days later, England were back at Twickenham in front of a capacity crowd of 60,000. On a dry, clear afternoon, England introduced several of their reserve squad into the team after playing virtually their Test side in the opening two Pool matches. This seemed a perfectly reasonable decision because England had beaten the United States quite comfortably in all three previous meetings and there were no grounds for suspecting this game would be any different.

As it turned out, the lack of top class competitive rugby for the newcomers may have been the reason that after a perfectly adequate first half, England

proceeded to play appallingly badly for the first 20 minutes of the second-half. The England selectors and especially the England coach must have been very concerned at the amazing ability of the whole side to squander almost unlimited possession during this third quarter of the game.

The forwards won almost twice as much line-out and loose possession as the Americans throughout the match, but at the start of the second-half the pack suddenly stopped driving and the backs, when they ran, lay far too flat and drifted hopelessly across the pitch, to make life absurdly easy for their opponents. They were repeatedly tackled in midfield and knocked backwards, often being bowled over man and ball at the same time; or else they were hustled into making mistakes.

With a healthy lead of 21–3 at half-time, it was understandable that England decided to take tapped penalties rather than kicks at goal in the second half in readiness for the more demanding tasks at

Richard Hill whips the ball away from an England scrum against the USA at Twickenham.

the quarter-finals stage. But it was embarrassing to watch them take a dozen pointless short penalties with seemingly little plan or idea of what they were trying to achieve.

There was no variety or imagination. The ball was tapped and passed to a forward who trundled at half pace towards the opposition before being hammered to the ground and a mad scramble began to win the rucked ball. It was all depressingly negative and was symptomatic of the complete lack of control and direction throughout this period of the game.

It was so bad that mid-way through the second half, I got the distinct impression that thousands of loyal spectators were fighting hard to stay awake. During this hiatus (or moratorium) it was hard to believe that Will Carling was captaining England for a record 22nd time, overtaking Bill Beaumont's previous record or that Rob Andrew and Richard Hill were the most experienced half-backs in English history; or Carling and Underwood were

two of the most exciting runners in world rugby; or that the loose forwards, Rees, Richards and Skinner had the experience of nearly 70 caps between them.

The Americans deserve credit for launching a magnificent rearguard defence but after their very sound first half, England should have been in a position to put them to the sword. They appeared to be tactically naive or perhaps they just lost their concentration because they already had one eye on the quarter-final tie against France in Paris eight days later.

It may, of course, be no coincidence that these American Eagles had reduced the mighty All Blacks to mere mortals three days earlier and they showed great resolve in raising their game once again in a short space of time. Kevin Swords was an inspirational captain and he had great support from his breakaway trio, Farley, Ridnell and Lipman and the half-backs, Pidcock and O'Brien.

They combined to set-up the American try with swift, crisp passing, which allowed Williams to make a clean break and create a double overlap. That allowed Ray Nelson to score with the luxury of an unmarked player outside him. Williams, who had earlier kicked a penalty, converted.

However, if the third quarter was dominated by the Americans, the rest of the game belonged to England and especially to Rory Underwood. He scored the first try and the fifth try, on each occasion chasing a kick to the corner and securing the touchdown. In between, Carling sliced through in midfield to score after a powerful break by Underwood, Skinner crashed over from a scrum near the line and Heslop scored by the posts after a blistering diagonal run from the wing which left several Americans flat-footed in his slipstream.

The Americans can be well pleased with their efforts in this World Cup and in particular their brave performances against New Zealand and England. In the past, they have often done well at the Cathay Pacific/Hongkong Bank Sevens Tournament, but now they look equally at home on the world stage at 15-a-side rugby. As for England, perhaps one of their players, Rob Andrew, summed it up best: 'It was a convincing victory, but not an impressive one.'

The Italians had been the villains of the piece at Twickenham; at Leicester in chasing the All Blacks every inch of the way, they were the heroes of the hour and in the final Pool 1 match, went down by only 31–21.

It was hard to believe that the Italians could produce two such totally contrasting performances in the same week. From negative no-hopers at Twickenham, suddenly there they were at Leicester carrying the torch of the underdogs with fierce pride. Their forwards through Favaro, Croci and Checchinato shared the line-out and they were just as fast and committed as the All Blacks in the open. The half-backs, Francescato and Bonomi played magnificently and Dominguez in the centre and Vaccari at full-back made enormous contributions.

In every chase they took the All Blacks on. They stood toe to toe in the forward battle and their backs tackled with the same ferocity and finality as the Western Samoans. The All Blacks played very much better than they had done against America but they simply could not at any stage take control of the match.

The attitude of the Italians was a revelation and they played throughout with a breathtakingly refreshing approach. They attacked and counter-attacked with rare enterprise and after all the insults they had to endure after their England match, the praise could not be too high for the remarkable manner in which they regrouped and conjured up one of the best performances ever from an Italian team. Their claims now to be given regular fixtures at full international level against the Home Unions can no longer be easily dismissed. Curiously enough, Italy could hardly have made a less auspicious start. In less than a minute New Zealand ran a penalty near the Italian 22 metre line and from a clutch of forwards, Zinzan Brooke emerged with the ball to discover the whole Italian defence parting like the Red Sea and he had a clear run to the posts to score.

Fox converted and a few minutes later, he made another little piece of history when he kicked a penalty. This meant that he became the third player, behind Michael Lynagh and Hugo Porta, to score 500 points in international rugby.

He kicked another shortly afterwards to make it 12–0 before Dominguez kicked a penalty for Italy. The last score of the first-half came with Innes scoring a try after a triple miss-pass from Fox to Tuigamala created the space. Early in the second-half Tuigamala scored a sensational solo try when he exploded through at least half-a-dozen tackles in a dynamic 50 metre run.

After another penalty to each side, Bonomi and Dominguez combined to make a try for Marcello Cuttitta but New Zealand regained their 18 point

A contest symptomatic of the match - Italy's Ivan Francescato and New Zealand's Zinzan Brooke contest the loose ball in a match where Italy took the mighty All Blacks almost to the wire.

lead with a try by new cap Jason Hewett. Appropriately, Italy enjoyed the last word. Dominguez kicked his third penalty and converted a final try by Bonomi. New Zealand won possession 30 metres from their own line but Fox dropped Hewett's pass. Bonomi scooped the ball up spectacularly in one hand to score between the posts.

It was all highly entertaining stuff, which was warmly applauded by the capacity 16,000 crowd. For the Italians, it was not quite a case for skipper Giancarlo Pivetta of 'Veni, Vidi, Vici' but very nearly. It was, though, in my opinion the best effort in the whole World Cup by one of the little teams from Lilliput against one of the giants from Brobdignag.

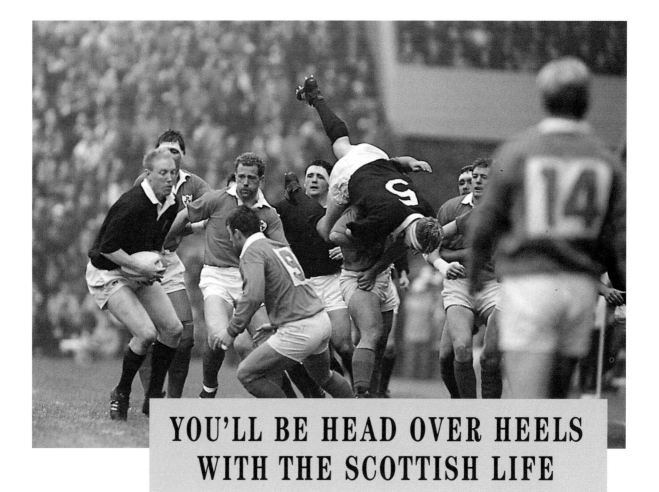

YOU'LL BE HEAD OVER HEELS
WITH THE SCOTTISH LIFE

*Pensions &
Mortgages*

THE LIFE TO LEAD

POOL 2

SCOTLAND COME OUT ON TOP AFTER EXTRAVAGANZA OF TRIES

BILL McLAREN

Whatever the cynics might say about the one-sidedness of some of the games, there is no denying that Pool Two of the 'up-and-under' World Cup produced by far the most spectacularly satisfying rugby, as the spawning of no fewer than 45 tries in the six games surely underlines.

True, there had never been much doubt that Scotland and Ireland would qualify for the quarter-finals, unless some earth-shattering result was achieved by either Japan or Zimbabwe. The only real question was over which of the two heavyweights would finish on top of the Pool Two table and so qualify for a quarter-final match against the dark horses, Western Samoa, at Murrayfield – the other would face Australia at Lansdowne Road.

Nor had there been any doubt about the style of play that would be embraced in those Pool Two games. The Japanese, hindered by lack of height and general physical dimension, know only one way to play. Theirs is a firecracker system of sweeping the ball away quickly from the congested areas so as to exploit the ability of, not only their backs but their forwards as well, to change direction and accelerate into top speed in a blink of light and to call on spell-binding dexterity in handling with the ball being flipped around as if it was a piece of red-hot charcoal.

Hence the description of one Scot that playing against the Japanese had the same effect as poking a stick into a wasps' nest. So the Japanese were conditioned to attack by handling from any point on the pitch and this they did with joyous gusto and on limited rations. The Japanese are good for the World Cup in that, with their their slick spread of play within the context of an adventurous approach, they provide a sharp, much-needed contrast to the more clinical percentage methods of the big guns of the rugby world.

The Zimbabweans, too, showed a refreshing desire to spin the ball and produced two sparkling tries against the Irish at Landsowne Road. They are handicapped at home by the enormous distances that have to be covered just to bring their squad together and there are financial as well as geographical restraints. The country boasts only forty-two registered clubs giving an estimated playing population of only 15,000 out of a population of ten million. Japan boasts over 100,000 players. Zimbabwe also is in dire need of more specialist coaches.

Both Japan and Zimbabwe have something in common – a shortage of the ball to play with so that each had to rely to a large extent on swift counter attack from breakdown delivery or, better still, from piracy. It rendered them very attractive to watch and had ensured that Pool Two would provide a lot of spectacle, and indeed, the highest scoring of the entire pools competition – 332 points.

It therefore came to pass that Scotland and Ireland emerged unscathed and with confidence restored to contest the top two places in the final Pool Two table. All had been sunk in a form of deep dejection in both countries as they stumbled through some hastily-arranged representative matches with the aim of honing match hardness prior to the start of the World Cup. An understrength Scotland had lost to the vigorous, rumbustious Canadians during their North American tour in May. A much stronger Scotland had succumbed to the Romanians in Bucharest. The final indignity was when a virtual full-strength Scotland lost to an Edinburgh Borderers Select XV crammed with eager aspirants intent on making a show and apparently in no way overawed by the illustrious nature of the opposition.

Ireland had lost two Tests in Namibia. It was little consolation that other teams had problems there. They just squeezed through against Malone, the club side, who came so close to what would have been a memorable addition to their club centenary celebrations; then the Irish ventured into the lion's den and were beaten by Gloucester before the baying hordes at Kingsholm.

A moment of Japanese delight at Murrayfield. Takahiro Hosokawa of Japan has scored under the posts, one of a barrage of delightful Japanese tries in the pool matches.

Of course, in the case of both Scotland and Ireland there were extenuating circumstances in the natural lack of match toughness at the start of their seasons and, perhaps, a subconscious desire on the part of some players to remain free of injury for the World Cup. Even so one wag did suggest that the Murrayfield quarter-final of the World Cup should feature Edinburgh Borderers and Gloucester.

Came the day, however, and Scotland and Ireland were back on the rails. Of course, they were fortunate in having their opening games against Japan and Zimbabwe, who could not quite compensate with their admirable zest, courage and commitment for deficiencies created, on the one hand by lack of physique, on the other by lack of regular squad sessions and continuous top international competition. At the same time there was no way that Scotland and Ireland were going to underestimate those opponents. Zimbabwe had emerged with a 100% record from the African zone qualifying although their opponents could hardly be regarded as out of the top echelon of international play: Ivory Coast (22–9); Morocco (16–0); Tunisia (24–13). In qualifying from the Asian–Pacific zone, Japan had beaten South Korea (26–10) and Tonga (28-16) before losing to Western Samoa (11–37).

Seiji Hirao, captain of Japan, has his progress impeded by Scott Hastings in the pool match at Murrayfield when Scotland controlled the match.

Scotland's 47–9 margin over Japan before a 40,000-plus Murrayfield audience was notable for its nine splendid tries, for thrilling ebb and flow and for a Japanese revival that drove home to the Scots that their 17–9 half-time lead was no guarantee of ultimate success.

The match was distinctive on several counts. For one thing, a Japanese player was cautioned for foul play. Personally, I had never seen that happen before. In some 40 years of covering rugby internationals I have regarded the Japanese as the best disciplined players in the world.

Perhaps it has to do with their strong hold on the amateur concept and with it, their retention of genuine sporting spirit; but I have never seen a Japanese player throw a punch or show dissent. They are an example to all in the way they just take the humps and hollows of rugby's fortunes in the same spirit.

So it was something of a surprise when Masanori Takura, their tight head prop, was given a right old finger-wagging by England referee, Ed Morrison, who made a stamping motion. I don't purport to know whether Takura understood Ed's reminder that if he was guilty again of foul play he would be ordered off but there was never any likelihood of a further offence.

One wouldn't be surprised, either, if Takura had the error of his ways pointed out by that delightful gentleman of Japanese rugby, Shiggy Konno. Shiggy is well aware of all that has become accepted on-field practice over the years but he is justifiably proud of the way his players deport themselves on the pitch and is not one to depart from what he believes is to the benefit of the game.

It was also heartening to note how often the Scots spun the ball wide. It stood to reason that they would want to launch their burly backs, the Hastings brothers and Tony Stanger, at their smaller opponents, in the wake of driving play involving their renowned breakaway trio, John Jeffrey, Derek White and Finlay Calder, and a hail of Garryowens from the educated boot of Craig Chalmers.

So they did, but the number of times the Scottish backs were launched was far in excess of recent experience and it served not only to lay before an ecstatic audience some real gems of interplay but also to establish the Hastings brothers, Gavin and Scott, as once again among the most trenchant runners in the game. They were right back to their old rumbustious form with the ball in hand and there was, too, some sinuous running at clever angles by Sean Lineen, watched by his parents, uncles and aunts, all over from New Zealand to watch the World Cup.

Scotland had the ideal platform in that the lanky Doddie Weir and the loose forwards took the lion's share of workable line-out ball, their scrummage was adequate and, after they had been held to just 9–3 at half-time, their loose forwards proved the spearhead to some surging drives which were interspersed with several inch-perfect miss passes by Craig Chalmers. These opened the way for the Hastings clan to revel in space.

And yet it wasn't until late on that the Scots could relax, for the Japanese demonstrated how lethal they can be when their full-back, Takahiro Hosokawa, shot in after a scrummage, with a move worked at cracking pace. In converting his own try after potting a drop goal, he scored all of Japan's points.

Their star, however, was tiny scrum-half, Wataru Murata, who scuttled about to considerable effect, like a demented ferret. But the Japanese were severely handicapped both at line-out and in fringe policing by the fact that not one of their loose forwards was over six feet. They just could not cope with the powerful bursts of Jeffey, White and Calder, even though the best of Scotland's seven tries stemmed from a White scrummage pick-up, a probe by Gary Armstrong and a thundering intrusion by Gavin Hastings, who left parts of the pitch like a casualty clearing station as sundry Japanese bounced off him.

The older of the Hastings brothers finished with 20 points and the other try scorers were Tony Stanger, Craig Chalmers (who also struck a penalty goal), Derek White, Scott Hastings, Iwan Tukalo and a penalty try (when Finlay Calder was high-tackled).

It was a heartening display by the Scots that was acknowledged by their revered coach, Ian McGeechan. He expressed admiration for their 'positive approach to both winning ball and using it well'. Their preparation, he said, had been geared towards the first game with Japan and they had managed to get it right when it mattered.

David Sole said he was delighted about the Scots' commitment but he hadn't experienced so many nerves amongst the side before a match. Shiggy Konno said, 'We were never able to get enough ball, especially from the line-outs, and we always seemed to need two players to tackle one of theirs.'

So for Scotland the outcome was something of a morale booster but they were in no doubt that it gave no true indication of how they would cope with the much stiffer examinations to come.

Andy Ferreira, the experienced Zimbabwe scrum-half, dive-passes the ball away before Phil Matthews, the Irish captain, can intervene.

Ireland, meanwhile, approached their opening game against Zimbabwe in much the same mood of nervous commitment as had the Scots against Japan.

The need for a convincing triumph was paramount in order to set aside their recent disappointments. Zimbabwe, after all, were something of an unknown quantity even though as near to being totally amateur as anyone in the game.

One surprise was the omission from the Irish side of their record try-scorer, Brendan Mullin, in favour of the burly Vincent Cinningham. There was also considerable pressure on the Cork Constitution fly-half, Ralph Keyes. He had gained his first cap against England in 1986 when Paul Dean was on the injury list but subsequently, had been in the wilderness for 33 internationals. He had been

recalled when Brian Smith opted for a rugby league career in Australia and had functioned effectively in warm-up matches with 30 points from the three games against an International XV, Malone and Gloucester. In the event, Keyes celebrated his return with a controlled performance and a new Irish record for points in an international. That had been held by Ollie Campbell with 21 against Scotland in 1982 and England in 1983. Keyes piloted home 9 of

Des Fitzgerald prepares to negotiate the tackle of Zimbabwe's Adrian Garvey in the pool match in Dublin. Ireland's forwards won the match, Zimbabwe's tries provided the entertainment.

his 11 goal attempts for 5 penalty points and 4 conversions and 23 points.

One surprising element of Ireland's 55–11 win was their almost total scrummage dominance. Scrummaging has not been an Irish strong point in recent seasons, even in the days of the world's most capped prop, Phil Orr. One recalls England's Dean Richards scoring two debut push-over tries against Ireland at Landsdowne Road in 1986 and being denied another when a penalty try was awarded.

The Irish scrummage, however, simply destroyed Zimbabwe. That craggy veteran, Des Fitzgerald, always has been a formidable scrummager and Nick Popplewell of Greystones was in his element on the loose head, even though opposed to the 17 stones of Brian Garvey. Popplewell risked being banned from the front row union by scoring two tries and, by curious coincidence, the 22-year-old Garvey was to do the same against the Scots.

Ireland's scrummage superiority was responsible in part for their big, blond number eight, Brian Robinson of Ballymena, equalling the world record for a forward in an international of four tries, a record created by the Australian Greg Cornelsen against New Zealand in Auckland in September 1978. Robinson also revelled in the freedom he was accorded by the Zimbabwean fringe defence. At least twice when he effected scrummage pick-up he found himself in a great void, with no tacklers. Ireland's other tries were by Simon Geoghegan and David Curtis.

Despite being put to the sword, the Zimbabweans showed admirable spirit and resilience and gave evidence that countries such as theirs are essential to the success of the World Cup. They brought the house down with two quite startling tries that were ignited from deep defensive positions and from where the so-called advanced nations would have hoofed to touch. Instead, the qualifiers from the African zone tilted their lances in commendable style and showed ball-handling dexterity and clever off-ball running to create lovely tries for right wing William Shultz and for their dynamo flanker, Brendan Dawson.

Having had the experience at the first World Cup in 1987 of playing their top side in all three pool matches and finding fatigue as a factor in their quarter-final defeat by New Zealand, the Scots management decided to rest eight of their first choice players for the second pool game against Zimbabwe, including the captain, David Sole, so

that the leadership was given to one of the most popular players in the Scottish game, Gala full-back Peter Dods.

It was an inspired choice for the 33-year-old Dods had captained the Scottish tour side to Zimbabwe in 1988 and rose to this World Cup occasion with another splendid performance, that included 16 points from five conversions and two penalty goals.

Yet even the unflappable Dods could hardly have envisaged a situation in which Zimbabwe would be very much in the hunt at just 12–15 down within five minutes of the interval. That was a surprise also to those who had watched the Zimbabweans train the day before, a session that was conducted at casual pace and with little physical contact. On the day, however, the Zimbabweans got into their top gear early on and were inspired, especially by their 22-year-old pack leader and No. 8, Brenton Catterall, and by the feat of their tight-head prop, Adrian Garvey, who showed a rare turn of pace in scoring two tries, both converted by captain Brian Currin.

One try came from an overhit Douglas Wyllie drop out and a surge by fly-half Craig Brown, the other when David Walters countered from a long Dods drop-out with a neat chip ahead and pass to Garvey via the lock, Honeywell Nguruve – Nguruve had been an 11th hour replacement for Chris Botha suffering a broken finger.

The Zimbabweans had restored their 33-year-old loose-head Alex Nicholls and so their scrummage, which had suffered so badly at Irish hands, proved a much more solid edifice to the Scots and should have pointed a warning to Scotland about their future scrummaging prospects. As it turned out the Irish provided a grim lesson at Murrayfield.

There were extenuating circumstances for the Scottish scrummage against Zimbabwe. On the eve of the match, David Milne (Herriots FP), who had replaced the injured Sole against Japan for his first cap and who was scheduled to play alongside his brother Ken against Zimbabwe, had to call off with a groin strain.

As Sole was injured Scotland decided to switch Paul Burnell (16 caps as a tight-head) to the loose head where he had functioned occasionally for Leicester. They then brought in at tight head for his first cap arguably the biggest prop ever to play in international rugby, Alan Watt of Glasgow High Kelvinside.

He is all of six feet five and just under 20 stones and had been converted from lock at the request of the national selectors, with a view to eventually doing the job that Ian Milne (Heriots FP) has done for Scotland in 44 internationals. Watt had already played in two non-cap tests against the U.S.A. and Canada on the Scots North American tour during the summer and had been receiving guidance, not only from Iain Milne, but from Scotland's most-capped prop, Sandy Carmichael, who is Watt's boss.

In the event Watt made an admirable debut as a scrummager and contributed some clattering bursts but a more accurate assessment of his propping capability would be made when perhaps he had to lock horns with the likes of New Zealand's Steve McDowell or France's Gregoire Lascubé.

Scotland used only sparingly their pivot five ploys, involving their loose forwards and halves, with a view to keeping moves under wraps for later challenges but they still mounted several thrilling passages of interplay in which forwards and backs interchanged roles and there was some beautifully creative play by Scotland's centres, Scott Hastings and Sean Lineen, especially in their adjustments to weight of pass to exploit sharp loop moves that stretched Zimbabwe's cover – in which their scrum-half, Ewan MacMillan, whose parents hailed from Perth, showed technique and courage in the tackle. Iwan Tukalo underlined his return to pristine form with three tries which took him to 15 and second place in Scotland's international try-scorers, behind the legendary 'Flying Scot', Ian Smith, who had 24 tries in 32 games.

A feature of the Zimbabwean's set piece play was their clever use of quick, flat throws-in to their front player, Garvey or to Michael Martin behind him. So it was irritating for them that Doddie Weir, Scotland's telegraph pole lock, should score one of Scotland's eight tries with a clean take of a Zimbabwean throw-in near their own line. He just had to catch and fall. The other Scottish try-scorers were Derek Turnbull, Scott Hastings, Tony Stanger and Derek White.

The theory expounded by the genial Zimbabwean manager, Sam Woldemar, and his two coaches, Ian Buchanan and Brian Murphy, that their comparatively young side had been quite stage-struck by the size of the crowd and the atmosphere at Lansdowne Road (their own national ground in Harare holds just 6,000) and had benefited from that traumatic experience, seems to be borne out by the manner in which they took the game to Scotland straight from kick-off and seemed in no way overawed by the Murrayfield situation.

The other underlying point to emerge, even from a 51–12 victory, was that Scotland's reserve resources are not desperately strong or deep. That had been evident from defeats by Japan in Tokyo in 1989 and by Canada during the 1991 summer tour, when the Scots had been understrength. It bore out the earlier comment by Scotland's team manager, Duncan Paterson, that Scotland would do well in the competition provided there were no injuries to key players.

So Scotland qualified for the quarter-finals and as they were doing so, Ireland were confirming their quarter-final place with a 32–16 win over Japan. Ireland also had taken the precaution of resting Simon Geoghegan, as well as six of their front line pack, but had Brendan Mullin back at the old stand.

Here too, there were doubts cast at Ireland's reserve strength for the Irish scored just four tries to three, were indebted again to the boot of Ralph Keyes for 16 points as well as a show of accurate tactical punts and at times were thoroughly discomforted by the resilience of the Japanese and their remarkable ability to come off either foot and reach top speed in a blink.

The Japanese won only 11 of their 26 throws-in to the line-out but as always, they made a little go a very long way and every one of their tries brought the crowd to its feet in admiration – sizzling break out, committed support, adhesive hands and unerring vision leading to the tries by lock Toshiyuki Hayashi, flanker Hiroyuki Kajihara and left wing Yoshihito Yoshida, the latter screeching down the left wing in minimum space before swaying inwards in triumph. Full back Takahiro Hosokawa had two conversions.

The match enabled No. 8 Noel Mannion to maintain his challenge for a regular first team Irish spot with two tries, the others coming from flanker Pat O'Hara and full-back Jim Staples.

When the Irish arrived in Edinburgh to decide who would be at home or away in the quarter-final, they exuded a quiet confidence reflected in the jocular comment of their bluff, wise-cracking manager, Ken Reid, that they should be given a home dressing room at Murrayfield in preparation for their quarter-final there a week later.

Both David Sole and Ian McGeechan had acknowledged at their Friday press conference that

Noel Mannion of Ireland thunders over in the right hand corner to re-assert Irish superiority in their surprisingly difficult match against Japan.

The seminal moment of the pool as Graham Shiel, the young Scottish replacement, dives underneath two defenders for the try which put struggling Scotland back on course to win the group.

when the two teams had last met, just seven months previously, Ireland had been singularly unfortunate to lose by 28–25 at Murrayfield.

This time, Scotland fielded 13 and Ireland 12 of those who had played in that match. The Irish rightly claimed that there was more pressure on Scotland in that the Scots had to win to ensure a home quarter-final whereas if Ireland lost, they would still be at home for their quarter-final.

Some cynics therefore suggested that it might pay the Irish to lose, but within the Irish party there

was a stern resolve to fight for a victory that would give them a considerable psychological boost for their quarter-final, even if it did have to take place

Brian Robinson of Ireland scores a clean miss as he jumps for the high ball as a wave of Scots chase in hope and expectation.

at Murrayfield. In a break with normal practice, too, the Irish decided against a Friday runabout. They had been delayed by fog on arrival in Edinburgh and felt that the strenuous session they had on the Thursday at 4p.m was all they needed. Scotland, for their part, had a mist-enshrouded session of enjoyable mini-games as the conclusion of their physical preparations.

The atmosphere at Murrayfield on the day of decision was akin to that of the Grand Slam decider against England in 1990. Some 15,000 Irish supporters lent their distinctive brand of laid-back humour and nationalism to the proceedings and they had much to warm their hearts in the opening 40 minutes, during which the Irish scrummage made Scotland's creak like a rusty hinge. Their line-out waxed strong, with Neil Francis setting out on one of his outstanding performances by giving the young Weir a lesson in line-out arts and practices in the middle.

On such a steady platform, Keyes began where he had left off against the Japanese with meticulous punting and four penalties as well as a drop goal off his left foot for a 15–9 lead soon after the break. The Scots, playing second fiddle, had been kept in the game by two penalty goals from Gavin Hastings (he finished with 13 points from three penalty goals and two conversions for a tally of 334 in 33 internationals), and by a drop goal from Craig Chalmers.

When Chalmers departed with a bruised thigh soon after the break to be replaced by his 21-year-old Melrose club-mate, Graham Shiel, the situation for Scotland looked dire indeed. Yet in one of those oft-recurring situations that are in the dreams of script writers, Shiel proceeded to mark his debut cap appearance with a try, converted by Gavin Hastings, for 15–15 and for a real shot in the arm for the Scots.

Unhappily there was an element of anger and disappointment over that score. Gary Armstrong had put up a Garryowen which Jim Staples, fairly harassed by Tony Stanger, failed to gather in. Finlay Calder, in follow up, appeared to hit Staples with his elbow. Stanger, at 5 feet 2 inches, reached higher than Keith Crossan, 5 feet 7, and gave the scoring pass to Shiel. Staples seemed concussed but stayed on.

Not surprisingly, another up-and-under by Shiel was spilled by Staples and Armstrong looped Stanger for a safety try that Gavin Hastings converted for 24–15. The Scots were incredulous at allegations that Calder had hit Staples, it would have been quite out of character.

Scotland had got themselves off the hook by their high degree of fitness and by responding to the inspirational qualities of Gavin Hastings and Gary Armstrong, the latter giving a remarkable performance incorporating tackle, harass, pirate, serve, drive and fall.

There was a post-match feeling that Ireland should have capitalised more on their set-piece delivery and well though Keyes punted, he did ignore at least three rare opportunities of giving his quick backs a run, augmented as they would have been by full-back Staples, who is quick enough to have played on the wing prior to switching to full-back.

Annoyingly for the Irish, their one promising attempted handling attack was from their own half and spoiled by a long miss pass that did not go to hand, when all that was required was orthodox handling – Geoghegan was roaring into mid-line from the right wing. There was, too, a lack of intuitive support for two thrilling breaks by Robinson and by Geoghegan.

In the post match chat Armstrong, typically modest, paid tribute to the composure of the new cap, Shiel, whilst Ireland's coach Ciaran Fitzgerald, made the point that there wasn't a great deal of spread of play because both sides knew so much about each other and it was bound to be a hard, very competitive contest. That it certainly was, but there remained the feeling that Ireland could have sealed it had they been just a little bit more adventurous when the opportunity arose.

The Japanese rang down the curtain on an entertaining Pool Two with a blistering series of attacks in an 11 tries extravaganza against Zimbabwe in Belfast. Japan scored 9 of them, the Zimbabweans unable to cope with the sizzling switches and elusiveness of the Japanese backs who registered eight of them – Yoshito Yoshida, Eiji Kutsuki, Terunori Matsuho (2 each), Masami Horikoshi and Katsuhiro Matsuo (one each) and one by flanker Ekeroma Tifaga, five being converted by Takahiro Hosokawa who also slotted two penalty goals. Zimbabwe had tries from Richard Tsimba and Honeywell Nguruve.

It was 52–8 as the Japanese said goodbye to the event in the scintillating style that is their hallmark, and that adorned Pool Two almost throughout.

Cathay Pacific.
The foremost exponents of non-stop flight.

Cathay Pacific offers you a better way to fly to Hong Kong. A non-stop London-Hong Kong service. With the care and attention provided by our Oriental flight attendants, it's the service you'll prefer. So now, when you want to touch down in better shape there's no stopping you. For full details of our services see your travel agent or call us on 071-930 7878.

CATHAY PACIFIC
Arrive in better shape.

POOL 3

WALES LOSE STATUS IN THE TOUGHEST GROUP
CLEM THOMAS

It was always Pool 3 which was going to be the toughest, a swamp full of alligators and no place for the weak-minded. So it proved. The pool was one of twanging tenseness with the result in doubt right up to the wire of the last game.

It contained the beleaguered Welsh and the joint favourites, Australia as its seeded teams, together with the intensely-combative Argentina and Manu (or warrior) Western Samoa.

Inevitably, it became the Pool in which most blood was to be spilt both in the literal and metaphorical sense, as the vigorous Western Samoans put six men off the field with their annihilating crash tackling (only one of which was a high tackle), and it was the only pool to produce a sending-off. For good measure, two players had first use of the hot water.

But there was to be even greater blood-letting in that Wales, one of the proudest and most skilful Rugby nations of the last 100 years, were to be pitched willy nilly out of the tournament in the preliminary rounds. This probably means that they will have to qualify with the rest of the minor rugby nations for the next World Cup and in the next four years may have to become accustomed to a different menu – like smorgasbord in Sweden, sardines in Portugal, unleavened bread in Tel Aviv and borsch in Russia.

Such a bitter ignomy for the Welsh was a product of laissez-faire leadership after the glory days of the '70s. A failure to put a competitive structure in place until 1990, a failure by the clubs to look after the young after the demise of so much school rugby during the '80s. A failure to appreciate how far and fast the rest of the rugby world had moved forward, not the least in the great southern hemisphere centres of New Zealand and Australia, but also in more unlikely places such as Canada, Western Samoa and Namibia.

The first rumblings of any danger to Wales in this pool came in the previous March at the Cathay Pacific/Hongkong Bank Sevens, where the Kiwis were muttering about Western Samoa being the All Black 'B' team. The New Zealand T.V. commentator, Keith Quinn, was relating how the Samoans were trawling through the New Zealand provinces for all their ex-pat players and even for those of Samoan extraction born in New Zealand.

There was also ample evidence of the sporting aptitudes and physical strengths of these Samoans, who are the very heart of Polynesia, a pattern of small islands north east of Fiji and north of Tonga with a total population of about 170,000 souls. They enjoy a high reputation for boxing and weightlifting in the Commonwealth and South Pacific Games. Greg Louganis, who won a gold medal at the Seoul Olympics after crashing his head on the diving board, is a Samoan adopted by American parents, while the 'dump truck', the massive 37 stone Sumo wrestler Konishiki, is of Samoan extraction.

Nevertheless, Western Samoa were still a fairly unknown quantity with only a recent win against the Australian Barbarians in July and a fairly heavy defeat at the hands of Australian Capital Territories, who even the Welsh managed to beat in the same month, as recent pointers of form.

Wales were therefore optimistic of beating Western Samoa, having also beaten them 32–14 in 1986 at Apia and 28–6 in Cardiff in 1988. Indeed Alan Davies, the new Welsh coach, had set Wales only the more realistic target of beating Western Samoa and Argentina in order to qualify for the quarter-final.

Alas! Even that was to prove beyond the capacity of a Welsh team that in recent years has sunk to the depths of mediocrity. Western Samoa, who were the first qualifying nation for the Asian Pacific group and the smallest country in the tournament with by far the least number of players to call on (which *pro rata* makes them the most talented players on earth) proved to be a lethal opponent. Western Samoa had also added to their strength by using the great All Black, Bryan Williams, as a technical director to strengthen and supplement the terrific work already done by their coach, Peter Schuster, brother of the All Black John Schuster.

They became a tremendously potent force and after they beat Wales in the first match, a New Zealander turned to His Excellency, George Fepulea'i, once the Western Samoan High Commissioner to the U.K. and now in Australia, and said, 'These guys are so good we might have a New Zealand 'A' versus New Zealand 'B' final'. The quick response came, 'You mean Western Samoa 'A' versus Western Samoa 'B'' referring to the tremendous input of Samoans in the current New Zealand team, including their star player Michael Jones, and also Graeme Bachop and Va'aiga Tuigamala.

The other underdog in the pool was Argentina, who like the Japanese are formidable guardians of the game's amateur ethic and have consistently refused to select many of their best players who have been part of a huge immigration to Italy in recent years to play quazi-professional rugby.

Like Fiji, the Argentinians enjoy a poor reputation as travellers and were not considered as serious contenders for further qualification. Nevertheless, many thought that they had the potential to beat either Wales or Western Samoa, for they are a proud nation, brave, tough and virile and in Hugo Porta (now his country's ambassador to South Africa) have provided one of the very greatest rugby footballers of all time.

For twenty years, Hugo was a colossus astride Argentine rugby. He provided them with many famous victories. They had also given the All Blacks a hard time in the first Test in Buenos Aires recently, losing in the end by 28–14 and losing the second Test more substantially, but only a year ago they had gone down heavily in 50-point drubbings by England and Scotland during their British tour.

They, too, were unlucky to be in such a hard pool and to be faced with such a difficult and morale-destroying game against Australia, which in the event turned out far better than anybody expected.

Argentina are always recognised as being extremely hard in the forwards and excellent scrummagers and once again, came with a powerful front row in Diego Cash, Ricardo Le Fort and the young nineteen-year-old Pampas bull Federico Mendez, who had already made a big impact in last year's tour of the U.K. He was sent off for flooring the 6′ 7″ Paul Ackford with a haymaker at Twickenham. They were also to be well served by Llanes and Sporleder at lock.

Argentina were not particularly strong at half-back, where they had to fill a huge gap left by the departure of Fabio Gomez to Italy. Consequently, they had to play two inexperienced half-backs in Camardon and the nineteen-year-old fly half Arbizu, who developed nicely as the pool progressed.

Argentina are currently team-building and frankly it showed. They will best be remembered for a splendid second half rally against Australia at Llanelli.

By virtue of coming third in the previous World Cup, Wales, ludicrously as it turned out, were the top seeded nation of their pool. During the four years which have elapsed since 1987, the Welsh have appeared to have gone into terminal decline. In the 14 matches played in 1990 and 1991, they won only two, both against Namibia, and had not won a match in their own citadel for $2\frac{1}{2}$ years.

Sadly, Wales were facing all those old chestnut jibes and cliches – 'What would have happened had you played all of Samoa' or 'Samoa of the same'. They were destined to finish third in their pool, but not even a win over Argentina could dispel the gloom that pervaded this once-great rugby nation, a nation once the pride and joy of Europe.

Throughout the World Cup, everybody has asked the same question: 'What has happened to Welsh Rugby?'. There is simply no easy answer. There are those who ascribe it to the closing of the Welsh coal mines (there are now only three pits left in Wales), and to the closing of so many steelworks. In fact, not that many miners or steelworkers played for Wales.

Then there was the teachers' strike some years ago and the consequent decline of rugby in Welsh schools. There was the matter of the decline of the Welsh chapel culture and consequently, of Welsh 'hwyl' (feeling). Some trace it to that notorious game at Twickenham in 1980. The resultant criticism, some say, led to the emasculation of Welsh forward play. Others blame the attitudes of Welsh referees, who have become far stricter on rough play than those in the southern Hemisphere and France. Then there are the depredations of rugby league, which have bled Wales of so many outstanding players in recent years, not the least being the best fly-half in the Northern Hemisphere, Jonathan Davies.

It is, of course, an amalgam of all these things, but is also much to do with the lack of leadership which saw Wales embrace a competitive league structure only two years ago, which was too little too late to combat the competitive instincts of the Southern Hemisphere and even of England and Scotland, who had a head start in this regard.

Certainly there has been too much complacency,

and a lack of strong leadership. Although much of the blame must lie with the recent administration of the Welsh Rugby Union, there is also fault with the first-class clubs who have neglected to foster young players by failing to run junior teams. Most of them, shamefully, only run one fifteen. Surely, after this World Cup is over, there will be some sort of a revolution in Welsh rugby.

After the nightmares in Australia, on and off the field, the Welsh had brought in, at the very last minute, a new management team to run their World Cup challenge. The Nottingham and England 'B' coach Alan Davies, and the highly-respected lock, Robert Norster, had no time for scrutiny and inevitably were on a hiding to nothing. They still managed to make a difference and perhaps saved Wales from being a totally demoralised rabble, for at least you could sense a little more spirit in the side.

After it had become clear that the Welsh had been dumped out of the tournament, the players, who had clearly recognised that Davies knew what

Martin Teran, the Argentinian right wing, has just scored his second try of the match against Australia at Llanelli after a dazzling back move. He turns to celebrate and David Campese can only watch.

he was on about, in terms of coaching and man management, (unlike many of his predecessors), begged him to stay on. Such was Davies' standing with the players that many of the more senior went as far as to say that without his help, they too would pack in international rugby.

Alan Davies should now be given a free hand and at least three years to re-ignite Welsh rugby and regain the high standards of play that have been endemic in Wales during the last 100 years.

People should expect little but continued failure for another couple of years, until Davies and Norster can develop a new side, using the talented under-21 Welsh squad. They are both confident that Wales can fight their way back up the rankings but to do that, they will have to practise against lesser sides, which qualification for the next World Cup already imposes.

Australia are the only team since the inaugural World Cup to have beaten all the senior International Rugby Board countries and have beaten the All Blacks twice in their last three encounters. Their killing field victories over Wales and England during the summer, and two successive wins over New Zealand, propelled them forward to be joint favourites with the All Blacks.

No country has invested greater effort towards success in the tournament than these Wallabies, who, in tandem with the Institute of Sport in Australia, have developed a rugby academy which has thrown up more good young players than at any time in their history. So much so that they no longer fear losing some of their players to rugby league.

This investment by the Institute of Sport and the production of an Emerging Wallaby side paid a huge dividend, not least in the discovery of magnificent young players such as the giant 6'8" lock John Eales, and the outstanding Tim Gavin, who sadly was lost to them because of a knee ligament injury sustained in a club match, and whose loss diminished Australian performances.

Like Buck Shelford in 1987, Gavin was the principal driver of the back row, the vital factor in the destruction of both England and Wales during the summer.

Furthermore, Australia developed the best young front row in world rugby in Daly, Kearns and McKenzie, had the best pair of experienced half-backs in Farr-Jones and Lynagh (though Bachop and Fox of New Zealand run them close), a terrific young pocket battleship centre in Tim Horan and,

of course, the inimitable genius of David Campese, who is the world's leading try scorer and one of the greatest players of all time.

Coach Bob Dwyer and his assistant, Bob Templeton, together with the technical assistance of Jake Howard, gives them a vastly experienced and innovative coaching set-up. They left not a stone unturned and brought to Britain fitness, diet and psychological experts.

They kept only four of the team who lost their home test series against the Lions in 1989 and for all their muscular forward play, the real charm of this new Australian side is their instinct for inventive play (not that they showed much of either in the preliminary rounds).

So the four teams in Pool 3, all from different cultures, were lined up for what they all knew was the hardest of the pools and the greatest rugby competition of all time, and to be played before the biggest-ever audience, variously calculated to be between $1\frac{1}{2}$ and 2 billion people. It was a staircase which would lead some down to the depth of despair and others up to the greater glories of the quarter and semi-finals beyond.

The first game of the pool was at Stradey Park, Llanelli, that lovely, intimate and most Welsh of all the Welsh stadia, alive with the club's scarlet colours and now replete with the new stand, where years ago the Tanner Bank used to be. How life moves on!

On every day but the one at Pontypool, the players in Pool 3 were to enjoy excellent weather and good pitches and Llanelli was no exception. A packed ground would see the joint favourites discomfited in their very first game and given a run for their money by the Pumas, who fought tooth and claw for most of the second half to reduce a half-time deficit of 16–7. At 20–16, Australia appeared to be in disarray and for 20 minutes they appeared to have found the first banana skin of their pool.

Perhaps where the Pumas surprised Australia most was at the scrum. The big Aussie pack, which has had its own way over the last 2 years, was said by the demonstrator of the 'Format Rhino' scrummaging machine to be by far the strongest scrummagers in the World Cup, ahead of the All Blacks and England, at least according to the measuring scale of the hydraulics on the machine. The Australians were comfortably held by the Pumas.

The Pumas also showed speed, courage and

tenacity, but in the end these traits were to prove powerless in the face of a scintillating performance by David Campese, who ran through his whole repetoire of considerable skills. Somebody needed to, for Argentina had shown real Latin fire and flair during the second half of what was generally regarded as a fine match.

The first half ended with Australia predictably leading by 16–7, but always struggling with the pace after a fairly long lay-off. And they were not

Michael Lynagh prepares to conjure up a backline movement with Tim Horan as Australia step up the pace in the pool match at Llanelli against the Pumas.

successful in putting their game together. Certainly, one area of their play was missing and that was their attack off the back row, a point which immediately created considerable doubt in the Australian camp.

Although Bob Dwyer attempted to cover Australian confusion by saying they were rusty and had still scored 5 tries though not playing well, there was still a huge concern in the Australian camp that they had not put Argentina away more clinically and completely.

The game also caused both Dwyer and his captain Nick Farr-Jones to observe that Argentina would beat both Wales and Western Samoa. They were to retract on both counts, particularly after they had played Western Samoa.

Although only a shadow of the side they were in

July, because they had lost their back row link in Tim Gavin they nevertheless kept their terrific determination and will to win, which was to carry them through a difficult second-half.

Predictably, the Wallabies took the lead with a superb try by Campese, which took him past three or four defenders using his famous goose steps and side steps. Two Lynagh penalties made it 10–0 as the raw power of the Australians took its toll. However, Argentina stemmed the tide and

responded with a well taken drop-goal by the young fly-half, Arbizu.

Good tackling and excellent play by full-back del Castillo, began to slow down Australia until Horan produced one of his hard, busy runs for a try converted by Lynagh. A quick-thinking diagonal kick by Arbizu saw another promising young Argentine player, Martin Teran, tearing into the corner for a try to make it 16–7 at half time.

Kearns scored another try with a rhino charge to make it 20–7 and now Argentina showed their tenacity with a tremendous fight back. Del Castillo kicked a penalty and then Teran scored the best try of the game, converted by del Castillo to make it 20–16, after a superbly sharp movement.

Danger was the cue for Campese to turn on the style and he took a short pass from Lynagh, coming in at an angle at speed, to score between the posts. Lynagh converted. Although Arbizu

A rare, rare moment of Welsh delight for Arthur Emyr and the Welsh crowd as Emyr crashes over to score against Western Samoa after taking a pass from Mike Hall.

took his second drop goal, another magic run by Campese had Horan beating three or four men for a try by the posts, converted by Lynagh, and Australia were home by a score that flattered. Argentina had given them some real 'hurry up' in the second-half.

This game led to the conjecture that Australia were vulnerable and that Argentina might be a force in the pool, but in the event Argentina had flattered to deceive and disappeared in their remaining matches. Typically, Australia took a good long look at themselves.

The next match was to be the crucial one – Wales against Western Samoa, two days later on the Sunday at Cardiff Arms Park. It was to be the one that was to really cook the Welsh goose. This was the game that the Welsh had to win if they were to get to the quarter-final. They knew that failure would bring the final denouement after 10 years of decline, and that its accompanying misery would break the rugby heart of the nation.

It was all so unthinkable, yet it happened. The French referee, Monsieur Robin awarded a try to Western Samoa when it was obvious that Robert Jones had got there first – an incident which normally would have started a huge controversy particularly as the final score was 13–16. There was, in fact, no complaint from any Welshman for they knew at the end of the game that they had been well and truly beaten by a country with a population less than Cardiff and without a fraction of the resources of Welsh rugby.

Although Wales still had to play Argentina and Australia, everybody knew instinctively that this was the end for Welsh rugby's World Cup aspirations and that they were facing the dreadful ignomy of having to qualify for the next World Cup.

If it was a sad day, indeed the apocalypse for Wales, it was to light a fire under the spirits of the Western Samoans. The news came through that they were taking their hangovers to church, after great parties in places throughout the Islands. It was a victory which was to put them firmly on the World rugby map.

It was a lovely still day and the crowd basked in bright autumnal sunshine but there was a nervous start by the Western Samoans, even though Wales were in difficulties at both the line-outs and the rucks. Half-time was reached at 3–3 with a penalty each mid-way through the first half, from Matt

Vaea of Samoa and Mark Ring for Wales. In the first half, Phil May was shattered in a tackle and left the field with a dislocated shoulder. In the second half, the Samoans began to desolate the Welsh with the power of their tackles and we saw two more departures from the field – Tony Clement with an injured knee and Richie Collins with another shoulder problem.

From here on, the Welshmen were constantly aware of the Samoan body-tackling which reverberated around the Arms Park, and was as hard as any ever seen by the Welsh supporters.

Early in the second-half came that crucial try, scored by scrum-half Vaea when, clearly, Robert Jones got there first. As the sensational and withering tackling of the Samoans continued to decimate the Welsh spirit, Samoa went further ahead with a try by flanker Simon Vaifale after a magnificent run by Tagaloa. Vaea converted. To their credit Wales rallied late in the game, as Emyr Lewis, by far the best Welsh forward in all the games, made a charge and Hall made a half-break for Emyr to score and Ring converted. A second Vaea penalty made it 16–9. Although a try by Welsh captain Evans at the death made it 16–13, everybody knew that Wales had been well beaten.

Western Samoa's most famous visitor, Robert Louis Stevenson, was perhaps a prophet, for many of his lines could be applied to this victory over Wales. How about – 'Fifteen men on a dead man's chest' or 'Under the wide and starry sky – dig the grave and let me lie'.

Although for the next week, Wales clutched at a corn stack of straws they really suspected that they were out of the Cup – while Western Samoa, regarded as the founding fathers of the New Zealand Maories due to their migration and navigation through the South Pacific, had achieved the unthinkable. They had brought down a senior IRB country in one of the great traditional bastions of the game.

There was some conjecture that the poor crowd at the Arms Park for this Sunday match was indicative of a decline of interest by the Welsh public. This was not borne out by the large crowds against Argentina on the Wednesday and Australia on the Saturday. It had more to do with the non-attendance of chapel-goers, and the fact that it was a 1.00 p.m. kick-off, unpopular with golf clubs, working men's clubs and pub-goers on a Sunday lunchtime.

The next games in the pool came three days later, on the Wednesday, when Australia played Western Samoa at Pontypool and Wales took on Argentina under lights at Cardiff. Neither game was to prove decisive, apart from guaranteeing Australia a passage to a quarter-final.

It was a shame that a game which promised so much had to be played in the only downpour of the group, and the glorious venue of Pontypool Park was concealed from the overseas visitors by low cloud and driving rain, which at times came down like stair rods. Astonishingly, however, we were to experience one of the most thrilling games of the whole competition. Never has anyone seen such incredible handling in such conditions as we saw from these amazing Samoans, who quickly showed the Wallabies that they were no South Sea bubble.

It was a totally absorbing match, which was to see the Australians breathing a huge sigh of relief. One would not go as far as to say that Australia were lucky, only that Western Samoa were unlucky and had no rub of the green, or much assistance from the referee. Only a team with the determination and resolution of these Wallabies would have withstood such an incredible onslaught. Strangely, Australia had never before

The Australians never subdued the Samoans in the gloom and rain at Pontypool Park. Matt Keenan, the lock, hangs on against all-comers.

46

played Western Samoa, who had beaten the Australian Barbarians at Manly back in July but then lost quite heavily to ACT, so there was a feeling that Australia might make the mistake of taking the opposition too lightly. However, Bob Dwyer, or Barb Wire as he is known to the Aussies, said after the match that not only had they had a nervous feeling and perhaps they should not have made as many changes from their full team, but that now Western Samoa were deserving of being brought into a full South Pacific round robin tournament.

They had every right to feel nervous, for against the Samoan tackling, Australia were to lose their captain, Nick Farr-Jones, with what looked at the time like a serious knee ligament injury.

Again the body-crunching tackles of the Samoans were not to the Australian liking and this, together with their extraordinary handling ability with a wet ball, discomfited the Australians. The game was to prove an uphill battle, settled only by Lynagh kicking three penalties to Vaea's one. In truth, had Vaea not missed three other eminently kickable penalties Australia would not have won. For a long period, the game was poised at 6–3 until Lynagh kicked another penalty in the last five minutes, and at the end Australia were generously conceding that they were lucky to have survived. Australia had learnt one more lesson and that was that their back row was still not firing and needed adjustment.

Although it had stopped raining, the late evening match between Wales and Argentina was of far lower quality and its only saving grace as far as the Welsh supporters were concerned was that it was, at least, a Welsh win and that if Argentina could beat Western Samoa and Wales could get a few tries against Australia, then it was possible for Wales to survive on the try count. If pigs could only fly! It also served to lift the Welsh depression for a while and to keep the interest in this pool alive right up to the final game.

The Arms Park is not what it was, a place of dread for visitors, for Wales had not won at home for eight matches, not since England were beaten in March 1989. Nevertheless, Wales came out to a marvellous supportive welcome from a surprisingly large late evening crowd of some 45,000, which perhaps showed that even in hard times, the Welsh public have not lost their love or appetite for rugby.

It was a game of frequent interruption as the

Kevin Moseley of Wales and German Llanes rise to do line-out battle with their supporting casts awaiting further developments.

French referee Monsieur Hourquet, in common with his colleagues throughout the competition, showered penalties against both teams.

Wales led 9–0 at half-time by virtue of three penalty goals by Mark Ring and although Argentina rallied in the second half, they could only manage a penalty goal by del Castillo before Wales increased their lead with a storming try by Paul Arnold and a penalty by Mike Rayer. Finally, Garcia Simon scored a try for the Pumas to make it 16–7 to Wales at the end of an undistinguished match.

And so we came to the final weekend and climax of this highly-competitive pool, with Wales versus Australia on the Saturday and Argentina versus Western Samoa on Sunday.

The Welsh, always the optimists, were still clinging feverishly to the dream of holding Australia and winning through on a try count. However, the Australians were now to produce their most emphatic and compelling performance of the pool so far. They were to score six tries in their remorseless progress to the quarter-finals and left Wales ruefully contemplating another set of record defeats; the heaviest at Cardiff, the most points against at Cardiff and the biggest points difference. In two matches against Australia within four months, they had conceded 18 tries without reply. It was another desperately demeaning moment for Wales but the most telling statistic, which emphasises the dreadful decline of Welsh forward play over the last ten years, was the line-out count of 28 takes to 2 by Wales. Not even the diminutive Japanese would have allowed that to happen without ringing the changes, but somewhere the Welsh forwards have even lost the art of being streetwise in the rugby sense. Never had an international team been cleaned out so disastrously at the line-out, where John Eales of Australia ruled.

Totally shut out from this primary point of possession, Wales were fortunate not to lose by more, for certainly, Australia still failed to press home many of their opportunities. The normally reliable Lynagh was off-form with his boot, kicking only six goals from 12 attempts and they could well have scored another clutch of tries. They only showed flashes of their skills in the summer and again, they were not convincing off the back row of the scrum.

Once more, there was a string of penalties, 18 to Wales and 15 to Australia, which was further confirmation that the referees were commandeering, even hi-jacking, the World Cup.

Australia scored six tries, two by Roebuck and one each from Slattery, Campese, Horan and Lynagh who also kicked four conversions and two penalties. Ring kicked a penalty for Wales. Once

John Eales, the Australian lock, who dominated the line-out against Wales, in typical aerial control of the ball as the Welsh defence closes.

again we were privileged, maybe for the last time (if he keeps his promise to retire to Italy for good) to observe the massive genius of Campese. His sniping runs, which continually discomfited and wrong-footed the defence, will remain a marvellous memory.

On Sunday, at Pontypridd, it was another glorious day of Indian summer which, together with the excellent staging of the game by the Pontypridd RFC, was to provide a marvellous setting for almost a capacity crowd to observe Western Samoa demolishing Argentina by 35–12, and deservedly winning a place in the quarter-final against Scotland at Murrayfield.

It was a game of considerable drama, as Jim Fleming, the Scottish referee, (who unusually had replaced his countryman Brian Anderson at half-time because Anderson pulled a muscle), was to send off the two locks, Pedro Sporleder of Argentina and more crucially, Mata'afa Keenan of Western Samoa.

It was a strange decision in the light of the fact that Fleming had already allowed a far more wicked tackle by the Samoan captain, Peter Fatialofa, on the Argentine full-back Guillermo Anguat, who 15 minutes later had to leave the field, to pass with only a wigging and a penalty.

It was a decision against which the Samoans appealed but it was turned down the following Wednesday by a tribunal chaired by Sir Ewart Bell, chairman of the disputes committee, Albert Agar, of the RFU and Doctor Malcolm Little, of the ARU. It was a delicate decision in view of the fact that it was the first ever sending-off of a Samoan at international level and because it was a Scotsman who sent him off – considering Samoa's next game was against Scotland in the quarter-final.

Western Samoa played with such pace and power that they demolished Argentina by four goals, two tries and a penalty to a goal and two penalty goals. The Western Samoan try scorers were Tagaloa and Lima, who got two each, and Bunce and Bachop, with Vaea kicking four conversions and a penalty. Teran got a try for Argentina, converted by Arbizu, and Laborde and Arbizu kicked a penalty apiece.

The pool had largely lived up to its great expectations of being hard-fought and dramatic. Australia powered their way through to the quarter-final against Ireland in Dublin but not without feeling a bit of pain and having to make adjustments to their pack. They seemed to be getting better as the tournament progressed but in common with New Zealand, they were still far from being convincing as joint favourites to win the Cup.

Unquestionably, it was Western Samoa who had really captured the imagination in this pool with their annihilating tackles and superb handling. Overnight, they had become the West Indies of rugby football with their feared tackling replacing fast bowling as an object of terror. They fully deserved their advance into the quarter-final at Edinburgh and their new status of belonging, at least for the time being, to that exclusive club of the superpower rugby countries of the world.

Argentina were far from disgraced, but they must now continue their rebuilding process and somehow endeavour to prevent their best players from going to play in Italy.

For Wales it was a calamity. Perhaps the final rock bottom, but such is the tradition and the love of rugby in the Principality, that inevitably one day they will rise again from the ashes, especially once they have reorganised and found some decent leadership.

Below: An unfortunate moment of the tournament as Matt Keenan of Western Samoa and Pedro Sporleder of Argentina are dismissed by referee Jim Fleming.

Right: Matthew Vaea, the brilliant Samoan scrum-half, sets the back division moving against Argentina at Pontypridd, where Samoa sealed their progress into the quarter-finals.

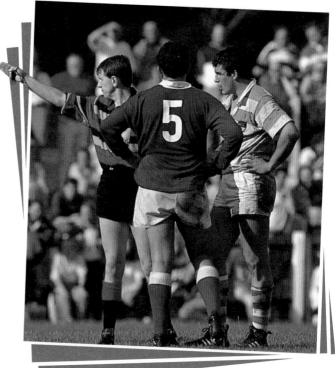

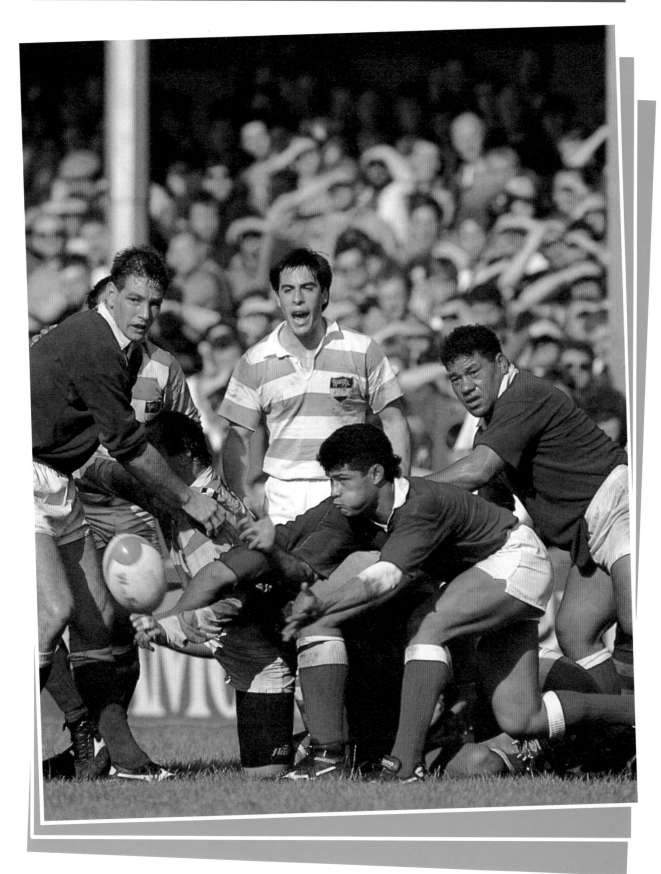

More non-stops to Asia's non-stop city.

POOL 4

FRANCE WIN THROUGH, BUT CANADA CHALLENGE
NIGEL STARMER-SMITH

This was always destined to be a highly competitive group of four nations from the moment the draw was made. Whilst everyone looked upon France as near-certainties to qualify for the quarter-finals, there was no common agreement to be found as to who would progress in the competition alongside them.

The fact that Fiji were seeded on the basis of reaching the quarter-finals in the first World Cup of 1987 was an irrelevance and quite absurd. More recent form must in future be taken into account. Imagine drawing up the seeding lists for Wimbledon based on the results of the same event four years beforehand.

What was therefore always bound to be a fascinating competition within a competition was made even more so by events in advance of the opening game between France, the host nation for this pool, and Romania on October 4 in Béziers. Uncertainty, apprehension and excitement were rife and the French rugby public was to be enthralled – though, it has to be said, ultimately to be frustrated by the absence of live coverage on television except on the subscription channel, Canal Plus.

Thus the vast majority of rugby enthusiasts who were unable to attend the matches in the South and West and who did not subscribe to Canal Plus, were forced to settle for occasional deferred coverage or highlights of a limited number of matches, in the early stages of the tournament, on the ubiquitous network channel TF1.

France were, quite reasonably, installed as hot favourites to qualify as pool winners for the quarter-final in Parc des Princes. But in the build-up to the World Cup there seemed to be anything but peace and harmony in the camp. The magnificent Grand Slam finale to the 1991 Five Nations Championship (in which France came thrillingly close to foiling England's bid at Twickenham with magical moments of unbridled skill and a try by Saint-André that will never fade

in the memory) augured well for their World Cup aspirations of going one better than in 1987.

But the months that followed did little to enhance their claims and further stiffen morale. First there was the 'clash at the top' within the new management team of Daniel Dubroca and Jean Trillo, the pairing who had provided such immediate success in international rugby after the Fouroux furore. But the harmonious partnership was soon to be rent asunder as Dubroca, the man with the final say, determined that no longer should France rely on the outstanding generalship and scrum-half skills of Pierre Berbizier, veteran of two Grand Slam seasons 1981 and 1987, and a key member of the World Cup Final side of '87. Thirty-three years old in June of 1991, Berbizier's outstanding career was done in Duboca's view – whilst Trillo, and just about the whole array of French backs, thought otherwise. The rift was entrenched but Dubroca would not recant, and France toured the USA without him on their World Cup warm-up trip.

That tour was a near-disaster. Acrimony, not camaraderie, was the hallmark of the tour. Off the field dissension, even, apparently, fighting amongst the players within the squad, and at times pretty appalling violence on the field in the tour matches (sparked by the Bègles-Bordeaux front row) hardly lent itself to the creation of the trust and friendship that usually accrue from an overseas tour.

With the exclusion of Berbizier from the World Cup squad Trillo once even threatened to resign. Questions were raised too about the continued eligibility of Abdelatif Benazzi for France, since he had played for Morocco, whilst injury worries surrounded the future availability of Philippe Sella.

Those anxieties apart, there was comfort to be gained from the return, under Trillo and Dubroca, to what Eric Bonneval described as the 'reinvention of French flair, the joy of taking risks, the adventure and the capacity to dare'. No longer were the French players and public prepared to accept France's attempts to emulate rugby 'à la Nouvelle Zélande'. It was never natural to their free spirits, nor their tradition.

The final warm-up with Wales on September 4 may not have produced a thoroughly convincing victory, but it did seem to mark a significant step on the road to rehabilitation and an end to the blood-letting – just in time perhaps.

Whilst disharmony and disagreement had characterised France's build-up Fiji had to put up with a mixture of good and bad news in their 1991 pre-tournament games. After various managerial comings and goings, Fiji reverted to the experienced triumvirate of Dr Josaia Taka, George Simpkin (released from duties in Hong Kong) and Samisone Viriviri, only for them to witness defeat (23–40) against Western Samoa in a three-way tournament in which they beat Tonga.

More heartening was the outcome of the matches with the England touring party in July. The Fijian B side overcame a top-notch England line-up 27–13 with the enigmatic fly-half Waisele Serevi announcing his return to his inspirational best. The full international produced an England victory, but not a convincing one. The scores were still level late in the game. But, as ever, there remained doubts about competence and capabilities up front, but none about the running and passing talents of a team who in successive years had run the rest of the world off their feet at the shortened game in the Hong Kong Sevens.

But having not played France since the World Cup of 1987, having not encountered Canada for 21 years, and having never played Romania at all, there were few pointers in the Fijian form book. But fresh in my memory were the inadequacies of Fiji away from home on their visit to Twickenham two years before, as they failed to cope up front and England, without the first rank front row, ran in 10 tries. It certainly seemed that it would take more than the comfort and inspiration afforded by their prayer and religious reading sessions between their matches in France, and the vows of chastity taken by the players for the tournament's duration as well as the liberal supplies of their familiar home foods, including their favourite quaff, cava, to enable them to cope with the forward battles that would ensue.

The capacity to beat any of their pool rivals in a game that was fast and loose and in which their forwards were not annihilated was always a possibility, but those two pre-conditions rendered the likelihood of their living up to their official number 5 seeding doubtful.

Romania's form is nothing if not erratic, and to assess the chance of the representatives of Eastern Europe in the World Finals was never going to be easy. How do you equate a first-ever victory over France, in France in 1990, and a 1991 triumph over Scotland in Bucharest, with a first-ever defeat by Italy in Romania in between times?

Turmoil and change on the political front was certainly reflected in the revolutionary events that characterised Romanian rugby in the post-Ceaucescu era. I will always recall the gloom and despondency of Bucharest and its people when England played Romania in 1989, to the extent that the sporting encounter seemed a total irrelevance under the circumstances.

No less so the visit of the Romanians, and another overwhelming defeat, at Lansdowne Road when Ireland won 60–0. The embarrassment I felt was nothing to do with the rugby match, but my shame on learning of the hardship that the visiting players were having to endure at home and abroad – penniless, kitless, cheerless. One could only marvel at their determination to survive against all the odds and keep their international rugby ties intact. Given the living conditions and way of life, small wonder that Romanian rugby was characterised by a dull, dour, style of play. It mirrored the environment.

The post-revolutionary era brought with it a new zest and self-confidence and, in rugby terms, a new freedom of expression. No matter a strong New Zealand XV scored over 50 points against Romania in the summer of '91, the Romanians did not capitulate and came back to score 30 of their own. The advent of new coach Petre Ianusievici inspired a veritable rugby revolution bringing a new purpose, a positive approach and a willingness to run the ball wide, attack and counter-attack, as never before.

The victory over Scotland was the first tangible reward, just two months before the World Cup; a result that gave promises of a real competitive edge to their campaign. If young half-backs Neaga and Nichitean could carry over this new-found self-confidence to the pool matches and harness enough ball from the pack, there was a real possibility that the new squad (with only three players over the age of 30, and 15 of them with less

One of the few Fijians to do himself justice in the tournament was Ilaitia Savai, the lock. Here he outjumps the Canadians for a line-out win in an otherwise disappointing Fijian effort in Bayonne.

over (albeit understrength) Scotland put Canada into a new bracket of international rugby reputation and respect.

Not by chance did this come about. In World Cup '87 when they received their first full international baptism, Canada emerged with an enhanced reputation – victory over Tonga and a superb 65 minutes against Ireland being the highlights. At the time I wrote that 'in four years' time Canada can prove themselves to be genuine challengers to the established order in international rugby'. The event proved a spur to renewed efforts in administration and organisation in succeeding years, with wondrous results, overcoming all obvious shortcomings of geographical distribution and paucity of players (about 15,000 adults in 200 clubs).

The combined efforts of Rugby Canada's 'workaholics' behind the scenes, from President Barry Geffin downwards, and more visibly from the coaching/management pairing of Ian Birtwell and Mike Luke, was rewarded by greater international exposure resulting in seven wins in ten matches since 1987. The lasting impression one has of Canada's performance in 1991 was of a squad newly-confident, thoroughly well organised and efficient, and with a commitment that lived up to the promise of a side determined to take its place in the top rank.

Crucially, they had made enormous strides in the area of play which is so often the Achilles heel for 'emerging' nations – front five forward play. They had players of top calibre in key positions up front and, behind, skilled footballers and tacticians at half-back, and good tacklers outside.

In France, Canada no longer showed promise that they might one day get there – they actually arrived!

There are few more imposing rugby stadia than the Stade de la Mediterranée, newly-built on the outskirts of Béziers and opened by John Kendall-Carpenter in 1989. From a distance, it looks like some vast grey concrete rugby ball that has been carved open and serrated at the top, rather as a tomato or melon on a dinner plate in a fancy restaurant. It stands high, dominating the skyline, and on this balmy Friday night it was even more the focus of attention of the whole community, as the battery of floodlights cut through the sky bringing daylight to the packed throng of 20,000 spectators.

than ten international caps) could make the next round. That is, if the newly-discovered joys of unlimited fresh fruit (including consumption of 10 kilos a day of grapefruit) available in their French hotels did not prove deleterious.

Unlike all other participants in Pool Four, Canada had enjoyed an almost uninterrupted stream of good news in the long run-in to World Cup '91. Twice winners over Argentina, a narrow defeat by Wales, a draw with Ireland, and victory

To describe Béziers as a hotbed of rugby union would be something of an understatement; suffice to say that it is the only town of its size that I have visited that does not even possess a soccer club. There were no empty seats – except when frightened souls leaped off them to avoid contact with a firecracker or Roman candle. Indeed, it was to be a noisy night.

France took the field with no surprises in their chosen line-up, though there was apprehension over the absence of the injured Philippe Sella, so long the mid-field general, who was replaced by Thierry Lacroix, Cecillon was also out through injury and there was the untried new scrum-half Fabien Galthié, just 22, from the unfashionable Colomiers club. His only international caps had been won against Romania and the USA.

France were hopeful of taking control up front from the start with the 'old guard' of Lascubé, Marocco and Ondarts, backed up by the massive physical presence and height of Roumat, Cadieu, Champ and Benazzi with Cabannes the new back row dynamo from the Racing Club.

As for Romania there was concern over the ability of the pack to withstand the French forward onslaught, particularly on the tight-head side where Constantin Stan, only 22 years old, was bound to find life hard on his switch from loose-head prop.

The setting then was perfect, conditions ideal, if anything a little energy-sapping in the 75° heat, and no wind. Sadly, rather as at Twickenham the previous day, the event did not match the expectation. The whistle of Les Peard and the whistling of the crowd were to be the dominant sounds of the night.

It was as though there was too great a tension, too much pressure, because for 60 minutes the match was strewn with mistakes and the spectacle spoiled. France failed to dominate the forward battle as penalty followed penalty, player followed player to the ground, and whistle blast followed whistle blast. It was the original 'stop, stop' game, a dour encounter. A sense of anti-climax heightened crowd hostility, drums pounded, horns blared and firecrackers made the nerves tingle even more.

Who knows what the course of the game might have been had not Romania's 22-year-old student fly-half Neculai Nichitean failed five times with mostly long-range penalty goal attempts in the first half whilst Didier Camberabero succeeded with

two kicks out of four? Sporadic breakouts came from Galthié, Mesnel and, in one classic moment, Serge Blanco in a run, tackle and roll-over – but these moments were either frustrated by sound Romanian defence or, as often, by careless handling errors.

The pattern of play changed little on the change of ends – and a four-man overlap for France, created in the first minute of the second-half, and wasted by an appalling pass, was symptomatic of so much of the action. Line-out obstruction produced another three points from the boot of Camberabero, before Patrice Lagisquet li.nped off, to be replaced by Jean-Baptiste Lafond.

That seemed to mark a watershed as France proceeded to step up a gear, and the ravages wrought by Lascubé on his prop opponent, Stan, began to show their effect. An exchange of penalties, and then, with 20 minutes to go, a penalty try for France as Romania collapsed the scrum on their own line. That was the beginning of the end. France took hold of the game up front and began to run, with Laurent Cabannes often the catalyst.

A sparkling combined move produced a try for Philippe Saint-André, then a slick move at the line-out, with a return pass from thrower-in Marocco to Roumat, made a second and Lafond rounded off a long cross-field movement to ensure a convincing score-line in France's favour. Yet the manner of its achievement was somewhat less than authoritative and impressive for so long.

Romania's inadequacies could not conceal France's shortcomings, a lack of cohesion and fluency up front and behind, an 'edgy' performance that did not augur well. There was nothing worth remembering until the last 20 minutes.

At breakfast the next morning Les Peard reiterated to me the requirement of the referees to do their utmost to ensure that players understand that they must stay on their feet, and not go to ground with the ball, if they are to remain unpenalised. I was already beginning to be concerned as to what the impact of the strict instructions laid down to referees by Peter Brook's panel was going to be on the whole World Cup spectacle.

On a lighter note, he remarked upon the retort from Serge Blanco when he enquired as to his well-being on being injured in the Romania game, 'I'm fine' said Blanco, 'but I'm an old man now!' By the end of France's World Cup run, some of us were indeed wishing that he had made the farewell to his magnificent playing career some seven months earlier.

It's a long, but spectacular, journey by road from Béziers to Bayonne. It's a drive that allows one to experience something of the geographical diversity of the French landscape, moving from the flattish hinterland of the Mediterranean coast, through the majestic scenery of the foothills of the snow-capped Pyrenees, to the southernmost edge of Les Landes and a region dominated by the Atlantic influence.

It takes you through a rugby heartland, as the signposts along the way point to Narbonne and Toulouse, Montauban, Agen, Bagnères and Tarbes, Oloron, Dax and Pau. Even the Autoroute restaurants mark the event by staging exhibitions with a rugby theme, photographs and memorabilia of famed clubs and players and the local speciality foods on display, from cassoulet to foie gras, in the wayside shops bear often the name of Spanghero on the tin.

I stopped at a café in Orthey, where the attention

of those drinking was consumed by the rugby action on the television. No, not World Cup affairs, but, live, the Currie Cup Final from South Africa.

The journey from south coast to west coast is also marked by the transformation from one climatic region to another – for in Bayonne it was not just raining, it was falling in torrents and the wind was blowing a gale.

It often does as the Atlantic air masses hold sway. But it's rugby that reigns most of all and explains why, elements disregarded, the Parc des Sports in Bayonne was bubbling with excited

Glen Ennis, the Canadian captain and one of the best forwards in the whole tournament, drives from the base of the scrum in the opening match in Canada's campaign – against Fiji in Bayonne.

anticipation in the midst of a downpour to greet two overseas teams. The crowd went home happy after a stirring display.

Here was a first chance to assess the form of the conquering Canadians, who came to this World Cup on a 'high'. Their own expectations were high of making the quarter-finals, and, it transpired, with justification. Their success began and ended up front, spearheaded by the massive, but muscular hulk of Norm Hadley, weighing in as the heaviest player in the tournament at 245 lbs, and the player whose role in the front row was crucial that night, loose-head prop Eddie Evans – a mere 235 lbs, who gave his opponent Epeli Naituivau a thoroughly uncomfortable evening.

Canada became the first country to beat one of the seeded nations in the 1991 World Cup thanks to the superb execution of a well-conceived game plan, in difficult playing conditions. Containment was Canada's watchword – denying the flamboyant Fijians possession and the chance to display their exceptional running and handling skills. So the Canucks scrummaged hard (taking one heel against the head), claimed the majority of line-out ball (including five, at least, from a Fijian throw-in) and cut the errors to a minimum. They also tackled like demons.

A heel against the head at a set-scrum in the first five minutes set Canada on their way, though Serevi's snap drop goal from a line-out put Fiji ahead. But if we were expecting only the Pacific Islanders to provide all the entertaining skill, Canada showed their prowess by coming back with a quite superb try from full-back Scott Stewart, which owed much to outstanding support play from Steve Gray and my man of the match, hooker David Spiers. It was a flip pass by Spiers, under pressure, that was the key to the try.

For Fiji, there were soon to be signs of frustration as Canada knocked them down and denied them possession by putting emphasis on the set piece, and closing down the Fijians close in. The containment job was working well. Gareth Rees, the former Harrow schoolboy and Wasps fly-half, kicked a penalty goal to make Canada's half-time lead 7–3. The harmonious chorus of Fijian supporters began to fade.

Canada's forward effort was unrelenting, and behind them Gareth Rees was doing what Serevi, his opposite number, had palpably failed to do in the first half – use the wind to kick his side deep into opposition territory. The odd break out from

Fiji – by Seru, Serevi or Nadruku – was all they could muster, whilst Canada's ever more effective forward superiority held sway.

Behind the front five, Glen Ennis, the outstanding Al Charron and Gord MacKinnon were winning the battle for the loose ball; Chris Tynan sniping at their heels. They never lost control and neutralised the athleticism and spontaneity of Savai and Tawake as the crowd willed more magical moments from the team who love to run and run.

The stark contrast of styles ensured that this would be a riveting contest until the final whistle – but one always sensed that Canadian efficiency and superior forward strength would win the day. Two further penalty goals by Gareth Rees in the final quarter were just reward, and made Canada safe in a spectacle that went a long way to making amends for the disappointments of the anti-climactic event 24 hours earlier.

It was a game that gave clear notice, too, that Canada had truly arrived on the world scene. Said Fijian manager Dr Josaia Taka afterwards, 'One thing's for sure, we can't play as badly twice in a row.' For Fiji the prospects looked bleak – the game is about possession of the ball, and in the ball-winning department, Fiji had been exposed.

As important as the stirring performance of the teams who produced splendid entertainment in difficult conditions was that of Australian referee Kerry Fitzgerald, who earned praise all round for his more sympathetic handling of the match, a greater tolerance in application of the advantage law that had disrupted earlier games in the tournament.

So, as the show moved across and up country, to the Alpine outpost of rugby in Grenoble, the pundits printed reams of comment in assessing the relative merits of the four pool contestants who had now been seen in action. On the reasonable assumption that the first ingredient of success is forward strength, already it was being mooted that Canada were the side best equipped to beat France for the top position in the group.

The approach to Grenoble from the south is magnificent as quite suddenly, you come upon the majestic ranges of the Alps all around as you drive into this principal rugby centre of central south-east France. The friendliness and informality of the French hosts in this section of the World Cup was again in great evidence, and

Right: Philippe Sella, the brilliant French centre, keeps Fiji at arms length during the pool match played in Grenoble. It was an impressive return after injury for Sella.

Below: Abdel Benazzi (with headguard) and Eric Champ initiate a rolling maul in a period of French ascendancy in the comfortable win over Fiji in Grenoble.

once more, too, the setting and the enthusiasm for the game was fully in evidence.

As one comes to expect at any venue south of Lyon, the weather and conditions were perfect. So, too, the ground itself with the Lesdiguières Stadium resplendent with a new 12,000 seater stand and, imaginatively, flags unfurled beneath the excellent floodlights, which not only cut a swathe of daylight brightness across the field, but attracted the night-flying moths, it would seem, from the whole of the region.

Once again there was a capacity crowd, and an intensity of noise to greet France on the day when the players and the public knew that a more consistent performance was required if they were to be deemed realistic challengers for the World Cup title. For Fiji it was 'make or break' time, and five changes smacked of panic as front row, back row, scrum-half and centre were all altered.

Memories were fresh of the tussle France had in subduing the Fijians (31–16) en route to the 1987 World Cup Final, but expectations were high that with Sella back at centre, and Lafond, ever the catalyst, keeping the place of the injured

59

Lagisquet, things would only get better. Surely the forwards would not be so careless as in Béziers four days previously?

The Fijian challenge thrown down in the Ciba (courteously looked upon by the French players, and received with acclamation by the crowd – to put the absurd sensitivities to such traditional 'war dances' in perspective) the game started ideally for the demoralised guests. A line-out infringement in the opening minute provided Koroduadua with an easy penalty goal – easy, that is, if one discounts the irritating barrage of noise that greets visiting kickers in France.

But that was the last time Fiji were to lead. From then on it was all problems, from the moment prop forward and captain Mosese Taga had to leave the field injured. French confidence and fluency blossomed thereafter – and was soon rewarded when Sella marked his return in spectacular style with a change of pace and a magnificent try.

For Fiji, once again, all was frustration and discomfort, as Derek Bevan had no choice but to penalise their forwards for persistently falling or diving over the ball on the ground. A Camberabero penalty to add to his touchline conversion gave France a 6-point buffer. The pack dominated possession and gradually one awakened to the fact that we were in the throes of witnessing a great midfield performance by Franck Mesnel and Philippe Sella, fed by Didier Camberabero and supported by Lafond and a rejuvenated Blanco. A Mesnel run, a Sella cut-back, and a supporting pack, created a memorable try for Lafond. Then Lafond scored once more, a try sparked by a magnificent 'gather' of the ball from the ground. It was 19–3 at half-time.

For Fiji it was rugby without the ball, mere scraps of possession from which the valiant Tawake at no. 8 and mercurial fly-half Waisele Serevi made occasional thrilling forays. But it was never going to be enough.

Forwards linking and rolling-off set up a try for Camberabero, superb interlacing of forwards and backs ensured a hat-trick for Lafond, and moments later Sella was through once more. It was mesmeric at times and a joy to behold. Alas, poor Fiji; a late, brave try by Naruma was small consolation.

This was France's night. Lessons had been learned from the Romania match; the tight five were rampant in the set-piece, and the platform perfect for an exhibition of those glorious skills that characterise French running rugby at its best.

Even new scrum-half Galthié had found his form and was razor-sharp. The only question in beating Fiji so handsomely was whether the size or style of victory really meant very much in the wider World Cup context.

Little was going right for Fiji – not even the broadcasting side, for the Fijian Broadcasting representative, Graham Eden, found himself debarred from the match in Grenoble as clearance for rights to radio commentary had not been fully given. Fiji did, however, hear the game live, reported by Graham down the telephone line whilst seeing the match on television in his hotel room. C'est la vie!

By the time the media circus moved to Toulouse for the fourth game in the pool, things had reached a critical stage for the pointless Fiji, and for Romania (who had drawn little comfort from their one defeat at the hands of France in Béziers) and for Canada (winners over Fiji). The outcome of the game at the vast municipal stadium would decide the two quarter-finalists should Canada win, or leave things wide open if Romania succeeded.

Toulouse has seldom been a popular international venue, although it has a 35,000 all-seated capacity. Even the attraction of France versus New Zealand in 1986 was insufficient to fill more than half the stands. For Canada v Romania, the attendance was little more than 4000.

A game that could be decisive then, and which brought changes to both team selections. From Canada's cosmopolitan squad – that included names emanating from Romania (Radu), Hungary (Szabo), Czechoslovakia (Svoboda), Scotland (MacKinnon), Netherlands (van den Brink), Denmark (Robertsen, though he is South African born) and the Bermudan-born Welshman, Wyatt. Mark Wyatt, who had suffered from a pulled hamstring in training, was at last able to take the field, whilst surprisingly, Bruce Breen was nominated in place of Al Charron, and Karl Svoboda for David Spiers.

Romania opted for Ioan Doja in place of Guranescu, whilst suspect defence by Sava against France resulted in the return of Nicolae Fulina.

For centre Adrian Lungu there was a Romanian record-equalling 70th cap. The omens for Romania were not propitious – as coach Ianusievici put it: 'France murdered us in the scrum... the team were devastated by the defeat because they honestly

Gareth Rees of Canada makes off with the ball in the match which confirmed Canada's status as contenders for the quarter-finals – the pool win over Romania.

believed they would win. In order to rebuild the side we had to find a way to rekindle the flame; so I began by emphasising the good things, player by player, that we had achieved in the first 60 minutes.

'I arranged to be interrupted when I was about to analyse for them the dreadful last 20 minutes. Deliberately I never restarted the meeting, but left the team with positive vibes, although I later spoke to individuals about their shortcomings, and as much as anyone to scrum-half Daniel Neaga.'

It was an interesting technique to apply, inspired by Ianusievici's sports psychologist wife, Viorica. Ross Cooper, the assistant coach, appealed to the players' self-pride and team spirit for this, their last chance.

For Canada's part, Mike Luke felt that his selection changes were required to fit the changed strengths of the new opponents. And from the start these strengths were evident as Romania began with effective use of the driving maul and at last found their more ambitious attacking style that had

deserted them against France. But a loose pass, a superb tackle (by Canadian full-back Wyatt) deprived Romania of early scores. The ferocity of the Romanian forward effort was certainly of a greater intensity and was only repulsed by brave Canadian defence. Yet with only their second foray into Romanian territory in the first 35 minutes, Canada took the lead through a Wyatt penalty goal after Dumitru was caught in possession trying to counter-attack in total isolation.

A dislocated shoulder compounded the hurt for the luckless full-back, but an equalising penalty by Nichitean levelled the score at half-time. But thereafter, it was once more the Canadian pack which grasped the initiative. An awkward bounce, missed in goal by Dumitras, let MacKinnon in for one try and kept Romania under persistent pressure; and gradually, the Romanian scrummage gave way.

It was a collapsed scrummage at which Ennis broke away for the second try. At 3–13, Romania went for broke and ironically played their best rugby of the tournament for, with Racean moving to full-back he launched a series of brilliant running counter-attacks, finally creating a superb try when linking with Fulina, who put Lungu through for the score – Lungu's 30th for his country, and Romania's first of the World Cup.

Undeterred, Canada re-established their game with typical efficiency and were rewarded by a huge Rees drop goal, before Romania were allowed the last, valiant word – Racean cut loose, linked with the forwards, first Dumitras, then Dinu, with the link to winger Sasu for a fine try.

Again, the reward was there when Romania found the confidence for the enterprising attacking style of rugby that we had first seen at work in August against Scotland in Bucharest. This time it came too late, but not before it had stretched the Canadians to the limit.

As Mike Luke put it 'this game revealed a side of Romanian rugby we had never seen before; spectacular, enterprising, a real confrontation'. In sharing the joy of his players and Rugby Canada in thus achieving their first goal of making the last eight in the World Cup, he also added pertinently: 'We are fed up with being patronised, having to suffer the condescending attitude of the so-called established nations. Who are they to give us a pat on the shoulder and tell us "Well done, boys!"' A fair remark.

For Romania, there was some consolation in knowing that they had gone down in style but as Ianusievici acknowledged afterwards: 'Our scrum again disintegrated; Stan is only 22, and a makeshift tight-head prop, though I thought the new cap, Viad, did significantly well for our scrummage when replacing Leonte in the second-half. We paid the price, though, for our naivety, and a bit of bad luck.'

Not surprisingly, the game in Brive three days later had lost some of its edge now that the two qualifying teams for the quarter-finals were known. For Fiji and Romania there remained only the incentive of pride and the earnest hope of salvaging a win from the pool matches. Nothing could really have been expected to assuage the hurt after high hopes in both camps, that a success would follow on the one hand for Romania after their real triumph pre-World Cup over Scotland and, on the other, after Fiji's severe testing of England the previous July.

With no chance of progressing further, there was much to commend Dr Taka's decision to select a side with nine changes, thus ensuring that every Fijian player in the squad would have taken part in a World Cup game.

Romania finally switched Stan to his normal loose-head slot, with Viad retained, and fellow newcomer Nicusor Martin, a mighty flanker from Constantia, replaced the injured Doja.

An added twist to the clash was provided by the respective team coaches from New Zealand: on the one hand, Fijian advisor George Simpkin, former coach of Waikato, and now coaching development officer for Hong Kong RFU; on the other, Romania advisor Ross Cooper, former coach of Thames Valley and currently New Zealand U19 coach, whose influence alongside Ianusievici had helped to change Romania's long-standing, dour forward-orientated style into something infinitely more appealing and enterprising, and who had taken unpaid leave from his school in Waikato to lend a hand.

Having seen the Romanians in training in their summer tour of New Zealand, he felt he could not just stand by and see them languish in the sterility of approach to their match preparations. Now there is a change – short, sharp and intensive pressure sessions – and within a year or two the rewards will come. Perhaps for Cooper and Ianusievici the compliment paid by Adrian Lungi is the most apt. As the veteran of the game took the field for a Romanian record 71st cap (surpassing the tally of Constantin Dinu), he said: 'I wish I were ten years younger!'

With the pressure valves released, it was likely that this farewell outing for Fiji and Romania would present a fine spectacle. It certainly proved to be just that, and even a little bizarre. A hatful of mistakes could not detract from the spectacular proceedings in a game in which there was no clearly identifiable pattern.

Turuva, replacing the lacklustre Koroduadua, kicked an opening penalty and Fiji went further ahead with a pair of monstrous drop goals from the diminutive fly-half Rabaka. In between, all was mayhem. Nichitean was having a nightmare, after running like a headless chicken without clear intent, and failing to perceive that something a little more clinical and less ambitious might suit his side rather better against Fiji.

Eventually, the Romanians reverted to what we know they can do well – good line-out possession, good driving play, tying in the Fijian fringers. The forwards called the tune and Ion, the hooker, rounded off a great surge begun by Marin, carried on by Dumitras, Ciorescu and Cojocariu, to score under the posts. Nichitean converted.

Amidst a plethora of mistakes and penalties awarded by Irish referee Doyle, Racean added a penalty for a 9–6 half-time lead for Romania.

As Rabaka landed another massive drop goal to level the scores, one was left to question whether the rugby world was turning upside down. Here were Fiji depending on kicks to score points and looking to attack by playing kick and chase and, paradoxically, Romania, so long respected for that particular art, having a disastrous day with the boot – first through Racean and Nichitean, and later from Nichitean's nervous replacement Ilie Ivancive – and resorting to the handling game as the only means of scoring points.

Turuva kicked yet another massive drop goal, then Dumitras responded by setting the driving example to his Romanian team. From a line out peel, Dumitras pounded up in support and with the goal line in his sights careered headlong like a charging rhino, bouncing would-be defenders in his path, for the try that put Romania in front for the first time, 13 points to 12.

It proved to be a killer blow for the Fijians, the brittle confidence cracked and the East Europeans rallied once more around Dumitras, who was playing probably his farewell international game. With another power drive, the ball passed through six forwards before the captain set it on to Sasu for the try.

But it was yet another disastrous day for place-kicking and there was still only a five-point margin, a slender lead that left a ray of hope for Fiji. Romania, time and again, failed to put their kicks to touch and gave a free ball away and at last, the Fijians came alive – sparked by the counter-attack running of the smallest man on the field, winger Kalaveti Naisoro. A Romanian defensive error, and a subsequent penalty goal by Turuva, was reward for unrelenting pressure.

Now there were three points in it and now Fiji were on the rampage – and surely a last-ditch triumph it would have been but for left wing Lucian Colceriu's try-saving tackle on full-back Turuva. It may have cost the Romanian two split lips and a broken nose – but it saved the game for his country. The final whistle came to relieve Romania, and to send the despondent, seeded Fijians home with scant reward – but many French friends.

It may not have been according to the plan of action but there was a smile on the face of the Romanian coach as he admitted, 'We asked them to play a tight controlled game, and not to run unnecessarily. The players did the opposite. They won – perhaps they were right!' And for Dumitras, some ultimate consolation, 'This is the first game I enjoyed. We peaked too early against Scotland. The players and I would like to start the World Cup right now.'

The Fijians weren't saying much at all. They are not great travellers, they are seldom at ease away from home, and yet again one shared their disappointment. Still, there's another Hong Kong Sevens on the horizon.

There was one small matter left to be resolved as the final match in Pool Four beckoned at the Stade Armandie in beautiful Agen. Here, many would avow, is the present day French home of rugby, not in terms of size as a rugby town or its 15,000 capacity stadium, nor indeed its historical connections with the Barbarians – the original ones who invaded the city in the fifth century AD. But rather for its local emphasis on rugby, the success of its club in the French Championship Final over the last 30 years, its ranks of illustrious international players from Guy Basquet to Philippe Sella, and an added focus of attention provided by the home presence of President of the FFR, Albert Ferrasse, for 30 years 'le roi soleil' of French rugby.

All that remained to be decided here was which of the two competing teams would face New Zealand and which would meet England in the quarter-final ties. Personally, being one of the very few who had for a long time maintained that the England threat was no less great than that of the All Blacks, I was far from convinced that the reward for winning, and the fun of playing England, was any reward at all.

No doubt, though, that France felt convinced that to be at home at the Parc des Princes against England was to be preferred to playing New Zealand in Lille, and that for both teams, most significant of all was the need to bolster confidence by the very act of winning again.

I gained the impression, though, that few Frenchmen had taken full cognizance of Canada's impressive form and did not countenance much of a challenge from the ambitious North Americans. They – and the French team – were in for

Above: Philippe Saint-André of France leads the field in France's hard-fought win over Canada in Agen. The match decided Pool 4 in France's favour.

Right: Laurent Cabannes injected much-needed pace into the French side in the tournament. Here, he bursts into the clear through desperate Canadian tackling in a generally poor French performance in Agen.

something of a shock. As Blanco was to suggest immediately post-match, 'It was a case of over-confidence.'

For Canada, success was no forlorn hope. Their pack had performed with as much discipline and efficiency as any I had seen up to that point in the whole competition. And what they might be deemed to be lacking in top experience and technical expertise they certainly compensated for in physical resources – sheer size — and those two aforementioned attributes.

Moreover, they were in my view the most 'together' of the 16 nations, knowing precisely what they were about and totally 'at one' with themselves. Quite simply, they knew they were pretty good and had self-confidence and no fear of failure as they approached the biggest game in their rugby history.

French coach Dubroca, no doubt, found it hard to instil in his troops the reality of the challenge –

but he, too, spoke before the match in slightly presumptuous tones, 'Canada is a little England. They play like the English and the game against them should provide France with a good general rehearsal for the match with England.' His words seemed to endorse the general French lack of respect for Canadian rugby. In the end, far from being a rehearsal, it was more like a fight for survival.

It started with the line-out, where Norm Hadley played the game of his life and gave Olivier Roumat a game to forget. Ennis also prospered at the tail and only Champ really enabled France to maintain a balance of possession in that set-piece.

So too in the set-scrum, from the moment early on that France attempted an eight-man shove, only to find themselves reeling at the Canadian push.

Over-enthusiasm, however, usually means errors and Camberabero kicked the penalty goal after the Canadian backs were caught off-side. Once more, too, Laurent Cabannes made his mark as France's most impressive forward in this tournament, supporting first Champ on the drive, and setting up Galthié through Camberabero, Blanco, and finally the ubiquitous Lafond arrived from the distant flank, to score on the left.

Ten minutes played, and with Camberabero's conversion, a nine-point lead established. One sensed then that the French presumed that the Canadian fire was already doused. But the Canadian effort proved itself throughout the World Cup to be rather like one of those birthday cake candles, that miraculously manages to re-ignite itself. Not once was their inner blazing desire and determination extinguished.

Over-confidence breeds carelessness and the French began to run in isolation and lose cohesion; Benazzi, for example, gave away the ball in a tackle; Blanco lost track on one of those romantic marauding runs. Lafond became the key 'tidy-upper' of many loose ends.

A French scrummage collapse provided Canada's first penalty goal points. The restored Chris Tynan, at scrum-half, chipped away with canny kicks and probing runs, and what some may have lacked in positional awareness they made up for in unrelenting effort.

A French offside, awarded by referee Stephen Hilditch, saw Wyatt off target again but Canadian confidence grew. They could see that France were unsettled, and the Evans/Svoboda/Jackart front-row combination lost nothing by comparison with the much-vaunted trio of Lascubé, Marocco and Ondarts.

It was France who proceeded to make the errors, and they reeled as a power-packed Canadian forward drive set up one of the best World Cup tries. A sharp feed by Tynan, clever midfield work between Rees, Lecky and Stewart, and Wyatt was over to score on the left. France 9, Canada 7.

Further worries followed for France as first Camberabero was crushed by a MacKinnon tackle. A cracked rib took him off the field and out of the World Cup, to be replaced by Thierry Lacroix. Soon after, Sella was in the wars and limped off the field to be replaced by Jean-Luc Sadourny, a new cap, who moved to the wing, with Saint-André moving into the centre.

In fact, it was from the centre position that Saint-André (of Twickenham try fame in the Grand Slam game of 1991) scored the second French try after a neat switch with Galthié and Lafond, which left the Canadian defence mesmerised. France appeared, finally, to take command as Lafond added a further penalty goal, and a Sadourny try would have spelt the coup de grâce but for a violent outburst by Pascal Ondarts, not for the first time in the game, which caused the 'try' to be disallowed – and Ondarts to be severely reprimanded.

Again, as if the incident provided the signal, back came Canada, with a newly-raised forward effort rewarded by a drop goal from Rees. The nine-point margin was restored to France by a Lacroix penalty goal, but appropriately it was Canada who had the final word with a Rees penalty that kept Canada within a converted try of France's total to the final whistle.

France had won the game, and the right to play England; Canada had won something even more precious – a place amongst the best nations in world rugby. As Mark Wyatt, Canada's captain, said succinctly: 'The days when the top eight nations could sit comfortably and patronise us are gone.' Mike Luke added, 'This was a clash between equals. This is our main achievement... It was an emotional game, exhausting, but this side is governed by a healthy calmness... Tynan's response to Ondarts' brutal attack, refusing to be intimidated by a heavyweight, that was the symbol of Canada's challenge.'

Daniel Dubroca said, 'This was a very good side. In a strange way, though disappointed with the performance of the French forwards I am happy that they suffered such a rude shock. It woke us up before the match with England. I have to admit that Canada is a fine side, very strong up front and resourceful behind, with excellent defence. Calm, composed, even serene.'

So Pool Four was done. Lille and Parc des Princes beckoned. France had achieved their first target, but without convincing me that they had the potential to fulfil their ultimate ambition of going one step further than in 1987. Romania had shown eventually with their new young squad that an exciting era could await them if they stick to their fresh approach; Fiji, once more had sadly failed to cope with the basics of the forward game, but left us, as ever, with some cherished moments to savour; but most important of all, Canada had earned universal respect and a place in the front rank of world rugby. The 'old order' would never be quite the same again – thank goodness!

IT WAS THE STRANGEST THING BUT, AS HE PREPARED

TO TAKE THE CONVERSION, HE FOUND HIMSELF REALLY

FANCYING A *Gordon's & Tonic* WITH LEMON.

THE PAIN OF ELIMINATION, THE JOY OF EMBARRASSMENT

STEPHEN JONES

The World Cup stories of the eight countries eliminated at the pool stage. Some subsided rather meekly; others made the supposedly elite teams fight for survival.

ARGENTINA

Argentina have threatened the old 'big eight' of world rugby nations more than any other country outside the supposed elite. Rugby in the country is strong, well-supported and well organised with a history stretching well back into the last century.

However, the timing of the first two World Cup tournaments was cruel to them – the 1987 event was too late, the 1991 event was too early. By 1987 the fierce and proud team they had built around the magical Hugo Porta, the fly-half and captain, was well past its best, was shocked by Fiji in the first pool game and never recovered.

Nor did the team recover quickly in the intervening years. The decision of the Argentina union to ban from test play those members of the squad who departed to play club rugby in Italy was a savage blow – if a brave one. The likes of Dengra, the prop, and Gomez, the scrum-half, are men of class.

However, the victory over the touring English at the Velez Sarsfield Stadium, Buenos Aires in 1990 in the second Test of a short series demonstrated some promise. By the time the All Blacks, forced to battle hard, had beaten the Pumas in the 1991 series in Argentina, it was obvious that Argentina were developing an outstanding young side; that if they could buy time till experience seeped in, then they were on the point of redevelopment.

Yet the World Cup showed that the side is still two years from any sort of peak. They have the world's most promising forward in the gigantic, teenage Frederico Mendez and two young locks of rich promise in German Llanes and Pedro Sporleder. They illustrated the possibilities when they shook Australia in the opening Pool Three match at Llanelli. They lost 32–19 but scored two outstanding

Lisandro Arbizu of Argentina boldly tries to check the progress of the formidable Peter Fatialofa of Western Samoa.

tries, both by Martin Teran on the right wing and indeed, if the Pumas had not started so diffidently they could even have won.

However, the inexperience began to show; first in disappointing defeat at Cardiff against Wales, when Argentina missed six penalties and a conversion and completely failed to build on the momentum of Llanelli. Lisandro Arhizu, the able fly-half, was unable to impose himself on a mediocre match.

Argentina would have made the quarter-finals if they had beaten Western Samoa in the final group match at Pontypridd but there was an air about the team, by then, which suggested that lack of experience was sapping self-belief; the Samoans, meanwhile, were far more purposeful and confident in their preparations. Samoa duly powered through,

with a late burst of scoring dumping Argentina to the tune of 35–12. Argentina, possibly unluckily, lost Sporleder, who was dismissed along with Keenan, his opposite number. Teran did manage another try but the team was overwhelmed and the early promise of Llanelli was a distant memory.

Nevertheless, the progress of the team will be watched with great interest in the next four-year cycle because the Pumas certainly have it in them to challenge strongly. Certainly, their pack will become a fearsome proposition. especially at home, if they continue to develop together. They played bravely, they had the skills. It was just that they did not know enough.

FIJI

The Fijians perform their Ciba as they signal the start of their World Cup campaign in Bayonne. However, they were to lose all three group matches and were the tournament's under-achievers.

Fiji is a paradise, and a paradise for followers of rugby. There are 600 clubs in the Fijian Islands, the largest concentration of clubs per capita of any country in the world. The players have outstanding natural talent and any time they take the field, there is always the chance of glorious running rugby and breathtaking skills, from forwards and backs alike.

Yet sometimes on tour, when the players are in culture shock and homesick for their homeland, they can be right off their game. In the French

Ivan Francescato of Italy is well supported by his forwards in the wonderful Italian effort against New Zealand at Leicester.

group, sometimes playing under unfamiliar floodlights, in bad weather, they never found themselves. They were fitful, tactically naive and they departed the competition without a win and with hardly a shot fired in resistance. They were the biggest single disappointment of the whole event because they have so much talent.

As they showed when playing the touring English in July, they also have a growing solidity in forward play as they try to marry natural talents with hard-nosed power. But in the 1991 World Cup, they never found the balance.

They never recovered from the Bayonne experience. They opened their campaign in Bayonne under lights and on a cool, wet and gloomy evening; for them, the conditions were alien and it showed. Against the powerful, pragmatic and motivated Canadians, they went down by 3–13.

Some of their play was desperate. For example, with the wet ball the obvious tactic was for Waisale Serevi, their fly-half, to hoist high kicks to test the defence. He actually put up six inch-perfect Garryowens above the Canadian full-back or wings. On five of those six occasions, either Nadruku or another following back gave away a penalty for interfering with the catcher before the ball arrived, missing five golden chances to win, at least, an attacking scrum and possibly even a try.

Taga, the giant prop and captain, and Savai, the lock, were at or near their best but there was no momentum or discipline or tactical plan.

They never looked like shaking off that disappointment. They moved on to Grenoble to meet France and were well beaten, by 33–9. It was their

ill-fortune to meet what was in many ways the best French effort of the whole tournament and there was to be no consolation win either because in the final group match against Romania in Brive, Fiji brought in all the players in their squad who were yet to appear in the tournament and they found Romania too keen and experienced. Romania won 17–15. However, at least there was some assured Fijian running in a match that was often delightful.

It was just that the final glimpses of what they could have achieved left them even more disappointed. They still have the ability to produce outstanding teams but they need to work on the marriage of the natural and the pragmatic. They need to become more worldly, more able to laugh off inconvenience of climate and surroundings. The world needs Fiji to be strong and a delight.

ITALY

Italy have never managed to capitalise on the strength of their clubs but this tournament brought clear evidence that they are the coming power in European rugby. They were in a desperately difficult group, having to play England at Twickenham and then the All Blacks a few days later at Leicester. Fresh in the memory was the 70-point drubbing they suffered in the opening game of the 1987 World Cup, against New Zealand.

But they coped wonderfully well, they provided some of the tournament's best moments and best players and no doubt, provided vast encouragement for the game in their country.

They had a superb half-back partnership of Ivan

Francescato and Diego Dominguez, the former a bustling, barking scrum-half and the latter one of the most talented tactical controllers in the tournament. They had a fine, competitive line-out man in Gianbattista Croci and outstanding young back row men in Roberto Saetti and Carlo Checchinato. Moreover, they had a powerful scrum and neither England nor New Zealand had much change from them in the tight play.

The front row depth of the squad was outstanding considering they did not even have to call on Rossi, the prop who played for the European XV in the Romanian relief match at Twickenham while elsewhere behind the scrum, there was competence and experience.

The Italians began the tournament in delightful fashion when they beat the United States in a storming and vastly entertaining match at Otley and they came through by 30–9. The highlight was a brilliant, individual try by Francescato, who shot down the front of a line-out, sidestepped violently off his right foot and reached the line.

The Italians complained that the backdrop of the Otley stadium was not the sort of scene to inspire TV viewers at home but they certainly enjoyed the warmth of Otley's welcome and their own excellence.

Their last pool match may well have been the high point of Italian rugby to date, because they held the All Blacks to 21–31 in front of a Leicester crowd which supported them unashamedly and which received two Italian tries – by Bonomi and Marcello Cuttita – with something approaching rapture and the determined Italian tackling stopped New Zealand in their tracks after the favourites had taken a commanding lead at half-time.

In between Otley and Leicester was sandwiched the date at Twickenham and this was a different story. The final score, 36–6 in favour of England, was just about acceptable to the Italians but the match left a sour taste. The Italians were penalised unmercifully by Brian Anderson, the referee, for what he and many others saw as the Italian attempt to kill the game by diving over the ball at rucks and creeping offside round the fringes. An astronomical penalty count shut Italy out of the game and also had them claiming that they were upset by the rush of penalties. It took the excellent effort at Leicester in a total contrast, to set the record straight.

Italy should become even more of a force in the FIRA (European) championships if they can build on this World Cup effort. The draw means that their

Doddie Weir, the Scottish lock, makes a magnificent clean take against the Japanese, who never really compensated for their lack of line-out capability.

prospects of reaching the knock-out stage were always grim, but at their best, they were accomplished and they were one of the teams to give the World Cup a special flavour.

JAPAN

The popularity of the sport in Japan, where rugby has been played since early in the century and where the top players have the same status as film stars, has been well-documented, as have two major problems of Japanese rugby – the lack of space for grounds, and the lack of size of their forwards.

Indeed, as teams around the world worked out their counters to the various Japanese line-out ruses, Japanese rugby at national level declined in the 1980s – they conceded a century of points to the All

Blacks in 1987. Their stature makes tackling a problem too.

However, in this tournament they had – just – enough size and power to scrape together some set-piece possession, usually through their own well-set scrum and the line-out efforts of Oyagi and Tifaga. They were still shut out of large periods of their games against Scotland and Ireland, which they lost 9–47 and 16–32 respectively and it was only against Zimbabwe in the final pool match that they won their share of ball.

Yet when Japan did win possession during the tournament, the effect was delightful and often, shattering. They played such a fast, alert and skilful short-passing game in the backs and they supported so assiduously that they created some of the most dazzling movements of the World Cup. They scored excellent tries against Scotland and Ireland, with a brilliant try out of defence created by a dazzling run from Yoshito Yoshida standing among the tries of the tournament. They made Ireland appear slow and stale with the vivacity of their play. Toshiyuki

Hayashi, the former captain and Oxford University prop, had an amazing game, appearing all over the field and running in a well-deserved try after a brilliant Japanese movement.

Against Zimbabwe, on more or less equal terms, the Japanese were nothing less than brilliant. They ran almost every ball, bursting with ideas and almost overloaded with support. They won, remarkably, by 52–8 and provided a rich treat for a large crowd at Ravenhill, in Belfast – it was the only match in the province.

Japan left with heads held high. They know themselves that for the forseeable future, they will have built-in problems. 'We always tried to develop big forwards of 6' 3'' and 6'4'',' says Shiggy Konno, the most famous administrator in Japanese rugby, 'But now that we are developing this sort of player we find that the world has moved on and the forwards are all 6'8'' and more. Still, we will keep trying.'

ROMANIA

Rugby in Romania was brought dramatically into the spotlight during the revolution in the country because the first man to lose his life in the fighting was, it is thought, Florica Murariu, the former international captain. Several other well-known players were also killed.

This connection with the game gave rise to the

Daniel Neaga, Romania's scrum-half, enjoys the rare luxury of good possession as he sends the ball out to his fly-half against the French in Béziers.

various Rugby for Romania fund-raising efforts and also put Romanian rugby under the microscope. The game was desperately impoverished during the Ceaucescu years and has remained so ever since – the upshot has been that sometimes, the preparation and morale of the team has been rock-bottom and they have been easy to beat.

Yet there has been the occasional flash of the true excellence of a country where rugby has been played for over 90 years. Romania gained a famous victory over France in Auch in 1990 and just a few weeks before the World Cup, they beat Scotland in Bucharest. They also coped passably well with a tough tour of New Zealand, where they finally began to shake off the old hidebound forward game and bring their talented backs into the action.

The key match for them in the World Cup, and the one which doomed them to departure in the pool, was that against Canada in Toulouse. They had already lost to the French and the Canada match was effectively for a place in the quarter-finals. Yet Romania were disappointing and never managed to cope with the beefy and highly-motivated Canadians. They lost 19–11.

They did finish on a high note when they beat Fiji in a match in which they played with some abandon and in which the virtues of the side were allowed to show through.

Overall, the Romanians had a satisfactory tournament. They lost by 30–9 against the French in Béziers in a night match but although the score is conclusive the match was far closer than that.

The French scored many of their points in a late rush and Romania competed hard for the first hour, could easily have set up a decent lead had not Neculae Nichitean, their young fly-half, not missed the target with a barrage of penalty attempts and had the referee, Les Peard, not awarded France a penalty try for deliberate wheeling of the scrum, a decision which looked extremely harsh.

Romania's inspiration was, as usual, the wholehearted Hari Dumitras in the back row. They had an effective pair of locks in Constantin Cojocariu and Sandu Ciorescu and a crop of new young backs, thriving in the new tactical freedoms. Romanian rugby will be watched with interest. If the potential can be tapped and the problems overcome, then they will return to the unofficial first division of world rugby.

UNITED STATES OF AMERICA

The massive logistical problems of preparing, selecting and developing a national squad of rugby players in the USA have been well-documented, as has the amazing dedication of officials and players in the cause of overcoming those problems and tapping the enthusiasm of American players.

At the start of this tournament, however, disaster beckoned for the Eagles. Realistically, the only match they had a chance of winning was the Otley clash against the Italians but when the Eagles crashed 30–9 they faced annihilation – they still had to meet, inside three days, the might of New Zealand at Gloucester then England in front of a giant, capacity crowd at Twickenham.

The way the Eagles pulled themselves round was a wonder of the World Cup. They lost 46–6 to New Zealand and by 37–9 to England but there were no astronomical scores conceded and indeed, they were unlucky in the extreme to go down by so many points at Gloucester.

The inspiration of their team in those two matches, in the absence of captain Brian Vizard, injured at Otley, was undoubtedly Kevin Swords, the lock who drove himself and his team back to respectability. The American forwards were not quite quick enough or talented enough but they fought hard throughout in the set-pieces.

Behind the scrum, they had some accomplished players. Ray Nelson, the full-back, was outstanding and there were two competitive and lively scrum-halves in Barry Daily and Mike Pidcock.

At Otley, the Americans were caught cold. Italy were too sharp and too tactically aware. The USA had no tactical controller on the lines of Italy's Dominguez, their forwards were a foot too slow and they had no luck whatsoever. They had control for some periods but their only try was a driving effort by Swords from short range.

The tackling and general heroics against New Zealand delighted the knowledgeable Gloucester crowd and for a time, it seemed that a New Zealand score in the lower 30s, a major achievement for the USA, was on the cards. However, New Zealand finished strongly.

The USA were not at all perturbed by the massive attendance at Twickenham. Their tackling in the back row and midfield was outstanding, helped by some poor play by the England backs. The USA also scored a memorable try, when Mark Williams made a searing break and put Ray Nelson over with a spare man running free outside. To score at Twickenham was a lovely memory for Nelson and his team.

WALES

The fate of Wales, and the realisation that they would be the major and most embarrassed victim of the pool matches, was sealed when they lost to Western Samoa in a dramatic match at Cardiff. They could not recover because they were not remotely good enough to raise the prospect of beating Australia later in their group and even a lack-lustre win over Argentina still meant that they had to rely on other results going their way.

Some people said that the Welsh failure to qualify represented the lowest point in Welsh history. Certainly, it was a disaster and could even mean that Wales have to play in preliminary qualifying pools for the 1995 World Cup. The crippling lack of

Right: Kevin Swords, the Eagles lock who, in the opinion of some leading commentators, was one of the most powerful forwards of the tournament.

Below right: The disasters are still in the future as Phil May of Wales cleans up line-out possession tapped back by Kevin Moseley. Long before the end of this match against Samoa, May's World Cup was over due to a shoulder dislocation and Wales were heading towards the exit as well.

big and athletic forwards and of confidence in the squad and country show no sign of easing and the 3–38 defeat at the hands of Australia at Cardiff was the worst they have ever suffered at Cardiff.

On the other hand, there is evidence that Wales had made a sort of slow progress since the shaming days of their Australian tour when they were abject in heavy defeats and in their post-match behaviour. It was the task of Robert Norster and Alan Davies, the new manager and coach, to re-build a side in time for the tournament which had almost ceased to exist. It was an impossible job and there was bad luck all along the line – Mark Ring, on whom Davies set great store, had a knee operation a few weeks before the tournament and never looked fit; Phil May, another key man, departed the tournament with a shoulder dislocation in the opening stages of the Samoa match; then, at a crucial stage, Samoa were awarded a highly-dubious try when Robert Jones of Wales seemed clearly to reach the ball first as it bounced over the Welsh line.

However, on the run of play the dedicated and crash-tackling Samoans deserved their sensational day. They were better organised, they won a surprisingly high share of the line-out possession and their tackling ruined Welsh attacking instincts. Wales did play well late in the game, at last establishing continuity, but they never really looked like catching up and they went down 13–16.

They struggled past Argentina in a floodlit match but the 16–7 win was not impressive and was due in part to the fact that the Argentinians passed up a host of penalties with poor kicking. Paul Arnold scored the only Welsh try.

The debacle against Australia was caused by an almost total lack of line-out possession. The likes of Robert Jones, Emyr Lewis and Phil Davies fought manfully, as they had done throughout, but Wales could certainly not have complained if the score had been higher. There was not a single department in which they matched the Wallabies, somehow a fitting Welsh farewell to the tournament.

ZIMBABWE

It was always on the cards that Zimbabwe, despite their dedication and their bright approach, would provide the weakest team in the World Cup and so it proved. They lacked experience and although they produced some marvellous passages of play and some exciting tries, they could not sustain it for significant periods.

They will be hoping to enrich rugby in their country with the experience and will also be awaiting the uplift in national fortunes which is bound to come when the full effects of the rapid spread of the game to the black population of Zimbabwe are felt. Already, the number of clubs in the country has increased by 50% inside six years and this broadening of the base of the game is critical. Zimbabwe qualified by beating Ivory Coast, Morocco and Tunisia in the African Zone qualifying tournament but less encouraging were defeats against Namibia in the run-up to the tournament. The biggest disappointment was unquestionably the massive defeat at Ravenhill, Ulster against the inspired Japanese. Zimbabwe were never going to beat Ireland and Scotland but they felt they had a chance to break their World Cup duck. They were never in the hunt although they did contribute well to a fast-moving and highly entertaining match.

They concede 50 points in all three group matches although they did throw up some impressive individuals – notably in Adrian Garvey, the splendidly-mobile prop and Brian Currin, the full-back. Richard Tsimba, the centre, is still one of the most talented backs in the squad but although he managed a try against Japan in Belfast, he was not at his best and suffered, along with his fellow backs, at the lack of quality possession which came his way.

Zimbabwe were unlucky to find both Ireland and Scotland in a situation in which they could show no mercy. Both Ireland and Scotland had endured miserable lack of success in their warm-up matches before the tournament started so both teams had some sorting out to do in the pool matches. It was Zimbabwe who were sorted out – although as both the Irish and Scottish camps agreed afterwards, the Zimbabweans were a proud bunch and they kept their heads and their tackling until the end. Zimbabwe are bound to bounce back stronger as their rugby gathers strength.

Zimbabwe's forwards are highest in this Dublin pool match won comfortably by Ireland despite some stern resistance from the Zimbabwe defenders.

RESULTS WITHOUT THE RITUAL

Pensions &
Mortgages

Scottish Life
THE LIFE TO LEAD

THE MURRAYFIELD QUARTER-FINAL

SAMOA'S GLORIOUS BOW AGAINST DOMINANT SCOTS
BILL McLAREN

In the entire World Cup no group of players proved as uninhibited as the Western Samoans and this, coupled with their high levels of skill and their obvious enjoyment in playing the game, made them the most popular bunch in the tournament.

For a comparatively young side – Brian Lima, their right wing, was only 18 and their first choice loose forwards were 24, 23 and 21 – they took the distinctive atmosphere of Cardiff Arms Park and Murrayfield in their stride. This was attributable in large measure to the fact that, although professional in their preparations, they were very amateur in the fun they had at practice and match play and in the totally unaffected manner in which they approached the strong challenges they faced from Wales, Australia, Argentina, then Scotland. They didn't seem to regard defeat as a national disaster – disappointing perhaps, but only that. Their progress was avidly followed by everyone at home in Samoa.

They came to Edinburgh for the first of the quarter-finals on a high, after beating Wales (victory over a senior IB country for the first time) and Argentina. Their forwards had played a rather tired match against Argentina but they eventually won with a bit to spare through the brilliance of their back play. But two days of relaxation rekindled their zest and restored tired bodies; and despite the most evil conditions of bruising gale and occasional biting rain they demonstrated their huge New Zealand influence in two training sessions in Scotland that were taken right out of the All Black handbook.

Scotland's coach Ian McGeechan, was in no doubt about the quality of their challenge: 'They are a typical New Zealand side, reflecting the number of players who operate regularly in New Zealand. They know what their priorities are. They are particularly strong tacklers and that seems to have surprised people who do not have experience of the New Zealand game, but their tackling really is no more than you would expect from New Zealand.

'We played some very tough sides last year on our tour of New Zealand so we know how they play and tackle. We felt a lot of pressure before our Japan game. It was so important to know that we could go out there and do it. Now, with the pool matches over, this is all so different. This is now a case of 80 minutes to decide whether you go home or stay in. We just can't afford any mistakes. It'll be very tight stuff.'

Sean Lineen's withdrawal with knee damage on the Friday morning meant that a centre partnership with Scott Hastings, that had been functioning in 20 internationals, was interrupted. It had come within three of equalling the world record for centres of 23, held by Brendan Mullin and Michael Kiernan of Ireland. Happily for the Scots, Craig Chalmers was declared fit so that he joined Gary Armstrong as Scotland's halves for the 20th time and with Graham Shiel winning his second cap for Lineen, Scotland had Chalmers and Shiel in the same five-eighth positions in which they play for their club, Melrose. The Samoans seemed somewhat aggrieved to lose their appeal against the one-match suspension on their front line-out jumper, Mata'afa Keenan, ordered off in the pool game against Argentina. This prevented him playing against Scotland. He was big, he had proved a useful number two jumper, he had played in New Zealand. He would be a big loss although his replacement, Eddie Ioane, was even heavier. But the committee were quite right in punishing a player who, after referee Jim Fleming of Scotland had blown more than once, still had aimed several blows.

The Scotland-Western Samoa contest demonstrated once again that (**a**) the best way in which to stifle opponents who seek to spin the ball about the paddock is to limit their ammunition supply and, (**b**) that, even in the dry, weather conditions can have a big influence on the style of game embraced.

In the opening 40 minutes and playing against the strong, biting northerly wind, Scotland put together such an amalgam of torrid forward play and craft in

Left: Brian Lima, the brilliant young Samoan wing, veers infield at Murrayfield

Below: David Sole, the charging Scottish captain, menaces Steve Bachop, the Samoan fly-half, during a typical run.

punting as to deny the Samoans opportunities to play.

There were those who questioned Scotland's tactics of exploding Gavin Hastings early on like a launch missile up the narrow side of scrummage and ruck, but the effect was beneficial to the Scots. They had appreciated the swiftness and field coverage of the Samoan loose forwards – Sila Vaifale, Pat Lam and Apolo Perelini. Those lads moved about like jungle cats. By launching the burly Gavin Hastings, Scotland committed those lithe fellows to unglamorous chores close in, so eliminating them from destructive work amongst Scotland's backs. There was, too, the psychological effect of letting the Samoans know that Scotland could absorb any Samoan tackling they liked to deliver and that the Scots, too, could jar on contact. Gavin Hastings certainly does that, and he obviously revelled in this role of blind-side battering ram. The idea, apparently, was hatched by Jim Telfer.

Scotland kept the Samoans on the back foot for much of the first half by taking them on round the edges and in not giving them sitting targets to hit. Ian McGeechan explained later that the plan had been to keep the ball moving: 'If you are a relatively static target, the Samoans quite enjoy that. Our aim was to try to keep the ball moving and launch a series of different targets coming towards them.'

David Sole, Scotland's captain, actually had opted to play against the wind in the first half and as Scotland's team manager, Duncan Paterson, said after the game: 'We took everything they could throw at us yet we kept asking them more questions.'

There was therefore a contrast in tactics dictated by that strong wind. Scotland opted against too much punting in favour of fringe driving, keeping the ball close to their forwards. There was little of the expansive play that had marked their work against Japan and Zimbabwe. It paid off in that they reached half-time with a 13–3 lead and the elements to come. They had been behind to a Matthew Vaea penalty goal for going over and lost 10 metres for dissent.

Gavin Hastings then slotted the first of his six goals. He ended on 16 points – his third penalty goal was one of the biggest kicks ever seen at Murrayfield, from fully eight metres inside his own half. It brought to mind the penalty goal from over 64 metres by Paul Thorburn against the Scots at Cardiff in 1986. That seige-gun effort by Hastings effectively killed off the Samoans at 19-6.

When the Samoans faced the wind they also decided against over-punting but, in contrast, they placed their trust in their flair for ball-handling expertise by spinning it about the field in a manner that set fire to the match as a spectacle and, in so doing, placed a question mark over some of Scotland's tackling. It helped them also that the Scots went fractionally off the boil. Perhaps their concentration faltered but as soon as the Samoans began to nibble some useable ball they underlined just how lethal they can be in handling sequences.

Frank Bunce, their second five-eighth from Auckland, made inroads by bouncing off a few tacklers, there was some snaky running and sweet distribution by Steve Bachop, the 18-year-old Brian

Lima gave one telling demonstration of his explosive qualities and the personality of the day undoubtedly emerged in the shape of the 15 stone left-wing who plays for Wellington, Timo Tagaloa. With his upright carriage, superb balance and a subtle body-sway at pace, he gave the 23-year-old Scottish wing, Tony Stanger, a very hard time, not to mention sundry other Scots as well.

Indeed, the Samoans created at least two good try-scoring opportunities which did not come to fruition because of badly delivered final passes. The Auckland no. 8 Pat Lam, also proved a powerful force.

One other big difference between the sides was in the deployment of their loose forward trios. Each of the Samoans proved hard to sink but their individual bursts were not well enough supported, whereas whenever one of the Scottish breakaways got up a head of steam you could be sure that the other two would be stuck to him like bits of fly-paper. Not only that, but the Scottish tight five would not be far away.

It had been an outstanding feature of Scotland's entire World Cup campaign that not only did they possess one of the most mobile packs in the competition but undoubtedly one of the fittest as well. Scotland's 'loosies' were immense, John Jeffrey playing one of the games of his life, apart from his two tries and a record 11 in internationals by a Scottish forward.

No higher tribute could be paid to Jeffrey, Finlay Calder and Derek White than that by the Samoan openside flanker, Perelini, who told Graham Law, Rugby Correspondent of *The Scotsman*, that the Samoans had been well aware of the experience of Scotland's breakaways, that as a schoolboy he had watched them on television and, after facing them he now rated them as just superb. He would always respect them.

So although the Scots had one or two testing moments as the Samoans swung the play right, then left, and as Tagaloa thundered among them to notable effect, drawing from Gary Armstrong and Gavin Hastings, in particular, some choice items of tackle and cover, a try count of 3–0 was sufficient indication of how Scotland had controlled so much of the exchanges.

The try by Stanger, his 13th for third place in the all time Scottish list behind Ian Smith (24) and Iwan Tukalo (15), was attributable to a Samoan defensive error brought about by the capacity 54,000 crowd swelling their roar of support. Chalmers hung up a deft punt. Lam, running back in defence, called for the ball as his full-back, Andrew Aiolupo converged, but the great wall of sound from the audience drowned Lam's call. It really should have been left to the full-back. Lam and Aiolupo got in each other's way and Stanger only had to gather in the bounce and fall over the line.

Jeffrey's two tries stemmed from forward stampedes. The first was launched by a Gary Armstrong tap-kick from which Jeffrey and John Allan, in great form, were at the head of a white tidal wave (Scotland played in white to avoid a colour clash) that ended with Jeffrey scooping up delivered ball for the try. Gavin Hastings converted with a splendid kick against and part-across the wind.

The second owed much to Doddie Weir's tap down that ignited consecutive thrusts by Allan, Sole, White and Chris Gray, with Armstrong putting in his penny-worth like a fired-up flanker before Jeffrey, once again, picked up and kept low enough in the drive to make the line.

WHAT THEY SAID:

PAT LAM
(Western Samoa No.8)

" I shouted to Andrew Aioluipo that I would take Chalmers' kick but in the din he never heard me and so we collided as we went for the ball.

" If the Scottish forwards play like they did against us and the crowd give the same kind of support I think you can beat anyone at Murrayfield, even the All Blacks. You could see it in the players' eyes that they were really built up and I knew we were in for a tough game. "

MARK BIRTWHISTLE
(Western Samoan lock)

" I thought it was Scotland's best display in the World Cup so far and I was most impressed by my opposite number Doddie Weir. He played very well and certainly made my job very hard. I think they have an excellent chance of going all the way.

" We were disappointed we could not get into the game in the first half, especially as we had the wind, but at least we played some good rugby after the interval. "

APOLO PERELINI
(Western Samoan flanker)

" We knew of the experience of the Scottish back-row. As a schoolboy I watched them on TV, yet after facing them what can I say? I will always respect them. They were superb. "

BRYEN WILLIAMS
(Western Samoan technical adviser and former All Black)

" I think the intensity of their forward effort surprised our fellows. "

JOHN JEFFREY
(Scottish flanker)

" I honestly believe that the first half of this match was the best 40-minute performance ever from a Scottish side. "

GAVIN HASTINGS
(Scottish full-back)

" I don't know if people appreciated just how big a factor the wind was. Rather than kick into touch in the first-half, and maybe only gain five or six yards, we decided to try to keep the ball close to the rucks and mauls. Maybe we should have done it even more, because a few kicks got caught by the wind.

" I'm just pleased to be making a contribution to Scotland's success and, of course, I'm delighted with my form. It comes from fitness, confidence and a lot of other factors. Most importantly, it comes from being part of a team that has such a good spirit it helps to bring out the best in individual players.

" Look at Gary Armstrong. After his performance against the Irish, he was just outstanding again on Saturday. In fact, there are a lot of guys in the Scotland side playing at the top of their form. "

And on his goal-kicking:
" It hasn't just happened by accident, I've practised very hard and put a lot of concentration into the kicking. It's a vitally important part of the game. "

Left: Graham Shiel, the Scottish centre, chips over the Samoan centres. Vaega (13) and Bunce were among the hardest tacklers in the event.

Sila Viafale has possession for Samoa yet a gang of Scots are closing on him.

All the Samoans had to show for some delightful play in the second half was a Bachop drop goal, struck with exquisite timing just as he had been doing in practice at Murrayfield on the previous afternoon. But, having given so much to the World Cup in their team-work and their *joie-de-vivre*, at no-side they provided one of those marvellous spontaneous acts – a lap of honour, and a repeat performance of their war dance, the Manu Samoa. Murrayfield had never seen the like before. They loved it. It brought the house down in the warmest standing ovation ever accorded a visiting side, and by the entire capacity audience.

Pita Fatialofa, the Samoan captain, said afterwards: 'We have been received so well in both Wales and now Scotland that I thought it would be fitting for us to thank everyone and show our appreciation of how we had been treated.' It was a delightful gesture and the Samoan spirit was further demonstrated by the volume of song emanating from their dressing room after they had departed the pitch, with applause ringing in their ears.

Bryen Williams, the 38-times capped former All Blacks wing, and so co-operative and friendly as their coaching director, (a position he accepted in tribute to his father, who had played scrum-half for Samoa and who had died of cancer some months before the World Cup) commented: 'It's been a great party but it's all over now. We failed to take advantage of the wind behind us in the first half and the Scottish forward effort proved too much for us, but we are still smiling.' And so they were.

CRISIS OF CONFIDENCE AMONG PLAYERS OF ABILITY

Robert Jones, *the Welsh scrum-half, digests the implications of the unsuccessful Welsh campaign and the Samoa effect.*

When I came back from Wales's disastrous summer tour of Australia, the last thing on my mind was the World Cup. I didn't even know if I wanted to continue playing international rugby. But despite the dreadful disappointment of our early exit from the tournament, I'm glad now that I decided to go on, and my experience during the competition – both playing in it and then having to watch it from the sidelines – has convinced me of my desire to stick around and help restore Welsh rugby fortunes.

Despite our defeat by Western Samoa and our

record home defeat by Australia, I am firmly convinced that there is still a strong nucleus of talented players with outstanding natural ability within Wales. What is lacking isn't so much ability – though of course we are deficient in certain areas – as confidence. To say that we were disappointed would be an understatement, but it was always going to be difficult to come back after the Samoan defeat. The thing was that we had prepared exactly right. The build-up to the game, everything that we did towards it, was positive and direct. The players had a belief in themselves again. In other words, it all went to plan until the kick-off. Our expectations were fairly high of even going further than the quarter-finals, which was our specific target when Alan Davies came in as coach: beat Western Samoa and Argentina and we were into the last eight. Then, and only then, would we need to start

Matthew Vaea of Samoa prepares to feed his backs during the Samoans' all-running second-half effort.

worrying about Australia. That was the theory, anyway.

The worst thing about going out so early was that the spirit we had built up during our preparations immediately evaporated because we were no longer together. Returning to your normal lifestyle when the rugby players that we know so well from the other home countries were playing on was agony, and there was no escape from it because it was on television and you couldn't help but be drawn to it. All the countries we thought would be there had made it through – apart from us. It was so different from the Five Nations' Championship, where at least you play on to the end like everyone else.

We all thought we'd turned the corner with our good performance against France at the beginning of September, a game we should certainly have won and would have won if we had possessed the confidence that comes from the winning habit. All the players would say that the work leading up to the World Cup, all the training camps, had been outstanding; we had learned more than we had done in the past and felt we had prepared properly. We knew exactly what we were going to do and although the Samoans were supposedly an unknown quantity, we knew full well that they would be physical and would tackle incredibly hard.

What went wrong once we took the field was that when we didn't win the stream of the line-out ball we expected we panicked a bit. We didn't stick to the game plan we had prepared and when we came back towards the end it was more in sheer desperation than anything else.

Afterwards, people didn't look at what happened throughout the game but, however good the Samoans may have been, you couldn't get away from the fact that we lost 16–13. The players were actually more disappointed in our performance than the result, because had we done what we originally intended we would have won. I was involved in the Samoan try that effectively won them the match. I was chasing back for a Samoan kick ahead and I believe I got to the ball first, a belief substantiated by the television replay. But when I turned round the try had been given. I appreciate it was a crucial time of the game and, yes, I was terribly disappointed, but there was no use shouting and bawling about it. Realistically, we couldn't take anything away from the Samoans; they definitely deserved to win the game overall. They were the better side and went on to prove they were a very good side indeed.

After the disappointment of Western Samoa it took us a couple of days to recover and to bring any continuity back into our training. Against Argentina, although we went out and perhaps didn't play particularly well, we just had to win. Coming off the field at the end after doing it 16–7 it wasn't a case of jubilation, just sheer relief that we were still in with a chance. We'd got a little pride back which would lift us for future matches. It wasn't done in style, it was just done, and to win again in Cardiff after such a long time was vitally important to us. I played a part in the Welsh try; Richard Webster drove off a scrum and I went up the touch-line, just managing to stay infield before slipping the ball inside to Emyr Lewis, who then gave it to the scorer, Paul Arnold.

Perhaps it was a false dawn but we did think we would do better than we did against Australia. I wouldn't say we were over-confident – we couldn't be – but we did feel if we went out with nothing to lose and gave it our best shot against a Wallaby team lacking Nick Farr-Jones and Tim Gavin we could cause an upset. Preparation was again second to none, but in the event we didn't win line-out ball and so didn't have enough possession to do anything. Having stuck to our defensive task relatively well in the first half, we were blown away in the second and lost 38–3. You can only go on defending for so long before you crack.

It's difficult to judge individual performance when you are part of a losing side but I felt things went OK for me personally. The biggest disappointment was that we didn't have enough possession for me to do the things I wanted to do, that I wanted to be good at and had worked out. I couldn't really express myself. I was always on the back foot, more often than not defending. When you look at our World Cup performances it's not so much a case of how well or not we played as how well or badly we defended.

What we need now is consistency of selection. We have to settle on who our best players are and give them a decent run and a chance to develop. Otherwise confidence will remain low. If players are good enough for the World Cup it doesn't mean they aren't good enough for the Five Nations Championship. The vast majority of this Welsh team have it in themselves to make a significant improvement. What they need is people to get behind them rather than knock them all the time, to be constructive in their criticism. Rugby in Wales, and the media attention given it, is incredibly

Iwan Tukalo, the Scottish wing, apparently on the route to glory. Tukalo crossed the line but the move was recalled for an infringement.

intense and in recent times the pressure this caused has had a detrimental effect on the players' confidence. They may try not to read the papers but if something is written or said about them, you can rest assured they'll find out.

I'm 25 and despite all the setbacks I'm carrying on. The urge to do well is as great as it's ever been, not just with me, and that needs to be encouraged. The 1995 World Cup is now my aim and, although it may seem a long way off, we have to improve much more quickly than other countries if we are to compete better than we did this time. The most important thing is that we still have the natural ability in Wales. Players have to learn to express that ability and have the confidence to do so within the national team. If we can find a way to do that, the next World Cup will be completely different.

SERVICE
is vital

Giving a first class service is vital to achieve success in Rugby
or in business.
At Friends Provident with more than one million customers our service
has proved to be just right.

FRIENDS PROVIDENT

ENGLAND GO THROUGH BUT THE GAME'S IMAGE SUFFERS

CLEM THOMAS

The quarter-finals in France were to bring a glorious end to Canada's marvellous run in the tournament at Lille, while in Paris, the French challenge was to end in tears. Not only were these two matches to be of grim intensity, with some of the hardest forward play of the tournament so far, but at Parc des Princes the occasion was to explode into controversy which was to provide the biggest news story of the tournament, when one of the world's top referees, David Bishop of New Zealand, was assaulted in the tunnel after the match by the French coach Daniel Dubroca of Agen.

The whole affair was to give the press a field day, especially when the chairman of the Rugby World Cup, Mr Russ Thomas of New Zealand, was to announce the next day at a press conference in Lille, that no action was to be taken over the matter. After indicating that he was aware of an incident, Mr Thomas said that no official complaint had been made and therefore no further action was intended. Thankfully, action was later demanded and Dubroca resigned.

Jeff Herdman, a former Swansea player and a Barbarian committee man, working as a radio reporter for the BBC, had gone into the tunnel immediately the game had ended and witnessed the attack on the referee by Dubroca, who called Mr Bishop a cheat and grabbed him around the collar. Furthermore, it was alleged that Dubroca spat at the referee and was dragged away still screaming insults.

The media were incensed that the World Cup chairman was so economical with the truth on an issue which they interpreted as a dereliction of duty to the administration of the game at large. If such a moment of anarchy, which could not be dismissed as merely a measure of the French frustration and deep disappointment, was to be allowed to go unpunished what then was the future, they asked?

Ian Robertson, the BBC rugby correspondent, asked Russ Thomas that very question when he asked what action the RWC committee would have

taken had the Canadian coach assaulted Fred Howard, the English referee, that afternoon. He received no adequate reply.

In taking no action at first, the World Cup administration was seen to be weak, cynical and guilty of bringing the game into disrepute, thus discrediting both the World Cup and the intelligence of those who were supporting it.

The matter also brought an outcry from the referees not involved in the World Cup. Roger Quittenton of England said that the whole future of the game had been damaged and that if referees at all levels were to be protected, then there should have been a prompt and searching enquiry into the incident. The French president, Albert Ferrasse, said that France too would welcome an investigation, but managed to prejudge by saying that Dubroca's English was not good enough to cry 'cheat'. Later in the week, Dave Bishop's colleagues in New Zealand were also to call for a full and frank enquiry into the whole affair.

It all proved to be the unhappiest moment of the World Cup and it was seen in the clear light of day as a murky piece of self-interest, a closing of the ranks by the rugby authorities to provide a cover-up. All at a time when rugby was supposed to be coming more into the open, certainly in places like Twickenham but apparently not in the International Rugby Board.

The normally responsible French newspaper, Le Figaro, the next day, was not only to comment on the fact that the referee desired an England/New Zealand final at Twickenham but furthermore that the Ango-Saxons wanted only to invite the French to take tea with them but preferred to keep the gala dinner amongst themselves.

In all these events, in the lurid headlines such as 'La Grande Desillusion' and in the racial inference by some of the French media, were to be seen the great depth of French frustration and disappointment.

On the following Tuesday, Daniel Dubroca, having

denied the charge at the post-match press conference, was finally to admit to his transgressions, including calling the referee a cheat, and apologised to the French Federation. He resigned four days later.

That this sorry affair was to overshadow and colour what were four magnificent quarter-finals was to be regretted, particularly as it could have been so easily diffused at the time if everybody had told the truth and made their sincere apologies.

It is also an indication of the character and tension of the game between England and France in Paris, which was charged with detonating and fulminating percussions of physicality, which would have made some mothers with young children turn off the television set.

England had taken the field controversially with a side in which their colossus of recent years, Dean Richards, had been dropped due to an inexplicable loss of form. The English manager and coach brought in Micky Skinner on the flank at no. 6 and put Teague at no. 8, totally against his current instincts, for having settled at blind side flanker since 1988, he was reluctant to be reinstated in his old position. It was a brave decision which paid a considerable dividend, for the power tackling of Skinner was to be one of the features of the match. One tackle in particular, on the big French no. 8 Cecillon who was driving around the back of a five yard scrum on the English line, late in the second half, like a crazed buffalo in a desperate search for the winning try, was a turning point. Skinner hit him with such force in a midriff tackle that he hurled him back several yards. It was an example that the England team responded to and in the last fifteen minutes wrested control from the French who, with the score at 10–10 for most of the second half, looked capable of running England out of the game.

Rob Andrew in his newspaper column in the *Times*, on the Friday before the game, had told us exactly how England were going to play: 'We plan a fairly restrictive pressure type game and we hope to squeeze them out. We won in Paris in 1990, with that sort of game and hope to repeat it tomorrow. The French don't like it, they love freedom. But we will try to stop them playing. I believe we have the firepower up front and the defensive power and strength in the backs to squeeze them'.

Prophetic words, for that was exactly the way it was. The only thing that Rob did not tell us was that he was going to hoist 16 of the 23 balls he

received while Richard Hill added a few more. Further confirmation of England's game plan came from Paul Ackford, one of England's heroes of the day who together with Wade Dooley mastered the line-out. In the *Observer* a day after the match, he wrote: 'Part of the game plan was to rattle the French early on, banking on the fact that the emotion of Serge Blanco's last international would

Below: The violent start. Nigel Heslop (14) has been punched to the ground by Eric Champ and Serge Blanco. Ondarts continues the hostilities.

Right: Jeremy Guscott brilliantly gets in his pass in Serge Blanco's tackle, and the waiting Rory Underwood is about to score the first England try.

tempt the temperamental French into moments of indiscipline. Indiscreet fists and a high tackle cost them an early six points and we were on our way.'

It was perhaps sad that Blanco in his last game for France did not go out in the blaze of glory that he cherished. Instead the old master gave an uncharacteristic display of histrionics and probably did more to unsettle his side by his punch on Heslop in the opening minutes than most people realise, as from thereon, the match lived on the brink of violence. As Stephen Jones said in the *Sunday Times*: 'If Keenan, the Western Samoan, deserved to be sent off the previous Sunday, then Blanco deserved to go as well.' Perhaps the referee's reluctance to send him off had something to do with Heslop's tackle being slightly late.

The French, who were forced to play without their midfield controller, the injured Didier Camberabero, were by far the most dangerous team in the opening stages, while England's hopes rested on a grim defence and denying them the ball.

France lost the match because they were wiped out in the line-out. Only Roumat, who apart from Cabannes, was easily the best French forward, competed in this department; his fellow lock, Cadieu, was simply too small and got blown away. The other two areas of French deficiency were the captaincy, where Blanco of all people had failed to remain cool and at scrum-half, where Galthié, for all his liveliness, which helped to make a French try, was a poor option-taker and passer of the ball.

Against the superior all round pace and wit of the vivacious French, the English pitted their more phlegmatic virtues of persistence, courage in adversity and a total refusal to cave in when the French in the second half looked to have the game won when the score was 10 all.

England preyed on French mistakes to go into a six point lead with two penalty goals by Webb in the first 10 minutes – the first from the Blanco punch and the second from a dangerous short arm tackle by Cecillon on Teague. Lacroix then kicked a penalty for France for offside in midfield, before England scored a try from a two man line-out. They moved the ball left, and Carling, who had one of his best games for England with his timing of the pass and his tackling always on target, pushed a lovely pass to Guscott, who in turn also showed his class by straightening the line to draw Blanco, to put Underwood over in the corner for a try. Another penalty by Lacroix made it a precarious but invaluable 10–6 to England at half-time.

Eleven minutes into the second period France levelled the score when a high kick by Lacroix rebounded off Webb's shoulder and Galthié gave a scoring pass to Lafond.

It was now all tremendous tension as the French rolled their mauls and constantly looked dangerous, but England began to play possession rugby.

The score remained level until six minutes from the end when Ondarts was penalised in the ruck, to his fury, which was further goaded by the English forwards, and when he was restrained he was seen to throw the referee's arm away. Webb made sure of the penalty goal. Finally, Richard Hill floated a high kick to the French line which was caught by Lafond. He was driven back over his own line by the English forwards, but it was Carling who sealed a fine afternoon's work by poaching the ball for a try converted by Webb and the French were undone.

England had achieved what their manager Geoff Cooke had described as his minimum objective, which was to reach the semi-final against the auld enemy Scotland at Murrayfield.

The French in defeat always show their disappointment and Jean Trillo, the French back coach and the finest of men, was to describe the match as the death of romanticism. A sentiment shared by the doyen of French rugby journalists Denis Lalanne, who announced that he was retiring after the World Cup when he said: 'It is time to go. Rugby is now all about big men and up-and-unders.'

He may well prove to be right, for there is now undeniable evidence that rugby is moving in the direction of the big battalions. You only have to observe the size of the Canadian and Australian forwards where 6'8" and 19 stoners are becoming commonplace and beginning to make even the All Blacks and England look small by comparison. One of the questions that the world rugby authorities will have to look at at the end of this tournament is whether the laws are creating only power rugby to the detriment of running and passing skills; and are we developing into the type of static game with only explosive moments – a game like American Football.

Serge Blanco safely fields the ball on this occasion but the match was an ill-starred departure for the giant of world rugby.

WHAT THEY SAID:

DANIEL DUBROCA
French coach

On allegations that he had assaulted the referee, David Bishop, in the tunnel after the game.

I simply congratulated the referee after the match. I said: "Bravo." If I touched him it was a fraternal gesture, as I know him so well.

ALBERT FERRASSE
FFR President

I am sure that Daniel's English is not good enough for him to abuse the referee seriously.

JEFF HERDMAN
BBC radio reporter

I was only a few feet from the scene. Daniel approached Mr Bishop angrily and seized him around the collar. He was pulled away and Mr Bishop was bustled on towards his changing room. He seemed very upset by the incident. As Daniel was pulled away he called out "cheat."

GEOFF COOKE
England manager

I was absolutely delighted by our control in a very difficult situation. Some of our line-out play was excellent and the way the boys responded was greatly to their credit and typical of the feeling in the current England squad.

WILL CARLING
England captain

Some of our best rugby of the whole tournament came when France scored their try to make it 10–10 in the second half. The French might have expected to step up a gear but it was England who stepped it up. The way the boys responded put us into the semi-final because we had control from the French try right up until the end. That 10 minutes after the French try was an important period and it kept us in the tournament.

BRIAN MOORE
England hooker

It is always rough playing in the Parc des Princes but this was a dirty, cynical game. Fortunately, we had resolved before the game that we would play them the way we have in the previous four meetings. You do not need to stand toe to toe slugging it out to prove your courage. It is much more impressive to simply take the kicks and the rakes and let the referee sort it out. David Bishop had his work cut out because the violence was fairly indiscriminate.

But there is always the extra satisfaction when you know you have been through as stiff a physical test as that.

THE PAIN OF DEFEAT

Serge Blanco, *the French captain, analyses the sound and fury of his team's exit in the quarter-final.*

Paul Ackford soars to win clean line-out possession in a match that was a triumph for England's locks.

Now that I have played my last match for France it is not a time for personal emotions. What does make me sad is that we had worked towards winning this quarter-final for six months and there will be four other countries in the semi-finals.

All that work dissolved in just a few minutes. Even so, this will not be the worst memory of my career. As for my son Stéphane, he was more sad than me. When I looked at him after the match it was clear that he was crying. I tried to tell him that in life one does not always win.

But Stéphane soon saw things differently because he said to me: 'Papa, I like it so much when you lose because we can get back to amusing ourselves together again.' The boy likes tumbling and being held upside-down by his papa.

Looking back to the match, I have never had so much difficulty in analysing the reasons for defeat and victory in my career. I suppose that the English team were well structured. They had domination in the line-outs. They occupied our territory and we could not play the game in the part of the pitch we wanted.

At the start there were two incidents affecting me.

93

Above: Another big leap by Wade Dooley, this time in triumph. Will Carling has scored for England in injury time, and they are through to the semifinals.

Right: A feature of the Paris quarter-final was the loud support of the visiting fans. The players felt that the support they received was a major factor.

On the first up-and-under I was under the ball and the English players treated me like a foot-mat. At the second I made a 'mark' and some hundredths of a second afterwards the English right-wing (Heslop) arrived, crashed into me and, it seems, with the intention of hurting me. Unfortunately, I reacted outside the rules of rugby. I have proved throughout my career that only the game interests me. England took the first step and I replied.

The referee, Mr Bishop, warned me that I would be sent off for another act of foul play, but he said also that he was a friend of mine and, though he was definitely very angry, he had a duty to see that I did not leave the field for the last time in such a way.

Of course, the debate about referees and interpretations could go on for hours because it is so difficult to decide on interpretations. My years of experience have shown me that you must always be aggressive and it is better to go forward without the ball than backwards with it. But this World Cup should have been a festival of rugby and has instead become a festival of referees. Matches have been dominated by referees. There were some bizarre situations today. For instance, I took a stiff-arm tackle and the decision was only a scrum. We were often embarrassed because the referee came into our dressing-room – with his smile – and asked us to play in a certain way. It is the first time that a referee has come into our dressing-room with instructions. He told us about scrums and line-outs, but he forgot to apply his rules about line-outs.

During the match I never thought that it would be my last – that in fact we would lose it. By contrast, the moment when I knew that I would not be playing at the Parc again came when we left our beloved Chateau de la Voisine and said *au revoir* to all the staff that I have known for so many years. There were people crying and that was when I knew that there was something special on this day.

One cannot say what one will be doing far in the future, but I don't think you will see me in a warm coat and a big cigar as a trainer or coach of the French team. I am not Michel Platini. I have filled many formidable hours. I have had joys and pain, but it has always been tense. I go back to my friends, my family and my work, paying a tribute to my sport.

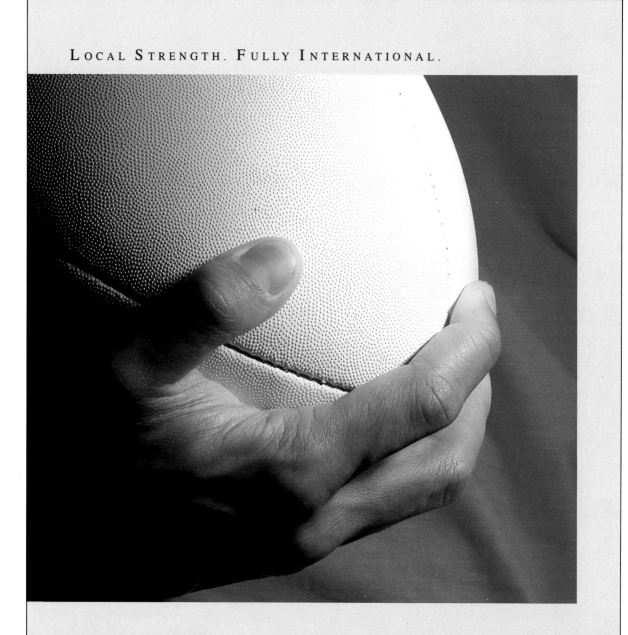

The top players have a number of things in common.

Experience of playing conditions around the world. A capacity to read the game. A sense of teamwork. Strength. Speed. And, above all, the ability to make fast decisions.

HongkongBank
The Hongkong and Shanghai Banking Corporation Limited

Fast decisions. Worldwide.

THE DUBLIN QUARTER-FINAL

IRELAND'S EARTHQUAKE SHAKES AUSTRALIA
MICK CLEARY

It was a quiet Sunday afternoon in the Centre for Seismological Studies somewhere in mid-Europe. San Francisco and Armenia were always worth keeping an eye on, but both areas had been stable of late. It was just approaching 2.30 and, after a full lunch, the duty officer felt his eyelids grow heavier. He suddenly shot bolt upright. It couldn't be true. Dublin appeared to have been struck by one of the biggest earthquakes ever recorded. But there was the proof on the screen before his very eyes – a blast registering 10.5 on the Richter scale. He turned to alert his colleagues throughout the world, not noticing that the needle on the scale flickered back down to zero almost as unexpectedly as it had sprung into life in the first place. Still, you couldn't really blame the poor bloke. How was a mere scientist to know the startling effect that 50,000 demented Irishmen could have had when they chose to jump up and down in emotional frenzy? Lansdowne Road shook to its ancient rafters as, with six minutes to go in the quarter-final against Australia, Gordon Hamilton took a pass from Jack Clarke and with half of Ireland in on the act with him, he raced to the line.

Even allowing for personal bias it was without doubt one of the great moments of the World Cup. Sport is about many things: courage, athleticism, beauty, commitment, hope and fear to name but a few qualities. But above all else it is about the shattering of expectations. The Big Upset makes sport what it is. No matter how heavily the odds may be stacked against an outcome, if we remove its possibility entirely, then sport loses its meaning.

And here at Lansdowne Road, that delicious scenario was unfolding yet again. Hamilton's try and Keyes' subsequent conversion put Ireland clear 18–15 with just six minutes to go. Those who had spent the previous three weeks counting the chickens heading for the semi-final showdown between New Zealand and Australia looked rather crestfallen. All Ireland had to do now was to catch the Australian kick-off and put it into orbit somewhere over Dublin Bay. On the basis of Murphy's Law – which states that you should always expect the worst to happen so that when it doesn't you have more opportunities to celebrate – the whole of Ireland was disappointed. The worst did happen.

The Australian kick-off was not even a particularly good one, landing deep inside the Irish 22, not far from Rob Saunders. Perhaps the Irish scrum-half was put off by the noise of a whole country screaming at the same time: 'Just find touch.' He missed. His attempted left-foot punt to the left touch was too ambitious on length. Saunders had gone for distance rather than safety – a poor decision which he won't need to be pointed out to him – and the ball landed close to Australian full-back Marty Roebuck. He too was on edge. In his haste to get his side back into Irish territory, he drilled the ball downfield for all it was worth. Chances are that his lowish kick would have shot straight over the Irish dead ball if it hadn't been for the athletic leap of Brian Robinson. The no. 8 could not catch cleanly but because he had touched the ball he had to go back into his own in-goal, and again there was the desperate sight of a player trying for all his worth to get the flipping ball off the park. How difficult it was proving. Again touch was missed. This time Australia made no mistake and set up camp in the Irish 22 from which they launched that last daring raid culminating in Lynagh's match-winning try.

(If you were a poor unfortunate watching the game on television you may well have missed the above sequence. Of all the times to show a replay, it is not when the opposition are restarting the game. So for perhaps the most significant few moments of any game in the tournament, viewers were denied live pictures, and were then not even updated so as to see what they had missed. It was a poor piece of television, noticed all the more acutely because it was a rare blemish.)

And so ended one of the most pulsating games of

the World Cup. The match wasn't touched by any great moments of lyrical beauty in which the ball was wafted through countless pairs of hands. The appeal was much more basic than that. Ireland set out to knock the living daylights out of Australia in order to neutralise their massive superiority in footballing ability. Now, if for a moment it appeared that Ireland were literally going to dent Australian confidence with an enormous punch-up at the kick-off, they soon resorted to more legitimate means of unsettling their opponents. Even so, you come to Lansdowne Road and expect to see a re-enactment of the Storming of the Bastille every time. However, the revolution tends to peter out after about an hour

and the aristocrats depart with their assets intact.

We expected a repeat of this oft-run classic. Just the week before at Murrayfield we had witnessed the same thing. For three quarters of the game Ireland had ripped the heart out of Scotland. Fifteen

Ireland stayed with Australia almost to the wire. Here, the powerful Willie Ofahengaue encounters strong Irish tackling.

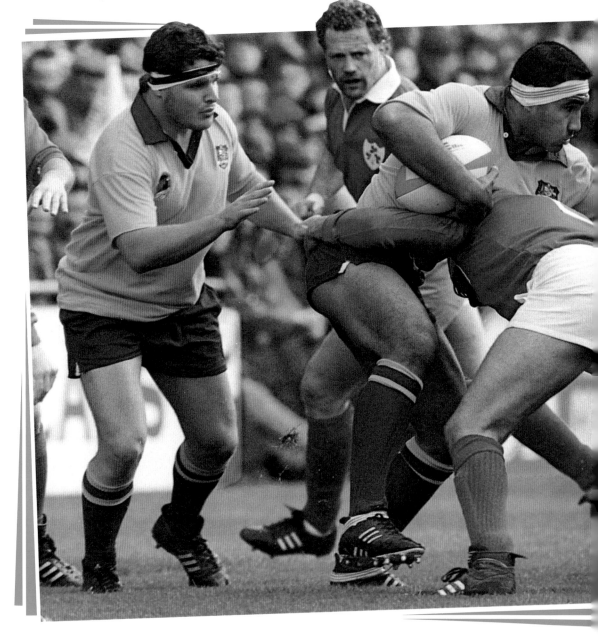

minutes into the second half, they led 15–9 and had dominated nearly all aspects of play. Then, they blew up. Never mind that Calder's tackle on Staples seemed to upset the full-back causing him to fluff a high take a minute later, the truth is that Ireland were beginning to fade away. They had the heart for the fight, but not the body.

It seemed we were in for a repeat performance here. How on earth could they hope to withstand the aggressive athleticism of the Australian pack to keep in check the potent dexterity of their three-quarters, Stem, by meticulous planning and unbending determination, both of these flows of attack, and there was still Campese to cope with.

Somehow, and from somewhere, Ireland managed to summon enough resources to extend their campaign from resistance to counter-attack. It was more than mere emotion which almost saw them through. Adrenalin will only get you so far. They matched the Australians for physical performance, keeping stride for stride with them round the field, matching them in the scrummage even though they ceded weight, and although they lost the line-outs by 21–12, they won the same percentage of their own throws as the opposition.

Ireland lost simply because Australia had far too much class in the three-quarters. That is why Australia felt confident enough to go for a try in the final few minutes when every other side in the world would have settled for a drop at goal to take the match into extra time. As Nick Farr-Jones, who had limped off after 15 minutes, said afterwards: 'Every time we get a scrum near the line, I feel we have a better than average chance of scoring with such a strong midfield.'

This is self-belief not arrogance, and was a view endorsed by coach Bob Dwyer: 'This is the best our back line has played all year and they did the right thing in running the ball wide when they did.' Dwyer did admit that even his confidence was beginning to teeter slightly: 'My knees haven't stopped shaking but a shot of Irish whiskey will help.'

Dwyer might also have had to resort to the bottle that night for two of his star turns were on the treatment table. Farr-Jones took an early trip back to the dressing room for the second time on tour as his damaged knee gave way. David Campese at least made the end of the match but was concerned later about a possible stress injury to his ankle similar to the one which hampered him in the 1987 World Cup.

The significance of the two players to the side cannot be overstated. Farr-Jones's replacement, Peter Slattery, is as competent a player as his captain which is no mean achievement. He has a sharp pass, a turn of speed and nose and aptitude for getting through a close quarters. However, he does not bring quite the composure to the side that Farr-Jones does. Australia were unable to work their way clear in this match, which possibly may have happened had Farr-Jones remained at the helm.

As for Campese, it's almost as difficult to describe his value as it is to tackle him. How can you put his worth into words? It's not just that his tries – 44 and 45 came up in this game with customary inevitability – put points on the board. It's the comfort he lends to team-mates who know deep down that no matter how much they might be on the rack, that any game is within their grasp if only they can somehow squeeze the ball to Campo. Quite rightly they've figured that there's little point in having to zap the ball all the way down the line in order to find their match-winner. Get him into the action as early and as easily as possible. That's how it happened here. Just a quarter of an hour into the game, Campese suddenly popped up in midfield, calculated his angle of running perfectly and shot through from 30 metres without anyone as much as laying a finger on him. The try was simple and precise, which proves that Campese is more than some simple showman who only gets his kicks from the outrageous. He has the clinical eye of the assassin also and knows exactly how to calculate the percentages. It's just that in Campo's case the percentage chances of a score are twice as high as for anyone else.

His second try, twelve minutes into the second half, was a simple matter of profiting from the fine work of the Australian centres, Horan and Little, whose midfield loop opened up the Irish defence. An easy try, until you realised that Campese had in fact run round from his wing on the opposite side of the field to score it.

Every time Australia managed to put the ball down the line, they looked threatening. It was difficult to work out how Ireland were managing to stay with them. It was, in fact, the old virtues of massive heart and huge endeavour which saw them hang on in there. Commitment is all very well but unless the scoreboard is also ticking over, the heads can soon begin to drop. In Ralph Keyes Ireland have found an outside-half in this tournament who brings reward for all the buckets of sweat expended. He outshone all the other kickers, his accuracy with the boot in this match yielding three penalty goals and a dropped goal to keep his side in contention mid- way through the second half at 12–15. Quite why Ireland allowed themselves to be duped into selecting Brian Smith defies belief on all sorts of grounds, not the least of which that Keyes is at least a good player and a far more damaging goal-kicker.

Australia always had the edge on Ireland, however, particularly wide out where Jack Clarke, a late replacement for Keith Crossan, looked out of his depth. Geoghegan managed to squirm his way through a few tackles on occasions, but these were rare moments of penetration from the limited Irish back-line. Nonetheless once again Ireland have surprised their critics and strung together performances of note. After a build-up of amazing ineptitude, they were within six minutes of the semi-final. Small wonder that Ciaran Fitzgerald should be moved to remark afterwards: 'Australia are the best in the world, which makes me very proud of my men. Perhaps now people will begin to appreciate that there is genuine talent in this Irish team. We did enough to win but just could not do it.'

His captain, Phil Matthews, was in equally buoyant mood despite the defeat: 'We put up a tremendous display. I have always felt that this is a good Irish side, capable of winning the Triple Crown. Certainly there is a great deal of optimism for the Five Nations Championship.'

And least now the seismologist might be prepared for that one.

Above: The master about to score. David Campese has carved up the Irish defence for his first-half try.

Left: Simon Geoghegan, the Irish right-wing, tries to burst down the left outside Marty Roebuck.

101

WHAT THEY SAID:

BOB DWYER
Australian coach

❛ My knees did not stop shaking for an hour after the game. When Ireland went ahead with only a few minutes remaining, it was worrying but I did feel that if we could win the ball then we could still score and the team told me afterwards that they felt the same. I would give Ireland credit for a tremendous team performance. We knew it would be hard to win in Dublin but possibly, we did not suspect just how hard it would be. On the other hand, the Australian team deserve credit because we never panicked. I always felt that we absorbed the pressure well. There were a few things wrong with the game that we need to work on but overall, I was pleased with the win on a great rugby occasion. ❜

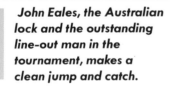

John Eales, the Australian lock and the outstanding line-out man in the tournament, makes a clean jump and catch.

NICK FARR-JONES
Australian captain

❛ I had to leave the field when I felt pain from my knee when an Irish player landed on me in a tackle. I do not believe that the injury is too serious and I had no worries about Slats (Peter Slattery) coming on as replacement because he has always done well for us whenever he has come on. However, we on the bench were very anxious after Ireland scored their try. Just for a few moments we felt we might be on the way out. However, we also have great confidence in the boys and the way they kept their cool and scored the try was fantastic. ❜

CIARAN FITZGERALD
Ireland coach

❛ I think that the way we played today answered all the criticism that we have received that this Irish side is a poor side and that we can only last for part of the match. The way we got together and the way we sustained our performance till the end was tremendous. There have been rumours that some of our players are considering retirement from international play but I feel that the spirit in the team will persuade them to stay on.
❛ The Australians are a fine side yet they only beat us at the end so today was a great achievement. Australia deserve credit for coming back at us so well. ❜

INCONSOLABLE IRISH TOOK AUSTRALIA TO THE LIMIT

Brendan Mullin, *Ireland's centre, looks back on a fervent Irish campaign and a glorious defeat.*

PHIL MATTHEWS
Ireland captain

❛ The first reaction of the boys after the match was one of extreme disappointment because we thought we might have the match won after Gordon Hamilton's try. But when a few days have passed I think there will be a feeling of deep pride at the way we played. The spirit in this Irish squad is tremendous and we showed all our critics a thing or two.

❛ The last time we lost narrowly to Australia at Lansdowne Road we went on to win a Triple Crown that same season and I feel that this time we have the potential to do that again in the Five Nations after Christmas. ❜

No one gave Ireland much of a chance in the World Cup but in the end we did better than anyone forecast and could be proud of our performances, especially in the quarter-final against Australia. At the end of it we were totally shattered, inconsolable really, after going so close. But when I sat back and thought a bit more about it I was tremendously satisfied to have taken part in such a marvellous game of rugby, a game that did an awful lot for the tournament as a whole.

In some games you go close to another team on the scoreboard but you aren't that close to reality, but I genuinely felt that with 10 minutes to go, just before we got our try, if we did get a score we would win the match. It was something to do with the way the Australians were composing themselves; there was a hint of panic setting in. Afterwards there was this empty feeling, having weathered the storm early on and grown stronger as the match went on. But on reflection there was satisfaction that we'd played well. We played to our potential; I don't know if the Australians did or not.

Our build-up to the World Cup had been terrible. As with a lot of sides, everyone was focusing on the tournament to the exclusion of everything else and if you look at other countries' preparation matches in the summer – England in Australia, Scotland in Canada and Romania as well as ours in Namibia and back home in September – minds were not on the job, they were on the World Cup.

That had a dramatic effect on our play. If Ireland aren't focused, which we weren't when we played those games in Belfast, Cork and Gloucester, it's a disaster. Other teams can get away with it; we can't, so we had terrible problems, winning three games unconvincingly and losing at Gloucester. A lot of people at that stage were mentally and physically tired, and then the worry about not performing in the World Cup set in. We were really stumbling from disaster to disaster.

But our coach, Ciaran Fitzgerald, and all the rest of us kept the faith. We stuck to our training programme and came good in the end. It had been specifically aimed at peaking in October at the World Cup. We underwent a rigorous time before we went to Namibia and the effects showed while we were away and right through to the middle of September. I suppose the fact that we got it more or less right when it mattered, actually during the tournament, shows that we planned it perfectly. In fact I felt we were at quite an advantage coming into a new season; the Australians and New Zealanders, coming from the southern hemisphere, had already had a long domestic season and had to struggle to peak again. Compare that with the 1987 World Cup when the home countries went down to Australia and New Zealand and struggled to find any form.

I missed our first match in Pool Two through injury, and it was my main personal regret that I was coming back to full match fitness only at the end of our World Cup involvement. I thought it was a good Irish performance in a very traditional sort of way against a very poor Zimbabwe team. The Irish team were very well prepared and Zimbabwe were 20 points down after 15 minutes and disappeared after that. It became a bit of a rout.

This was a major encouragement; you have to recall that we struggled against Namibia and had had a very hard time in the Irish press during the September warm-up games. A lot of people weren't convinced, but to win by a convincing margin got rid of any doubts the players had, as well as rallying public support. If we'd beaten Zimbabwe by, say, 25–0, people would have been much more worried but 55–11 seemed to unite everyone, players and supporters, behind the cause.

I came back in against Japan after watching Zimbabwe from the stand. We were aware that they would be stronger than Zimbabwe and were also very aware that it was a game we had to win to secure our place in the quarter-final. The Irish management took a brave decision to make eight or nine changes and there was a small amount of apprehension. But we started well, were always in control and managed to beat them quite well, although the Japanese displayed good form and scored a couple of good tries. At 32–16 it wasn't quite as convincing as against Zimbabwe but this was much better opposition, as the Japanese showed when they trounced Zimbabwe in Belfast. Our team

had had a specific job to do: to qualify for the quarter-final, though I admit there was relief rather than rapture after we'd done it.

People had been talking about the Scotland-Ireland group match in Edinburgh ever since we'd played a wonderful game there in March and there was always going to be a carnival atmosphere about it. Scotland were very determined to remain at Murrayfield by winning this game and we wanted to win because we wanted to top the group, though it was a double-edged sword because defeat would see us back in Dublin. It was very difficult; for the first half I felt we were very much in control, playing a good game, and the Scots seemed a bit rattled by the whole thing.

But after about 10 minutes of the second half I suddenly sensed the Scots moving up a gear and us struggling to keep up with them. That was a testament to their fitness and in the end they came through to beat us 24–15. It was a very hard game physically, which made us realise we were getting down to the serious stuff, but even so I felt too much was made of Finlay Calder's tackle on Jim Staples. It was much ado about nothing. In the five minutes preceding that incident the Scots had stepped up their game and were pushing hard. I didn't think too much of it at the time; the Scots stayed within the laws, if only just, and were wily enough to play the game to the limit. There was a lot of fuss about an incident that was normal, the sort of thing that does happen in a tough international. I never thought it was the turning-point as some have suggested.

We were happy enough in that we knew we were going back to Lansdowne Road. My own philosophy was that we were going to have to beat one of the two major teams at some stage but it's not unfair to say we would have preferred to play Western Samoa, as Scotland did, rather than Australia. When you get down to a knock-out, Ireland are as good as any other team in terms of having a one-off game against any opposition. We were very confident about it. No one in the Irish party didn't think we could win the game. We were well aware that the Australians were favourites – but the Australians did as well, and I think it may have affected them. It's certainly a dangerous thing to say and think, as some if us were doing.

They nearly had to eat their words. The first incident was a kerfuffle among the forwards – as traditional an Irish welcome as you can get – and the Australians knew immediately they would be in for a tough match. We never let them get away and by the time Gordon Hamilton got his try I already felt that one score would have been enough to finish them off. We were six minutes (including injury time) away from the end of the game. We were competing so well up front that if we could have kept it tight and got the ball away we'd have held out. The opposition can't score from the fifth row of the East Upper, so that's where the ball should have been put. But as things turned out the Australians came back and scored and won 19–18. I couldn't believe it. Two minutes earlier, the place had been pandemonium; suddenly there was an eerie silence.

Our aim had been to get at least to the last four and we came within a whisker of that. It's fair to say that, had we got through and played New Zealand in the semi-final, Dublin would have gone crazy. We would have had nothing to lose, just the same as against Australia. But it's easy to speculate on what might have been, and from the Irish point of view the tournament was a success. The inexperienced team that came together last season had to mature very quickly and in my opinion there's a Triple Crown and championship to come from that side in the next two or three years.

The interest has been phenomenal and the effect on rugby in Ireland has been highly significant. For a team given no chance before the start to go so close to beating the joint favourites has done a lot for the game here.

It was disappointing to miss the first match, but after that I was pleased with my own form. My regret is that I didn't score any tries and that Ireland didn't score that many either. The 1987 World Cup was a bit of an anti-climax for Ireland and for me but this one was superbly organised and had a far greater sense of occasion, perhaps because we were at home. I'm still only 27 but, although I intend to continue with my international career once I've sat down and had a think about it, I definitely won't be around by the time of the 1995 tournament. I can see conflict now between the time required for my family and my job as a Dublin stockbroker and the time required to compete at the top level of rugby. Other countries have been putting in this level of commitment for years. I've learned over the last year or two that if you want to compete with the best you have to prepare just as thoroughly as they do. It's become a professional commitment.

Right: Rob Saunders fires the ball away with the old-fashioned dive pass, watched by Jeff Miller of Australia.

Left: Was it the most thrilling moment of the whole tournament? Gordon Hamilton, running on to an inside pass from Jack Clarke, has held off Campese and is about to score. The crowd went hysterical; yet Australia saved the match.

105

One try and you'll be converted.

Wherever you are, whatever you look for in a hotel, there is one choice you can make with confidence. "Take me to the Hilton." Stay with us once, and you're hooked. With a standard of service that is respected worldwide, the Hilton combines friendliness and efficiency in a way which is appreciated by our guests, whether they are travelling on business or following their favourite sport. For information and a brochure on Hilton Sporting Deals 1991/1992, phone 0923 246464. For personal hotel reservations in the UK, phone 071 734 6000; and for Hilton International hotels overseas, phone 0800 289 303.

HILTON
INTERNATIONAL

THE HILTON · THE HOTEL

CANADA FIGHT PROUDLY AND NEW ZEALAND PREVAIL
CLEM THOMAS

The game at Lille between New Zealand and Canada was largely overshadowed by the pre-match announcement that a press conference was to be held by the Rugby World Cup Chairman, Mr Russ Thomas, concerning the previous day's events in Paris. Yet the match was, nevertheless, far from being an anti-climax for it was to be an occasion of remarkable interest, played with a great deal of heart and no little skill by those delightful dark horse Canadians, who like the Western Samoans, had used the World Cup as a vehicle to put their country's rugby on the world map. The Canadians ensured that the maple leaf fell proudly in its golden autumnal glory.

In coming a convincing second in their pool, by beating such established countries as Fiji and Romania and by giving the French the hardest of contests, Canada showed that their game was not only built on vigour but also on a deep intelligence.

In the previous 18 months they had beaten Argentina and a strong Scottish XV and now they had arrived at Lille in the last eight of the World Cup tournament to attempt to topple New Zealand, the current World Champions.

Considering that they have only some 33,000 players, only 12,000 of whom are seniors, (the rest being youngsters and women) based mostly in Ontario in the east and British Columbia in the west, it seemed that they had no chance against a country where rugby is an obsession and played by a quarter of a million people.

It was a great pity that the day was to be so wet and the pitch so waterlogged with standing water, but in the event, the Canadians gave the All Blacks an extraordinary examination in courage and commitment, far in excess of what many more senior and established rugby countries would have achieved. This was due not only to the fact that Canada were astonishingly some 10 pounds heavier than the All Blacks and had the biggest forward on the pitch in Hadley, who is 18 st 4lbs and 6'8", but

also to their determination and the vigour of their forward drives.

There was virtually a full stadium at Lille, largely expecting to see these new upstarts take a beating from the mighty All Blacks. However the sheer size and spirit of the Canadians was to confound everybody and that we saw a real match showed that Canada are far more than being mere sparring partners, showed that they were contenders in their own right.

The principal difference between the two teams was always that the All Blacks consistently were more streetwise in the use of the ball and like the Western Samoans in Edinburgh, Canada tended to be caught cold in the first half, when the All Blacks went into an overwhelming 21–3 lead. In the second half, Canada actually outscored the All Blacks by 10 points to 8.

The All Blacks were distinctly disconcerted by a ferocious opening onslaught by the Canadians, which few other sides could have withstood and which prompted the Canadian coach to say that had they scored then, the course of the game might have been so different. But no team soaks up punishment better than the All Blacks and they were quick to settle into that composed posture which wins so many matches for them and they were soon gathering scores with orderly method against these frenetic and tough opponents.

Injuries meant that Timu, a wing, had to play at full-back where he promptly proceeded to show the world what a marvellous and capable footballer he is. By hardly putting a foot wrong in such an exposed position in these terrible conditions, and by scoring two splendidly-taken tries, he now looks set for a very long run indeed in the All Blacks team.

In the first half Timu scored the first try, (as he did the last) by supporting Innes. Then came a clever Bachop dummy run and a back row pick up by Zinzan Brooke, which put Bernie McCahill over for a try. Fox converted both. Fox then kicked a

107

penalty goal and New Zealand were comfortably out of reach.

Mark Wyatt, a great servant of Canadian rugby and playing his last Test for Canada, also kicked a penalty before Brooke stormed over from another decisive back row move with Bachop. Fox converted.

It had been a brave performance by Canada but of no avail against the enduring methods and finishing of the All Blacks. Nevertheless, in the second period Canada were to surprise everybody by more than holding their own and outscoring New Zealand. However, it was the All Blacks who were to score first in the second period, with a power try by Kirwan down the narrow side, which gave the wing his first try in the World Cup. Most other teams would have crumbled at this point, but not these hard-headed Canadians. They not only stuck to their guns but increased their rate of fire and had they not spilled so much ball, then their second half offensive might have reaped even greater rewards.

A huge drive in which Van Den Brink was prominent was rewarded when the tenacious and lively scrum-half, Tynan, bolted through the All Blacks for a typical and well-taken try. The All Blacks responded with another clever try by Timu who, spotting the danger of being tackled by a covering defender, cleverly slid on his belly and slid some six yards over the line for a try, that was both brilliantly executed and highly amusing.

Canada continued their defiance with two marvellously taken tapped penalties which ended in a try by the flanker Al Charron and Wyatt kicked the conversion. Canada's principal fault is that they still tend to rely too much on physical attributes and therefore do not allow the ball to do enough work. The Canadian manager said in the press conference after the game that the World Cup had given Canada a structure and a measure of where they stood in world rugby. Mark Wyatt, their captain, after announcing that the match against the All Blacks was the end of his international career, said: 'We are delighted with what we have achieved and we thank all those Canadians who have supported us at considerable expense. All 31 World

Cup games have been seen on Canadian television, which in itself is a tremendous achievement, and this can do nothing but good for our rugby back home.'

The Canadian squad was extremely well managed by Mike Luke, who is a professor in French, and well coached by Ian Birtwell, who before this tournament had taken them to five wins in six internationals. After each game he provides his players with a written in-depth analysis which runs to five or six typed foolscap pages. These two men have made Canada believe in themselves.

The immediate Canadian dividend from the World Cup was that Albert Ferrasse, the President of the French Rugby Federation, invited them to make a full tour of France. No doubt other offers will follow.

The All Blacks were delighted by the fact that Canada had given them such a hard game. Both their captain Gary Whetton and the manager Grizz Wyllie said that it was the perfect preparation for their climactic semi-final match against Australia in Dublin the following weekend.

Above: John Timu, New Zealand's full-back for the day, scores the first try at Lille despite the tackle of Tynan of Canada.

Right: Brian Anderson, the referee, steps in with a warning as behind him, Canada's Norm Hadley, who had an outstanding tournament, prepares to jump.

WHAT THEY SAID:

JOHN HART
(New Zealand coach)

❛This was an extremely hard physical contest in which the Canadian forwards kept the pressure on the All Blacks and stretched us the whole 80 minutes. It was exactly the sort of match we needed, a week before playing Australia in the semi-finals. In my opinion, the Canadian pack was just as good as the English forwards and with no disrespect to the Americans and the Italians, it was the sort of tough challenge we needed to sharpen us up.

❛We lost our concentration occasionally against both the Americans and the Italians and we could not afford to do that against Canada. Our forwards were not at their best in the pool matches and it was very encouraging to see them play well in the dreadful conditions here in Lille. ❜

GARY WHETTON
(New Zealand captain)

❛Although we have to pay full credit to Canada for playing so well and crossing our line twice from close range, for good tries, I can live with that as long as we score five tries, which we did today. But, having said that, as we approach the last two weeks of the World Cup our defensive organisation, which is normally very good, needs tightening up . ❜

MIKE LUKE
(Canadian manager)

He was asked if the Canadians might be offered tours by major International Board countries after their excellent showing in the World Cup.

❛The press obviously have a very good grapevine because one or two countries have already made initial enquiries and tentative offers (including France) so we're hopeful something will come of it in the not too distant future. In fact, we might try to fix something up next week because we're not busy and neither are France! ❜

New Zealand's experienced front row of Richard Loe, Sean Fitzpatrick and Steve McDowell were given a hard match by their Canadian opposite numbers.

IAN BIRTWELL
(Canadian coach)

❝ We were very pleased with our performance against France, where we lost narrowly, and we feel we did Canadian rugby proud again with this great effort against the All Blacks. The World Cup has created a framework for countries like ourselves and it has given us a measure of where we stand in world rugby now and it has shown that we have made considerable improvement between the last World Cup in 1987 and this World Cup. ❞

MARK WYATT
(Canadian captain)

On his team's lap of honour after the New Zealand match.

❝ It was a spontaneous gesture at the end of a very hard match. We were all pleased that, considering the awful conditions, we had played to the best of our ability and succeeded in giving New Zealand a good game. It was our way of showing how much we had enjoyed being part of the World Cup, our delight at reaching the quarter-finals, our chance to thank the army of spectators who had been loyal to us throughout our four matches in France and it was our way of saying goodbye. ❞

DREAMS FULFILLED ON A LONG ROAD

Mark Wyatt, *Canada's captain, on his team's outstanding performance in the tournament.*

When you look back on Canada's achievements in the World Cup, you have to look back a long way. We began our build-up over two years ago with the qualifying stages. Although we were guaranteed a place in the last 16 because there was a place for all three countries in our qualifying section – Canada, America and Argentina – it was very important to try to win our group and secure a place in Pool Four.

The Canadian team has felt that the critics have sold us short in recent seasons, and we were not surprised to learn that nobody gave us much chance of beating Argentina in Buenos Aires and we won the return match in Vancouver. We beat America at home and even though we lost a disappointing match in Seattle to the United States, we still finished top of our qualifying group.

In a sense, you can say that we began our giant-

Left: Eddie Evans has the ball but is about to come under pressure from Allan Whetton and sundry other All Blacks.

Above: John Kirwan managed to escape this tackle by Al Charron and run to score near the right-hand corner

killing act with our two victories over Argentina. From the onset we had a series of goals and topping our group was the first achieved. Furthermore, most of our players are from British Columbia who celebrated their centenary in 1989. This meant that we had several extra matches as part of the celebrations.

New Zealand, Australia and Japan all played games, on their way through Canada to tours in the Northern Hemisphere, and along with regular fixtures, we were able to gain valuable experience against top-class sides to see where we stood in the world pecking order – and in what ways we needed to improve. All these matches in 1989 also helped us select and finalise our very best squad and work with them for the next 18 months up to the World Cup.

In March 1991, our second big goal was achieved, when we had a hugely successful run at the Cathay Pacific Hongkong Bank Sevens Tournament. This is, without question, the best organised and the highest standard of Sevens competition in the world and it has always provided a wonderful platform for emerging nations like Canada. This year, we beat the full Scotland side, with all their famous players taking part – Scott Hastings, Craig Chalmers, David Sole, John Jeffrey and Derek White – and this gave us tremendous confidence.

Hitherto, we had often lifted our game and played

really well against the major International Board countries but, now, at the biggest and most glamorous Sevens competition in front of a global television audience, we had beaten Scotland.

In May, we achieved our next, equally important, goal when we beat Scotland at fifteen-a-side rugby in Vancouver. It may not have been the full Scotland side but it was a very strong team and it meant a great deal to us that we won. This victory was a major breakthrough. A huge psychological barrier had been broken and we were now ready to take on anyone and everyone.

Our first match in the World Cup was against Fiji in Bayonne, and in terms of motivation and mental preparation this was our single most important match. Fiji were one of the seeded sides and we had to win to reach the quarter-finals. We knew that to do so, we had to resort to tremendous driving forward play and hard first-time tackling, because the Fijians are lethal with the ball in their hands and room and space to operate. Although our try, by Scott Stewart, was scored out wide it was our superb close-quarter forward play which helped us to win the match.

After a decade in the Canadian squad, this match will always remain one of the great highlights of my career. It was also a turning point, a watershed in Canadian philosophy. It was the first time we had beaten a big international team and the atmosphere in the changing room was: 'What's next, lads' rather than 'wasn't that just amazing and unbelievable.' At long last, we knew we were up there with the best in the world. We deserved to be, we had the confidence and we were not in any way overawed by it.

With this self-belief, we were always in control of the match against the Romanians and that victory put us in to the quarter-finals. We really thought that we could beat France in our last pool game in Agen, and we came within six points of producing a real shock result for the host nation.

I think we surprised a lot of people with the way we played against France and we knew that we were fully capable of running New Zealand very close. In fact, we came extremely close to scoring in the opening five minutes, twice being stopped or held up on the All Blacks line. We then saw the All Blacks at their best for the next 20 minutes. Their forwards drove at us non-stop, sucking in all our loose breakaways, and sometimes our half-backs as well, before launching rolling mauls down the touchline and then in field. We defended flat out,

tackling, covering, and supporting each other as wave upon wave of black jerseys swept towards us. It was pretty desperate stuff and very high pressure. Twice we missed tackles, and twice they scored.

We tried to compete with them up front and we came out of the battle with a great deal of credit. Our scrummage held up well, Norm Hadley and Ron Van Den Brink shared the line-out and I thought our loose forwards, Gord MacKinnon, Glen Ennis and Al Charron, were outstanding. The conditions were absolutely dreadful, with a strong wind blowing straight down the field, driving rain, a wet ball and a sodden pitch, and we adapted to this lottery just as well as the All Blacks. Our backs tackled well and did everything they could in attack. We played to our potential and we can't ask for any more than that. We showed that we can compete with the best in the world and I hope that as a result rugby will become even more popular in Canada over the next four years. The reaction from the country is highly encouraging.

Our ultimate goal had been to reach, at least, the quarter-finals and we achieved this. Our next long-term goal will be to reach at least the semi-finals at the 1995 World Cup. In between, we will try to maintain our improvement and momentum to justify our new-found status. I am sure we will do that, and I know that this whole squad will also take great comfort in the months ahead in looking at the experience of a lifetime, when we did Canadian rugby proud by finishing in the top eight of the 1991 World Cup.

We rubbed shoulders with the world's greatest players and we survived the comparison. We fulfilled our dreams and can look back with a lot of satisfaction at wins over Argentina in Buenos Aires at the start, wins over Fiji and Romania in the Tournament proper and highly-respectable defeats by France and New Zealand at the end. Canadian rugby can look forward to the future full of hope and confidence.

Wyatt and Woods of Canada are shaken up in the tackle of New Zealand's Henderson, who deputised on the flank for Michael Jones.

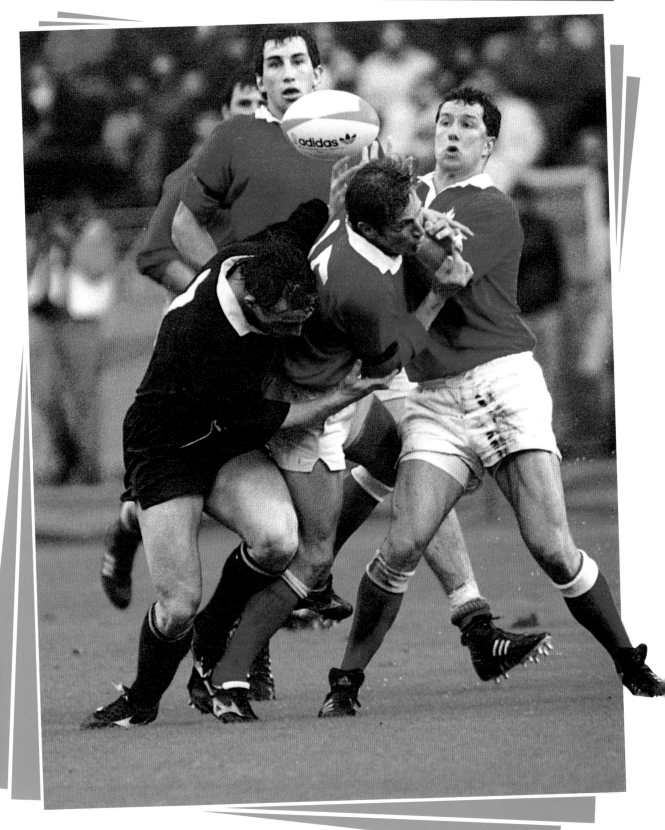

PERFORMANCE
is everything

Over the years, Friends Provident has been well
worth applauding.
We equally applaud the performance in the 1991
Rugby Union World Cup and look forward to 1995
when once again performance will be everything.

FRIENDS PROVIDENT

ENGLAND THROUGH BY A KICK AND A MILE!

BILL McLAREN

No scriptwriter could have created a more alluring first semi-final than that between the oldest of rugby union international rivals, Scotland and England, whose meeting at Murrayfield on Saturday October 26 not only ensured that a northern hemisphere country would be represented in the final but sparked off such enthusiasm for attendance at the game that, on the Tuesday, hundreds of supporters actually braved the fog and chill of a perishing night just to trouser one of the 1500 tickets remaining.

The demand was unprecedented and rendered it regrettable that the building of new stands, when coupled with the Safety of Sports Grounds Act, had reduced the capacity of Murrayfield to a mere 54,000 whereas in 1975 it had housed 104,000 for Scotland versus Wales.

Whilst the media gradually built up the hype as the weekend approached, both squads remained relaxed and in low profile. After their Friday practice sessions, England gave a model press conference that was amiable, informative and fair. Geoff Cooke, their manager, said that whilst England hoped that they might have a slight advantage through having had two very hard games against New Zealand and France which Scotland hadn't had, they knew that they would have to play very, very well to win. 'If we don't,' he said, 'we will lose. It's as simple as that. Scotland are a very good side. A lot of teams have come to Murrayfield and thought they could win but haven't done so.

'The Scottish back row have caused us many problems. We have a lot of respect for Gary Armstrong, who makes the Scottish side bubble. Goal-kicking will be crucial. We mustn't give away any penalties. We got very close to our top gear in Paris. This time we are up against a very good side playing on their home ground.'

The Princess Royal flanked by the two presidents, Gordon Masson of Scotland and Peter Yarranton of England (right).

On the subject of southern hemisphere referees and the fact that the Australian, Kerry Fitzgerald, was to be in charge of the game, Cooke said that the England squad now were much more experienced in the ways of the southern hemisphere referees, having played seven games in Australia with them in charge: 'Kerry has slight differences when compared to David Bishop and he may make some mistakes, but we just have to get on with the game. No amount of shouting or bawling will change that. The players are aware of it.'

Ian McGeechan, their coach, sought to play down the fact that Scotland were regarded as slight favourites: 'England have developed as a very strong side who will ask us a lot of questions. We have respect for them. At the start of the 1989 season, they still had a lot to learn in terms of experience of world rugby. Now all those players are much more mentally aware and harder, especially in the build-up to important games.'

Came the day, dull but dry and carrying a threat of the continuance of the early morning misty haar that did not materialise, and never before had Murrayfield held such a cosmopolitan audience. There seemed to be folk from all over the world in the capacity crowd, that included her Royal Highness, The Princess Royal, patron of the Scottish Rugby Union, and her children, Peter and Zara, who met the teams before the starting-gun sounded.

One unusual feature of the pre-kick-off events was that neither side was led on to the field by their captain. Rory Underwood emerged at the head of the England team in recognition of his achievement as the first Englishman to reach the 50 caps mark, which had brought from his captain, Will Carling, the previous day, a handsome tribute to his dedication, his consistency and his loyalty to the team, not least. Said Carling: 'He is such a help to me on the field.'

The Scottish team had John Jeffrey leading. It was to be his last international at Murrayfield and, indeed, having gained his 39th cap as Scotland's most capped breakaway forward of all time, he announced after the game that he would be retiring from international play after the World Cup. The 'White Shark' has been an adornment to the Scottish game, one of the great predators, utterly brave and an integral part of one of Scotland's most successful breakaway trios, alongside Finlay Calder and Derek White. Jeffrey was also still in possession of the Scottish record of tries in internationals by a forward – 11.

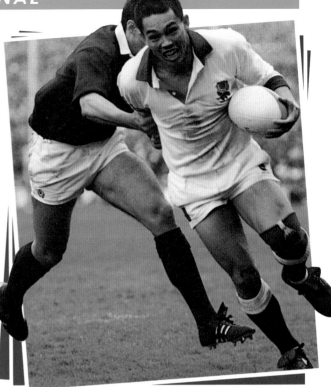

Rory Underwood celebrated his 50th cap for England with this brilliant break.

The singing of both the national anthem and Scotland's rugby anthem 'Flower of Scotland' was quite inspiring as a prelude to one of the most fascinating contrasts in strategy of any international.

Scotland anticipated scrummage problems. They had had them against Ireland, had repaired the damage against the Samoans, who were no great scrummagers, but were badly in need of that massive cornerstone that is Iain Milne, whom injury had precluded from the World Cup squad. Paul Burnell has proved an able deputy, not least in mobility and tackle chores, but he is not a Milne as a scrummager and with such a telegraph pole as the 21-year-old Doddie Weir behind him at right lock, there was clear vulnerability in that Scottish edifice, especially against such a power-house pack as that of England. As a result, Gary Armstrong was keen to get the ball in and out of the scrummage as quickly as possible and although John Allan defended his own put-in very well, the hinges of the Scottish scrummage squeaked frequently, so that it was difficult to ignite the kind of pick-up ploys that had been requisites to Scotland's recent success.

The line-outs were some study. What with Scotland shifting their personnel, so that no one line-out resembled the one before it, with Weir not always marking Wade Dooley but operating often as number 2, opposite Paul Ackford, and with England taking a leaf out of Scotland's book of 1990 by often placing Mick Skinner at 2 so that Ackford dropped back to 4 and Dooley presented a massive block at 6 to Scotland's desire to use the tail, it was all very confusing but interesting. The end result was that Scotland did reasonably well in getting some first touches but the quality of England's service was that bit higher. Dooley has become one of the great deflectors, just as Delme Thomas used to be for Wales.

With their scrummage channelling with chocolate bar slot-machine delivery and their line-outs pretty

well controlled, England ensured that scrum-half Richard Hill would have something akin to an armchair ride in the set positions. It meant also that Gary Armstrong, a renowned scrummage harasser, just couldn't get at Hill.

Scotland clearly reasoned also that the fewer line-outs into which England were able to throw, the better for Scotland's chances. Thus the Scots only punted to touch in an emergency or in desperation. At other times they hoisted a series of high punts across the breaking forwards into quite spacious areas, and that brought out of Jonathan Webb and Simon Halliday especially some hurried but competent cover.

The English had practised the previous day dealing with such aerial bombardment and their gathering at the dropping point was sharp and collective. One wonders what might have happened if Craig Chalmers had feinted to kick high, then

Right: England had the better of the line-out battle with Wade Dooley outstanding.

Below: The English forwards offer total protection as Mike Teague feeds his scrum-half.

had swung out a spin pass to his centres, perhaps running against an already-turning defence. Gavin Hastings placed a series of such massive high punts into some of England's panic areas but the value of having such flying machines as Rory Underwood, Jeremy Guscott and Carling in their back division is relevant not only to attack moves, but to getting back that yard quicker in defence. England coped.

Scotland even used two ploys that are very seldom, if ever, seen at the top international level nowadays. At one shortened line Jeffrey was positioned as the scrum-half just inside the 15

Above Right: Gary Armstrong caused England a few problems with his sniping runs.

Below left: Gavin Hastings breaks through the English defence, always looking dangerous.

Right: The heroics of Hastings and Armstrong gave the Scots supporters plenty to shout about.

metres line but ran into an ample gap between his two specialists, leapt high and caught the throw-in and made quite a dent. That caught England on the hop. It was an example also of how the Scots were keen to reduce the number of conventional lines when once, within three metres of their own line, John Allan threw a beauty right over the line-out which Jeffrey and Chalmers gathered in, but England managed to smother their attempt at clearance. On other occasions when Allan's throw cleared the line-out England's centres twice thwarted the move.

Scotland also made sensible use of Gary Armstrong, standing in the five metres area as the hooker, when England threw in. Armstrong is also a pirate of some note and the idea was for him to hassle and harry his opposite number, Hill, at those

line-outs. He came close on occasions but, as at the scrummages, England's control and direction made it virtually an impossibility.

The match was disappointing from the spectacle point of view. England adhered strictly to their game plan of kicking for position, keeping the ball within easy reach of their big, rumbustious pack and barely ever spinning the ball along their back division. They had a class architect in Rob Andrew, with his adhesive hands, and a weight and accuracy of punting that, as at Twickenham last March, broke Scottish hearts. It wasn't pretty to watch but it was efficient, clinical and effective. England also had the argument that they never did have a cushion from which they might have given it a twirl. They might have had a launch pad but Jonathan Webb missed three penalty goals in the first half and eventually finished with two out of six.

Scotland, indeed, led 6–0 from two penalty goals from Gavin Hastings but it was the burly Scottish full-back who unaccountably missed the simplest goal kick of the afternoon. The great man pushed it fractionally wide. Scotland could have taken a 9–6 lead with just 18 minutes to go. The psychological advantage that would have been Scotland's therefore swung England's way – the humps and hollows of rugby fortunes. Hastings played so well throughout but that was a crucial miss.

Scotland, however, had to survive a series of scrummages in their panic area and England excelled in frequently getting in a fractional nudge that earned them vital scrummage insertions. It seemed in every sense appropriate that the player whose right boot was inspirational to his side should also use it to pilot over from a scrummage the match-winning drop goal. It was Rob Andrew's 14th drop goal for England in internationals, just one behind the world record of Jean-Patrick Lescarboura (France) and Naas Botha (South Africa).

As Finlay Calder was to slip back into retirement after the third place play-off against New Zealand he can reflect on his splendid World Cup comeback, including as it did a desperate lunge that blocked Rory Underwood's pass to Brian Moore who would have scored – all very much in the Calder 100 per cent mould.

Whilst it had been a hard, bruising confrontation with deeds in defence to mortar bomb attacks that were quite exceptional and with a nerve-tingling quality because of the closeness of the scores throughout, many folk in the ground expressed disappointment that there had been so little back play other than chasing after Garryowens and tackling. That thrilling and lethal runners such as Underwood, Guscott and Carling should have been on such short rations seemed an indictment of the English style. But in defence of that style, Geoff Cooke had made the point before the match that whilst England would like to play a more expansive game they had to be in the right situation to do so and their supporters would not thank them for a handling error that might cost them the World Cup.

So England churned their way into the final, deservedly, having ended Scotland's run at

The final difference between the two teams – Rob Andrew's perfectly struck drop goal.

Murrayfield of 13 consecutive wins. Apart from Underwood's 50th cap and Jeffrey's last international appearance at Murrayfield, Hill equalled Steve Smith's record for an England scrum-half of 28 caps, Will Carling came within one cap of equalling Paul Dodge's record for an England centre of 32 and Carling and Guscott formed England's centre partnership for the 16th time, beating the record of Mike Weston and Malcolm Phillips. David Sole led Scotland for the 18th time, one short of Ian McLauchlan's record of Scottish captaincies in cap internationals. All of which simply added up to Scotland travelling to Cardiff for the play-off (is it really necessary to tag on that extra game that means little to players disheartened by defeat in the semi-final?) whilst England set about preparing for the final. As Brian Moore said after the Murrayfield match: 'We reached the final hardened up through three desperately hard games. We have enough left for one more big match.'

WHAT THEY SAID:

GEOFF COOKE
England manger

❝ This was a very satisfying win and it proves that we are moving forward. We have made the final and have every chance to win it. The players have improved in every game of the tournament.

❝ People may say we did not win in any great style but kids believe in winners. We would have loved to cut Scotland to pieces but that is not always possible, especially today. Scotland are a very good side and no one wins by a lot of points at Murrayfield. ❞

ROGER UTTLEY
England coach

❝ We met a side which was prepared to give everything. They had us rattled for long periods of the game and they were exerting tremendous pressure out there. I was very pleased with some of our control of the forward play. ❞

WILL CARLING
England captain

❝ I was a little worried at one stage because Jon Webb was missing a few kicks. We thought of asking Rob Andrew to take over at one stage but then we were awarded an easy penalty near the Scottish posts. It was the ideal chance for Jon to get his confidence back and he put the kick over.

❝ It is a great feeling to be in the World Cup final. It is a great achievement because very few teams could have gone to Paris and Edinburgh in successive weeks and come through. Now, I am sure that we have one big game left in us. ❞

IAN McGEECHAN
Scotland coach

❝ England played act-piece rugby and kept us on the defensive. At times, we were close to playing well against a team that can dominate set-piece possession, but as the game went on, they were trying to strangle us and we were trying to bring it alive. I like to think that we would have played a fast and attacking game if we could have controlled more of the ball.

❝ We had to make them change their game, make them do things differently. If we could have maintained a certain momentum then they would have had to change.

❝ However, I am proud of the whole Scotland squad. The positive way in which the players have approached the whole tournament has given me the greatest pleasure. The World Cup has been a great success in Scotland and the repercussions will benefit Scottish rugby for years to come. This has been the best group of players that I have been associated with. ❞

THE DUBLIN SEMI-FINAL

CRUSADING WALLABIES SHATTER THE CHAMPIONS

CLEM THOMAS

We had travelled from Edinburgh after the English semi-final win knowing that England had earned an inalienable right to a place in the final after fighting their way through the minefields of Parc des Princes and Murrayfield. However, we would have liked to have seen them score a try or two in Edinburgh, particularly in view of the amount of ball they had won and the control they had exercised in the scrums and the line-out.

Dublin, however, was to light the touchpaper of huge interest throughout the world for the cup final at Twickenham the following Saturday, when Australia and New Zealand captured our imagination with a crackerjack game.

It was the game which in everybody's perception was the true final of the competition, largely because the seeding arrangement had contrived to bring these two great Antipodean teams into the same half of the draw and because they were the teams of the moment in world rugby. They did not disappoint us.

It was the fair city of Dublin's good fortune that they should have promoted such a tremendous contest and provided the arena for what was the most powerful and significant match of the 1991 World Cup. For whatever Australia and England, who had won the semi-final at Murrayfield, were to say, this match in Ireland was the game that most judges believed would provide the winner of the tournament. Even though, so far, neither team had played in this World Cup with much style or with any great conviction.

New Zealand had not been fully stretched, apart from their opening game against England which they managed to win by a mere six points. For all the gallantry and commitment shown against them by Italy and America in the pool games, with Italy surprisingly holding them to 10 points, and by Canada in the quarter-final, the results of these games were never really in doubt.

Australia on the other hand had been engaged in those fierce pool matches in Wales, which had

Argentina rallying fiercely against them in the second half to reduce the gap to 20–16 with only 22 minutes to go, before Campese again decided to take a hand. While in the pool game against Western Samoa and then in that excruciatingly exciting quarter-final against the fighting Irish in Dublin, the Wallabies might well have been gone. Instead of being in the semi-final they could, (most Irishmen will say should), have been sunning themselves back home.

It had become obvious throughout the British summer and in the pool games that the All Blacks were not the annihilating force they had been under the captaincy of Buck Shelford four years ago. There was none of that fearsome drive off the back row which had been instigated by Shelford himself.

For their part, Australia had shown against Wales and England in the summer and in three Tests against the All Blacks in a year, which had them winning two and conceding only one try in the three matches, that they were building something special. However, the loss of form by the Australian forwards, especially in the back row, where they were sadly missing the power and understanding of the injured Tim Gavin, was a niggling worry for the Australian coaches Bob Dwyer, Bob Templeton and Jake Howard.

The Australian coaches therefore read the riot act to their tight forwards and even at this late stage had the nerve to change their back row against the All Blacks, restoring the 19-stone Troy Coker at no. 8, putting Willie Ofahengaue back in the number six jersey and dropping Miller, with the remarkable and redoubtable Simon Poidevin taking on the role of openside flanker and rear gunner at the line-out.

By comparison, the All Blacks were in far deeper trouble. They were unable to play 'never on a Sunday' Michael Jones, even though they tried to convince him that 2.30 p.m. on a Sunday afternoon in Dublin was early Monday morning in Auckland. Courageously, Michael stuck to his religious principles. In addition, they had Terry Wright out of commission with his leg injury and the reserve full-back, Philpott, was also grounded.

They therefore turned to Kieran Crowley, who had flown in as a replacement but who had not played any rugby for six weeks, having retired and thrown his boots away. Furthermore, Gary Whetton had been ill with flu in midweek and was probably far from his normal self. The absence of the pace of Michael Jones and Terry Wright was to prove disastrous.

In the event, this semi-final exceeded our expectations as it became a contest not only with the hardest competitive edge, but produced a game which expressed the style and passion of rugby football and which was additionally graced by the genius of two individuals.

Above all, it was a match which fully exorcised the minds of the Australian public from the

nightmare of that dreadful error made by David Campese in the final Test against the Lions in 1989. This was to be the 29-year-old David Campese's finest hour in his distinguished Test career, which has brought him 46 Test tries – easily the world record.

All through the tournament, Campese had looked as if he was determined to fight a personal crusade to win the World Cup. Again, it was he who brought the unconfined joy of rugby into the tournament, with the magic of his running which brought that dazzling opening try; and not satisfied with that, he proceeded, with the assistance of Lynagh, to conjure up the try of the 1991 World Cup.

That first try was perhaps the one that the All Blacks feared most. Campese, moving into the fly-half position, took a rifled pass from Farr-Jones and spotting that he had only two New Zealand forwards and Kirwan to beat, took off on a diagonal run, whose subtlety in changing pace and an awareness of space and time baffled Kirwan. The All Black wing only managed to tackle him as he went over the line, for what was a huge psychological advantage.

The genius of David Campese's brilliant running captivated Lansdowne Road.

Left: All Black wing John Kirwan also had an outstanding match with his explosive bursts.

Below: Willie Ofahengaue leads another thundering Wallaby charge.

It was the second Australian try, some six minutes before half time, after a Lynagh penalty had made it 7–0 after 13 minutes, which was to bring down the safety curtain on the All Blacks, to finally end their utter dominance of world rugby since 1986. This try captured the imagination of countless millions of people on television, who could only gasp at his sheer artistry and instincts, and pure genius. It was surely the try of the tournament.

It all began with a narrow side move by Farr-Jones and the invaluable Lynagh, who put one of his delicate probing kicks into the no-man's land between Crowley, the full-back and the rapidly-approaching Campese. The bounce may have been kind but you felt that Campese had a magnet. At full throttle, he feinted outside and then inside the remaining All Black defence before throwing an outrageous blind pass over his head, without looking, for he knew exactly where the skilful centre, Tim Horan, was going to be. The rest was a formality as Horan ran to narrow the angle for Lynagh's conversion and at half-time with Australia winning 13–0; New Zealand were virtually dead and buried.

It will always be remembered as Campese's match, but one should not disregard the impact on the game of another magnificent player, Nick Farr-Jones, who had remarkably recovered from his serious knee injury during a pool game.

The Australian captain was at his authoritative best, and if the try scoring was by courtesy of Campese it was Farr-Jones who looked after the nitty gritty. Whereas Australia won convincingly both in terms of the score and by virtue that they locked out the All Blacks in defence, it was nevertheless not one-sided in terms of possession or territory.

In fact, it will surprise most people to know that in terms of overall possession from the forwards, the All Blacks were miles ahead of the Wallabies. They convincingly won the first half line-outs and overall, from set-pieces and broken play throughout the game, New Zealand made the ball available to their scrum-half 75 times to Australia's 43. Strangely, this was a pattern in most of Australia's matches apart from the Welsh game. It was also true that Australia had scored eight tries from set-pieces and the week before against Ireland all three of their tries had come from set-pieces.

It therefore followed that the All Blacks, with plenty of ball, enjoyed as much territory as the Wallabies, but made the worse use of the ball by the backs that one could remember from them. They were continually overwhelmed by the swarming defence of Farr-Jones, Lynagh, Horan and Little, not to mention the wings, Egerton and Campese. Indeed, Timu gave up running in the direction of his counterpart, so efficiently had Campese gobbled him up in defence.

The All Blacks showed no guile whatever in attack, and were sadly short of pace. They had not one player who could inject speed or wit into the attack, so the loss of Terry Wright as an attacking full-back and Michael Jones on the flank were critical factors in their defeat.

With the game won in the first half, Australia seemed to sit on their lead in the second period,

merely making sure that New Zealand could not cut loose. They had few worries for the All Blacks seemed to have no idea of how to crack the Australian safe, apart from the futility of running into the steel-hard Wallaby defence. Neither did New Zealand help their cause by dropping so many passes behind their supporting men. Apart from a Fox penalty two minutes into the second half, at no time did New Zealand look like pegging back the arrears. Another Lynagh penalty mid-way through the half finished off Australia and although Fox kicked a penalty eight minutes from time to make the final score an unflattering 16–6 to Australia, it was irrelevant.

Other key players in Australia's performance were the back row, who for the first time began to look an effective unit. The reintroduction of Troy Coker at no. 8 was a revelation and it also allowed the powerful Ofahengaue to play in his preferred position, where he was able to block that well-trodden New Zealand path down the blind side of the scrum.

The All Black defeat was their first in 11 World Cup games and only their third since 1987, since which time they had won 31 and drawn one from 35 Test matches. Two players, Sean Fitzpatrick and Gary Whetton, played in all 35 matches.

For the Australian half-backs, Farr-Jones and Lynagh, it was the 40th time they had been paired at half-back for Australia and it was the 21st time that both Simon Poidevin and David Campese had played against the All Blacks, another record.

Typically, the All Blacks took their defeat well, generously conceding that Australia on the day were by far the better team. They thought that perhaps they should have introduced more young blood into their team like Australia and there were already arguments raging about the advisability of appointing two coaches who, it was well-known, were incompatible. The Wyllie supporters were quick to point out that the forwards had won enough ball to win the match twice over and that it was the back play, or lack of it which dumped the All Blacks out of the Cup.

It did not take long for the antipodean sledging of England to start with the New Zealand coach, John Hart, saying that Australia deserved to win the final because they played great rugby. Campese, who had already shown antipathy towards the English players and their rugby on the Wogan show the previous week, said how important it was to score tries and that the kick and chase game adopted by

Above: The mighty All Black pack produced plenty of driving forward play but the Australian defence was superb.

Right: A searing diagonal run results in Campese's opening try.

England was not going to win games or do rugby any favours.

It was wonderful for rugby in Australia. For years, they have been virtually ignored by their own media, who devote acres of newspaper columns and hours of air time to their isolationist sports such as Australian Rules and League, while totally neglecting rugby union. Now at a stroke, they had beaten the world champions to reach the Rugby World Cup final, thus achieving for Australia more honour and publicity than any other sport except, of course, cricket.

In two successive games in Dublin they had achieved fantastic wins with a style and an elan that was the toast of the rugby world and which was to switch on a record television audience in the British Isles, let alone Australia.

WHAT THEY SAID:

BOB DWYER
(Australia Coach)

❛ One of the reasons why we came through is our defence. I thought it was superb in the second half when we were under pressure. I believe our centres are outstanding defenders and that Jason Little is the best outside-centre defender in the world.

'This was a great day for Australian rugby because New Zealand are always the standard by which we judge ourselves. This would have to be the best day of my involvement with Australian rugby because of the respect which we have for the All Blacks. This is an outstanding Australian squad which has worked hard together and I was delighted to come through such a fine game of rugby today.

❛ We do not play attacking rugby necessarily to entertain. We want to be a well-tailored suit, not a frilly dress. Yet when you have players of the talent of David Campese it is silly not to bring them into the game. ❜

NICK FARR-JONES
(Australian captain)

❛ I was delighted with our play in both halves – running up a lead over the All Blacks is a real achievement, then our defence in the second half when, as expected, they came back at us was excellent. It was our swarming type of defence which kept them out, especially among our midfield backs.
❛ Our back row was also excellent. Simon Poidevin was an inspiration and I think he is playing better than at any other time. To beat New Zealand at any time means a lot to Australians; to beat them in the semi-final of the World Cup is a great feeling. This is also Bob Dwyer's best year as coach. ❜

ALEX WYLLIE
(New Zealand coach)

'We played our best and we were beaten by the better side on the day. Some of our play went well but this is a very fine Australian side. We got enough of the ball from line-out and scrums but they defended very well and we could never cash in.'

GARY WHETTON
(New Zealand captain)

'We were very disappointed because we wanted to win desperately. You simply cannot give a team like Australia a start of 13 points and expect to come through; and not many teams would have been good enough to hold out under the pressure we were exerting in the second half.'

Tim Horan crosses for the second Australian try, made by Campese.

ROLLS
R R
ROYCE

In the New World of international travel, these are the limousines.

CATHAY PACIFIC
Arrive in better shape.

CROWDED CARDIFF SEES REAL TEST ACTION
STEVE BALE

If it is true that the third place play-off is a dead end match between reluctant participants, New Zealand and Scotland obviously had not heard about it. Of course they would have preferred to be at Twickenham and it took a prodigious effort to raise bodies and minds after the disappointment of semi-final defeat but if the All Blacks and Scots were indeed reluctant they did not show it in their play. This was another memorable World Cup match, won 13–6 by New Zealand, a modest enough score given the open nature of the contest. Forty-eight thousand, a very decent Wednesday afternoon crowd, were at Cardiff Arms Park to see it.

As they won, it was acceptable for the New Zealanders to complain about having to play the match – more than could have been said for Alan Jones, then Australia's coach, when his side lost the 1987 third-place match to Wales in Rotorura: 'I do think that third-place play-offs have a limited value and they should certainly be played on the Thursday or Friday before the final and not on the Wednesday.' John Hart, the All Blacks coach, said: 'The play-off probably has commercial value rather than sporting value.' Without doubt an opportunity was missed when it was decided not to utilise the magnificent new Arms Park floodlights and it could hardly be claimed that the game suffered from over-promotion. Had they played it during the evening, the place would have been full.

Amid the splendid rugby, Gary Armstrong was the talk of the Arms Park, just as he had often been of the World Cup, when one of the television pundits announced he was about to sign professionally. As is the way of these things Armstrong later denied it, just as Widnes already had, but there was no denying he was a player rugby league would love to have.

The Scotland scrum-half has developed enormously since an educational visit with the Lions to Australia in 1989. His vastly-improved skills, strength in the tackle and ball-retention are qualities in any player that would obviously be coveted by the other code, just as in Armstrong's case they have been enjoyed by Jed-Forest and Scotland.

In the World Cup as a whole Armstrong provided not so much a revelation as simple confirmation – albeit on a world stage – of his supreme talent. In the third-place match he was, as usual, a fearless and heroic figure, ending up with a fearful raking by Richard Loe before hobbling back undaunted into the fray for further punishment. He and the Scots took a fearful pounding in the first half but somehow held their line and it was not until right at the finish of the second half, after they had weathered all else the All Blacks could throw at them, that they finally cracked. Scotland's record against New Zealand now consists of 13 defeats and two draws going back 86 years.

Whatever the value of these play-offs – Wales enjoyed theirs well enough when they beat the Wallabies in 1987 but neither of the beaten 1991 semi-finalists thought a great deal of it – it did not prevent New Zealand and Scotland combining in rugby as full-blooded and physically punishing as anything in the tournament. What the game lacked in spectacle (which actually wasn't that much), it more than made up in ambition and effort.

This was a testament to the fitness and continuing desire of the two teams, who had plumbed the depths of disappointment the previous weekend when England beat Scotland 9–6 and Australia beat New Zealand 16–6. Scotland had no compunction about playing their defeated side again, the only question being raised over Doddie Weir, the elongated but lightweight lock who had been paired as first choice with Chris Gray in the hope of acquiring more line-out ball than would have been supplied by the alternative, the 1990 Grand Slam veteran Damian Cronin. Sean Lineen, Scotland's Kiwi whose father Terry played 12 times for New Zealand from 1957–60, and was in Cardiff to have his loyalties divided, and Scott Hastings played together at centre for the 23rd time to equal the Test record of the Irish pair, Brendan Mullin and Michael Kiernan.

New Zealand, on the other hand, showed six changes, some voluntary and some enforced. Injury removed John Timu and Grant Fox from contention, but as balance Terry Wright was passed fit to return at full-back. Now if he had been able to face Australia and inject his pace into the threequarter line the All Blacks might well have won. And if they had had the nonpareil Michael Jones on the flank, their chances would have been even better. Jones had missed the Pool One match against Italy, the quarter-final against Canada and the semi-final because all took place on Sundays, and to have played would have been contrary to his religious belief. Wednesday was acceptable, though, and Jones was back, with Andy Earl coming in on the blind side instead of Alan Whetton. Bernie McCahill had a hamstring injury but would have been displaced at inside centre by Walter Little anyway, and Timu's place on the left wing went to the powerful Va'aiga Tuigamala. The winger was replaced at half-time by Shayne Philpott after tearing a hamstring; for Scotland, the wing Tony Stanger was replaced by Peter Dods early in the second half after pulling a hip muscle.

The Scottish forwards mounting a brave rearguard defence near their own posts

From the All Blacks – not least when trying to bounce back from unwonted defeat – you would expect no different, and no side playing them can afford to give anything less than total commitment, which was fine for the Scots as they never do. Thus New Zealand did their utmost to run the Scots ragged in the first half and failed to do so mainly because of an astounding defensive performance in which Scott Hastings' last-ditch tackling saved two certain tries and the improving Weir performed a minor miracle to save another.

The All Blacks won most of the best line-out ball and their waiting backs were given complete freedom to attack. Scottish tackling was the vital preventative measure, but there was also some

extremely bad New Zealand outside passing reminiscent of their semi-final performance in defeat by Australia and there was far too much crash-ball running by the outside centre Craig Innes, who does it well but to excess. And even locked in deep defence, the Scots forwards refused to be overawed by their New Zealand opposites; Finlay Calder showed as much by taking a lunge at Sean Fitzpatrick which might, in another setting, have sparked considerable controversy.

Ultimately, though, constant defence cannot win a match and although they broke away later on, Scotland spent too much time on the back foot ever realistically to consider victory. They have still never beaten the All Blacks but there is a respect between these sides going back to last year's tour by Scotland, who were unfortunate to lose the second Test in Auckland after scoring two tries to one – a game that provoked the sacking of the New Zealand captain, Wayne Shelford. 'It was a pleasure to play against a side with a progressive attitude,' Hart said, presumably drawing comparison with the England strategy he had so disparaged during the course of the tournament. 'Scotland competed tremendously well. I particularly admired their defence. We could have scored three or four tries before half-time and it is great credit to Scotland that they managed to keep us out.'

In addition, New Zealand's passing was sometimes as ineffective as Scotland's cover was effective, and all they had to show for their overwhelming first-half superiority were penalties from 50 and 40 yards by Jon Preston, deputising at fly-half for the injured Fox, to one from 50 yards by full-back Gavin Hastings, which had given Scotland an early lead on what was to prove a rare foray into All Black territory. Hastings, as he had been in the semi-final against England, was a towering figure under the most intense pressure.

Preston had come into the All Black side when Fox withdrew with a pelvic condition that had troubled him ever since New Zealand's summer tour to Argentina. Fox had had to have constant injections, intensive physiotherapy and massage just to keep him going and in the end, with no World Cup left to play for, he started the extended rest which he had been told was the only cure. At home, Preston had played most of his rugby at scrum-half until he succeeded Stephen Bachop, now of Western Samoa, into the Canterbury side as half-back partner to fellow All Black Graeme Bachop, brother of Stephen. In the second half he extended his side's

133

Finlay Calder leads a Scottish assault with John Jeffrey in support. This was the last Murrayfield international for both players.

modest advantage with his third penalty from six attempts, this one from 45 yards, before Scotland mounted a ferocious, but temporary and unrequited, comeback. Hastings – shades of his semi-final miss from 20 yards against England four days earlier – was wide with a straight 30-yarder and when a storming attack up the right was halted close to the All Black line, the Scotland captain David Sole could not force himself across. Eventually, with time running out, Hastings added a third, much harder penalty on an angle from 35 yards.

New Zealand's last word was emphatic. Thirty seconds of injury-time had passed when Little, a second choice all through this World Cup behind McCahill but comfortably the most penetrative New Zealander during the first-half gadding about, linked with Graeme Bachop, the replacement wing Shayne Philpott and full-back Terry Wright before popping up again and accelerating past the outside of the last of the Scots defenders, Derek White. The

try had in effect been created by Scotland's desperation; as Armstrong sought to run out of defence the ball was freed by a thundering tackle by Zinzan Brooke and with the Scots sucked in at the point of breakdown the All Blacks at last had room to manoeuvre. 'They are,' reflected Ian McGeechan, the Scottish coach, 'still one of the top two sides in the tournament and they're still one of the sides you've got to beat.'

In 1987 Alan Jones complained that the third-place match was one his players never wanted to play (especially after the monumental semi-final they had just lost to France in Sydney), and of course it showed in their play. Australia were beaten by a Welsh side who had just been trounced by a record score in the semi-final by New Zealand, which undoubtedly meant the Wallabies presumed victory just as they had presumed securing a place in the final. There was no such bad grace four years on, though McGeechan did say: 'It was very difficult to lift the players for a second international inside a week.' On the other hand, he also said: 'It was worthwhile because we were playing the All Blacks.' And though Hart had his reservations, his co-coach Alex Wyllie called it 'a tremendous game'. Whatever, it was certainly a noble way for the great Scots John Jeffrey and Calder, not to mention a great generation of All Blacks, to bid farewell to Test rugby.

SCOTLAND'S WORLD CUP: PRIDE AND THE PRESSURE

Gavin Hastings, *the outstanding full-back, recalls the Scottish effort.*

It was a great honour to take part in the World Cup, even though it ultimately ended in disappointment for Scotland when we were knocked out by England in the semi-final. The standard was so much higher this time than last time. New Zealand stole a march on everyone else in 1987, when they were so far ahead of every other team. Even though they didn't make the final, our experience against them when we lost the third-place match told me that they hadn't gone back; it was more a question of other teams having come up. Although we were disappointed, it was an achievement to reach the semi-final and I enjoyed being in a position that comes along once in a lifetime leading the back pages and stealing a march on football. The World Cup created a huge amount of interest and the following for our team in Scotland was quite unbelievable.

We had a game against England that we knew would be extremely difficult, but our feeling was that, given our success in the 1990 Grand Slam match, we could reasonably expect to do the same providing we were at the peak of our form. I suppose you have to look back and say we were fairly comfortably beaten up front and it was difficult to play off scraps of possession. Credit must be given to England for doing that; they did tremendously well winning in Paris one week and Murrayfield the next. They had learned over the previous 18 months. We tried to combat their strengths up front with a bit of quick-wittedness and sharpness but it wasn't good enough. We went into the third-place play-off and were playing what I firmly believe to be, if not the best, then the next best side in the world. We badly wanted to become the first Scotland side ever to beat the All Blacks but we didn't achieve it. Of course this was another disappointment but we have to be realistic and given the numbers of players that play in Scotland I suppose a top-four spot has to be seen as a success. Within the team, the squad and the coaches we'd set standards which we felt made us capable of at least getting to the semi-finals – which we did.

At the same time, we have to be self-critical. We showed a lot of commitment and passion. That's fair enough but the squad, through the standards we've set over the last few years and with our record at Murrayfield, have maintained quite a high level of performance and even so we failed because our performance was not up to scratch on the day. Obviously England were one of the reasons; there's no getting away from it that they put us under tremendous pressure. It's difficult to set up moves off the back foot and winning a limited supply of line-out ball.

After the semi-final there was a feeling of let-down. The New Zealanders would agree that in the 24 hours after the semi-final the last thing you want to do is play another game three days later. But when it comes down to reality in the light of day, it is very important that you go out with an extremely positive attitude. All right, we weren't in the World Cup final but what a compensation there would have been if we had beaten New Zealand for the first time. We didn't want to undo the positive work that had been done for the World Cup and, with the team breaking up, we felt we owed it to John Jeffrey and Finlay Calder, and also to coaches Derrick Grant and Jim Telfer, to do our best to go out in style. We were as positive as we could be after only three days' 'rest'. Actually there was no way it was a rest; it was three days' intense preparation. Anyone who has played three international rugby matches in 10 days will tell you it's a desperately tough thing to do and my body felt the full effects.

In the pool matches our initial target had been to ensure we played our quarter-final at Murrayfield. The last time we played Japan was in 1989 and, without the Scottish guys who were on the Lions tour of Australia, they pulled off a surprise victory. The Japanese prepare very well for games, we were conscious that they had given Australia a fright in their first game of the '87 World Cup and that they had an extra four years' experience. They had to be taken seriously and from a backs' point of view we ran the ball fairly well and from reasonably deep

135

positions. Our strength, speed and angles of running were quite good.

I didn't play in the next game against Zimbabwe, Peter Dods coming in and giving a fine kicking display. In the first half that was extremely important because Zimbabwe came out with real fire and unless Peter had been on song with his kicking we might have struggled a bit – though we never thought we were going to lose. Once the game progressed our greater fitness, team-work and spirit shone through and we ran in quite a few tries. This was an opportunity to rest some players, which coaches felt they had to do to avoid the experience of 1987 when we played more or less the same guys through to the quarter-finals. In World Cups you just can't afford to do it.

The big pool game, as we always knew, was against Ireland. They'd come to Murrayfield last season and run around, although we managed to end up winning. This time it was again extremely tough. They tended to do very well in the line-out and play their typical harrying game. We knew what to expect but eventually we overcame it. I was worried at half-time when we were behind but the guys picked themselves up and, to their enormous credit, played much more powerfully in the second half and deserved to win at the end of the day.

In the quarter-final Western Samoa were Western Samoa in name only. We were very conscious of the fact that the vast majority of their players lived and played rugby in New Zealand, so we felt they would be the equivalent of a strong New Zealand provincial side – and from our own experience there last year when we played Wellington and Canterbury on successive Saturdays we knew what

The fantastic Scottish covering and tackling thwarted New Zealand on so many occasions.

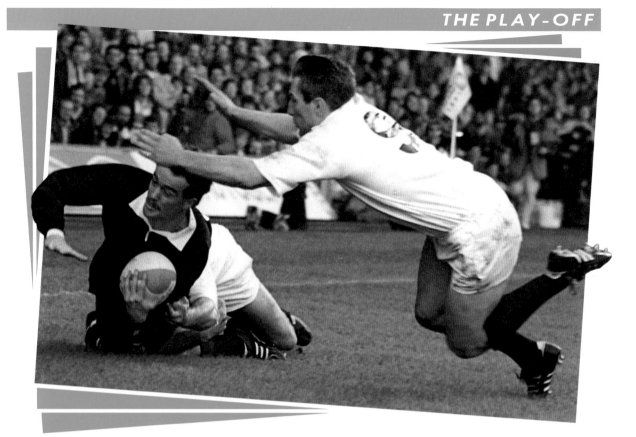

Terry Wright is squashed by a double tackle from Scott Hastings and Gary Armstrong.

we were up against. A lot had been written about their physical tackling and aggression, their constructive defence which would put us on the back foot. We decided the best way to combat that would be to meet it head on. Our first-half performance was probably the finest half of the tournament from Scotland's point of view. We felt that if we could drive at them close in and win the rucks and mauls we'd get the crucial nudge going forward. Jim Telfer had sussed it out and it worked a dream. This is why I was used standing off and driving in; when the forwards get their heads up and see one of the backs running full bore at the opposition it gives them a tremendous lift and target to aim at. That is where a great coach comes in.

My preparation for the World Cup was more intense than anything I've known. Although people react differently, a lot of guys were in need of a rest at the end. I was looking forward to going home and getting stuck into a new job. I felt it would be

difficult to keep motivated in terms of the club scene but we've come off Lions tours before now and picked ourselves up, and I was keen to put a lot back into Watsonians, draw on my own experiences and try to encourage others to reach their best level of performance. I'll certainly be playing in the Five Nations' Championship this season but I'm not one to look after that. We aren't like England, New Zealand or Australia; we'll always struggle against any side we meet unless we are absolutely right and raring to go. We have very few players to choose from and as a result we find it hard to raise our performance unless it absolutely matters.

This explains our poor displays before the World Cup. There was always that feeling that when it came down to the wire the Scottish team would perform, but I do remember the way I was feeling when we lost to Romania in Bucharest (when I didn't play) and then the feeling when we lost to Edinburgh Borderers a week before the tournament. It was extremely difficult to get motivated. Nonetheless, New Zealand would never lose a game like that. Scotland cannot afford to take any side complacently, if only because of the low standard of our club rugby. The Western Samoans, for example, play a very much higher standard of rugby week-in week-out than any of the Scottish guys.

137

To finish with that penalty I missed against England: to be honest, I have thought an awful lot about it. What I'd like to say is that the annoying thing from my point of view is that we will never know how the game would have turned out had that penalty gone over. Perhaps people will remember the game for that missed kick. It was a part of the game which had a significance that was apparent. Of course, Jon Webb had missed some kicks for England as well and, although I'm not making excuses, possibly if they had gone over England might have been out of sight by the time I missed. That moment will live with me but I don't wake up in the middle of the night screaming and crying and wanting to jump out of the window. When it comes down to it, these things happen.

Tuigamala added power, pace and penetration to the All Black effort.

THE ALL BLACKS: NEVER FOR EVER

Grant Fox, *New Zealand's fly-half, looks back at the eclipse of his team and forward to an uncertain future*

It is the end of an era and, although I feel sad about it, all good things come to an end. It's a cyclical thing; other countries have had great eras too, and they never last for ever. If there are All Blacks who retire – and I don't want to pre-empt anyone's decision – it may be the start of another one. We

may not have won the World Cup but we can be proud of our achievements since 1987: in my 35 Tests there were 31 wins, one draw and only three losses, all to Australia. From a New Zealand perspective, I'd like to think the All Blacks can start straight back up again next year, but it may take longer than that. We have the talent at home, but what we don't have is the experience at international level that other teams have.

The World Cup has changed the face of rugby and I would hope, having fallen at the semi-final this time, we would already be planning for the 1995 tournament. Take Australia: I believe through 1989 and '90 they built their side for this World Cup and, while they were doing so, losses were acceptable. But to the New Zealand rugby public and the All Blacks, losses are not acceptable in any shape or form. I'd like nothing better than for the All Blacks to continue to be successful, even if I'm not part of it, but if they suffer the odd loss while they are rebuilding, people will have to be more patient and understanding.

The trouble for me is that I haven't been through it. I don't know whether accepting defeat is really the right thing, because for our team since 1987 defeat was simply never acceptable, whether the World Cup came into it or not. Success at Test level is possibly more important for New Zealand than any other rugby country and I have a feeling that, despite the World Cup, for us Test rugby will not be lessened in significance. There has been comment that the Five Nations' Championship, for example, may not be as important but I hope that's not the case because Test rugby is the ultimate level – though obviously the World Cup is the ultimate level of the ultimate level!

To lose the semi-final to Australia was a shattering blow. We had clearly set ourselves to get to Twickenham and certainly didn't contemplate going to Cardiff for a third-place match. We had great confidence in ourselves. We always talk in terms of winning, never of keeping scores down – which is a guaranteed way of ensuring you lose. I experienced only three defeats and this one should have hurt the most because it was a World Cup semi-final. But I felt that in the other two we let ourselves down, whereas this time the guys gave everything but even in defeat we did ourselves credit. We tried as hard as we could.

I want to acknowledge that these Australians are a very good side and on the day they deserved their victory thoroughly. We have to face facts: at the moment they have caught us and overtaken us in overall rugby standings. I saw in the intensity Australia were able to generate in Dublin what I felt the All Blacks were like in 1987, '88 and '89.

In our build-up to the tournament we toured Argentina, which was very successful when you consider that no side had gone unbeaten through that country since the 1976 All Blacks. But although the results were good, in terms of performance it probably wasn't up to the standard we would demand of ourselves. No one puts more pressure on the team to perform than the players themselves. There is an expectation and demand from the New Zealand rugby public that we win matches well because we have set the standards. On the other hand, the pressure is so great that in a sense we can't win: if we win well, the opposition are deemed to be no good; if we win unconvincingly we didn't play well; if we lose, heaven help us. But we created the monster ourselves because of what we started in 1987 and continued through 1988, '89 and most of '90, so I suppose we can't really complain.

When the World Cup started, we were happy just to get a victory against England at Twickenham. We felt we played reasonably well. We went out to attack England with ball in hand in certain areas where we thought they would suspect but it didn't work, so we were forced to revise our tactics and that meant kicking the ball a lot more than we had intended. We were only ever six points up, never enough of a buffer to open up the game, though in the last 20 minutes we always had things under control. It was important to get the win under our belts and start planning for a quarter-final in Lille, rather than the daunting prospect of facing France in Paris.

I didn't play against the United States at Gloucester. It was not a satisfactory performance at all. There were some basic errors where we let ourselves down. By our own high standards it was most disappointing because we always talk in terms of quality, not quantity of performance. It didn't matter that we scored 40 points; the All Blacks played badly. I returned against Italy and although we scored fewer points than against the US and the margin was relatively narrow, we were happier. We

felt we weren't too far from cracking it. To be fair, Italy have come a long way since 1987, and we weren't very pleased with the way the referee, Kerry Fitzgerald, let them get away with persistent offside.

Then it was on to our quarter-final in Lille. Of all the sides who participated in the 1987 World Cup, Canada have improved the most – to the stage where International Board countries are asking them to tour, which is a mark of respect to Canada and their development. They were a big, strong side and we played them in very difficult conditions. We were very satisfied with the way we played because, despite the weather, when we got ourselves into scoring positions we generally took advantage. We played the game in their half, which was essential on a day like that.

When we came to Australia in Dublin, there was no doubt that pace was the significant factor. They did have a distinct advantage over us in that area. They spent a large part of the first 30 minutes in our half, applying pressure and, although we absorbed it for a while, they eventually managed to turn their pressure into points. That period just before half-time was vital: if we had scored at that stage when we were on their line it could have turned out very differently but, once we'd missed out, 13 points was too much to catch up. The need to play 'catch-up' was a Catch-22 situation: we spread the ball more than we envisaged and were forced into making 50–50 passes because we were trying to create that little bit extra that we needed to break them. If we'd been closer we'd have held on to the ball a lot more and created more second-phase possession. We tried everything and the forwards did a great job winning us the ball. I don't think the backs let them down – the Wallaby defence was superb.

I was terribly disappointed to miss the third-place game in which we beat Scotland. I was desperately hoping to see it out. I'd set my heart on Twickenham but I still wanted to play in Cardiff. But I'd carried a pelvic injury since the tour to Argentina and the only known cure is rest, the one thing I couldn't allow myself with the World Cup coming up. Through the fantastic efforts of our medical team I'd managed to keep myself playing but it had been a painful experience and dreadfully hard work. I'd had injections, intensive physiotherapy, massage, everything that could be done so that I could carry on playing.

I don't think it affected my play but I'd never been totally free of it, always been aware of it while I was on the field every time I had to run or kick. I think my form was OK given what the team wanted me to try to do. People may suggest that as an individual I didn't have quite the same sort of impact I perhaps had in the previous World Cup but my role was different so I wouldn't accept that. Finally, the injury took its toll and I had to miss out against Scotland. I couldn't stretch out; I could jog and that was about it. I had no idea how long it would take to clear up but it needed complete rest.

I've been giving my future a lot of thought. I haven't made an ultimate decision because I have to be away from a rugby environment, away from the disappointment of defeat against Australia, to come to a sensible conclusion. There are other factors. I have a young family to whom I desperately want to give more time. I have a job which I enjoy. My employer has been very good to me over the years and I'd like to put more time into that. Probably the biggest part of it is whether I actually want to continue playing and, to be perfectly honest, at the moment I'm looking towards not playing.

The World Cup is essential for the promotion of world rugby. In terms of quality, I don't think the 1991 tournament got anywhere near 1987. In 1987 we were clearly dominant, whereas now a lot of sides have done a lot of work to come up – but we still didn't see so much quality rugby as a spectacle. A lot of games were boring. Maybe there's too much emphasis on winning as the overriding factor. I still don't know whether that's right or wrong but it didn't help to uplift the style of football that was played. Maybe there's simply too much pressure on amateur sportsmen.

Walter Little capped a great game with the only try in injury time.

ONE TEAM IS CHANGING THE FACE OF BRITISH SPORT.

Over the next few years stadia in the U.K. will change radically.

The paying customer demands it. The Taylor Report insists on it. But how can stadium owners fund major redevelopments?

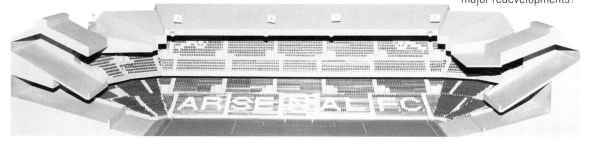

HIGHBURY STADIUM, LONDON

IBROX STADIUM, GLASGOW

This is where The Carnegie Partnership can help.

That's because we specialise in individual financing projects for the redevelopment of sports stadia.

Dorman Jeffrey, one of Scotland's leading corporate law firms, will advise upon the special and complex legal issues involved.

Our unique and comprehensive service covers every aspect of funding, implementation and project management.

Arsenal, Glasgow Rangers and the Scottish Rugby Union have already benefited from our expertise.

Perhaps our team could help your stadium. Call Graham Watson on 031-225 7773 or Brian Dorman on 041-221 9880 for a confidential chat.

Or drop either of them a line.

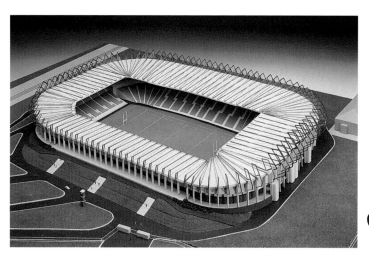

MURRAYFIELD STADIUM, EDINBURGH

THE CARNEGIE PARTNERSHIP
business management for sport

THE FINAL

AUSTRALIA'S GLORIOUS TRIUMPH OVER HEROIC ENGLAND
CLIFF MORGAN

Sound the trumpets, clash the cymbals, beat the drums and make a joyful noise throughout every land for this sporting battle was genuine and worthy of an honoured place on the world stage. It was an immense struggle, overwhelming even, in its heroism and its heartbreak. Above all else, in its spirit and gallantry. Wrapped up in one eighty minute parcel was the skill and style, the power and the turbulence of brave men who were dedicated to making a man's game something to wonder at. The 1991 World Cup final had integrity and it was a flourish of triumphant rugby.

It was a day calculated to make us sit up. The undeniable fact is that at the end of a pulsating match we all stood up, along with the Queen, and applauded and cheered and cheered again as, first the vanquished and then the victors, drained of oxygen, climbed slowly up the slope of the grandstand to receive their medallions. By this time it was impossible to see one blade of Twickenham's green grass for it was hidden by thousands and thousands of deliriously happy Australians trying to outsprint the English for the best vantage points in front of the Royal box in the West Stand. There was frantic jostling for position but no loutish behaviour, no rancour or bitterness that too often, these days, disfigure great sporting events. The fans simply wanted to be close enough to let both teams know that they cared, that they appreciated the fact that they had been witness to a mighty struggle. It would be a bonus if they could touch even the hem of an English or Australian jersey and they could say, in years to come, that they had actually run on the field where the gladiators had produced a truly memorable sporting confrontation.

Twickenham has never in its long history seen a day like this – not even when England defeated France to win the Grand Slam earlier this year when the team and the fans were justifiably proud and happy. Although England were beaten there was spontaneous and loud renderings of 'Swing Low Sweet Chariot' and 'Land of Hope and Glory' which rang around this majestic stadium as Will Carling shook hands with the Queen, who obviously understood and shared his anguish. Even in defeat there was natural dignity as England's captain turned to the crowd below and put on a brave smile which masked his bitter disappointment – not only for himself but for a team that had served him and his country so loyally and often brilliantly for three years. The glittering gold prize was almost theirs. Second best is not as sweet. Despite the certainty that this had been England's best performance of the tournament, and indeed, probably their best ever, they were always just that touch away from the all-round class of a terrific Australian team, which displayed that precious, creative charge on the field. They were, in all their matches, restless and first-rate.

And first-rate is how I would judge the performance of the England pack. As they dragged their tired legs up the steps to claim their medallions you reflected on the inspired leadership of Brian Moore, who had a storming game. Later he took a verbal swipe at David Campese because he felt that the Australian wing had deliberately punched the ball forward and thus prevented a try by Rory Underwood. Moore thought the referee should have awarded a penalty try. 'Campese proved today that he is not what he says, the saviour of rugby, but he's as cynical as the rest of us.'

Pale-faced and pretty well spent came Wade Dooley and Paul Ackford, still upright, as they always have been, as England's middle-row men. Both gave exceptional performances in the line-out and in the tight and broken play. One storming run by Dooley made the heart leap. Prop forwards Jason Leonard and Jeff Probyn looked as if they had been in the thick of a titanic struggle. Peter Winterbottom who had shown tough persistence all through had played his best game in an England jersey and Mick Skinner, bold and aggressive, had stormed the field like a hungry panther. Then there was the no. 8,

Mike Teague, who had shown England supporters why he had been nominated 'Player of the Series' during the Lions tour of Australia. The England forwards must have felt that they had done enough to win. Were they for or against the English backs attempting to spread the ball wide? I would essay a guess that they would sooner have played the type of game that took them to clinical, hard victories over France and Scotland.

Rob Andrew, who early in the match had trouble with one of the contact lenses he wears, looked numb. He could not believe that out of the 41 times he had received the ball and passed it to his threequarters on 26 occasions, England failed to score a try. Rob's kicking, save for one slice at a drop goal, was top class. Jeremy Guscott, head bowed, probably remembering the moment, late on in the game, when he so nearly got away and another when he seemed to take the wrong option. 'If only' must have been running through Rory Underwood's mind. Once when he was free and was thrown what turned out to be an uncatchable pass and again when Winterbottom's pass was knocked on by Campese – he may or may not have made the line but, 'if only'. Simon Halliday, with limited ball, played his part and at scrum-half, Richard Hill did what he was there to do. He fed fine ball to the backs and revelled in the close play too. Jon Webb kicked two out of four penalties. The two he missed were beyond his range. Seldom was he able to join the threequarter line to effect. Like the rest of the England team he was inevitably trapped in the spider web defence of Australia which held firm.

There was a din of delight when Nick Farr-Jones – for me the best back in the world – was handed the Webb Ellis Trophy by the Queen. The colourful crowd struck up 'Waltzing Matilda' in three or four different keys at first but they soon got their act together. It was a tribute, not only to a fine man but to a team that had played the most adventurous rugby throughout the tournament. Farr-Jones, the protagonist, lifted the trophy high above his head, turned to the crowd and smiled. It was a moment to savour and one of relief, I am certain, for Australia's captain knew in his heart that England had helped his cause by spilling too many rushed passes. He didn't fancy extra time.

The day itself began with the groundsmen putting the final touches and Twickenham was shaved to a one-inch length – its closest crop ever. It was 10 o'clock and programme stands, hamburger and coffee stands – even chip stands – were doing brisk

Above: Will Carling creates a gap.

Right: Wallaby lock John Eales could jump, run, pass and, as we see here, tackle.

trade. The hospitality tents looked opulent – Silver Service here. Television and radio people from all around the world scurried about the village of vans, testing circuits and satellites. More than 2 billion people in far flung places on the planet would be tuned in for this match.

Tradition dies hard in the West car park and picnics had already started before noon. This is the place where old internationals meet and long-standing supporters park their cars and eat their goodies in the same spot, year after year. A few Rolls-Royces and Land Rovers and champagne and smoked salmon but many more with beer and wine

Simon Halliday tries to escape the clutches of Tim Horan.

and pies. This is a wonderful cocktail of human beings. It is full of character and colour. Unlikely ladies in England jerseys and a sea of gold and green sported by the Aussies. A couple arrived with faces painted in the Australian colours. 'Where do you come from?' 'Merthyr Tydfil. Now Wales is out we're supporting Australia. Anybody except the English!' Ancient rivalries die hard! Britain's finest 400-metre runner, Roger Black, arrives. Says he was a rugby player before becoming an Olympic athlete. He'd love to be out there today. Mr and Mrs Carling – Will's mum and dad. Parents share the trials and tribulations as well as the glory. 'When I watch, I hope Will doesn't get hurt,' says Mrs Carling. Nothing like a mother to get down to reality.

Half past one and the Massed Bands of Her Majesty's Royal Marines strike up. They sound and look wonderful. Precision is their business. Mini rugby and New Image rugby played by the little ones entertain the swelling throng. The pitch is perfect, a few clouds in an otherwise blue sky and the pulse races as the teams take the field. The preliminaries are on as Her Majesty The Queen and Prince Edward and the Princess Royal walk the red carpet and shake hands, and the National Anthems ring out. The moment of truth has arrived. The referee, Derek Bevan, looks around, blows and with a flourish of a Welsh arm the final is on.

Understandably it is a nervous start, diamond cut diamond and Rob Andrew does well to clear the line. To the delight of the crowd, England let the ball out and threaten the Australian defence but Michael Lynagh, with delightful attacking kicking, swings the pendulum. For the first 20 minutes the England pack seem quicker to the ball but lose momentum by giving away a penalty which Lynagh fluffs. Within two minutes Jeremy Guscott is put in a clear attacking situation but grey gloom descends as he takes the wrong option.

Within 60 seconds came the lightning flash of invention from David Campese. Seemingly from nowhere, he arrived to take the ball well in his own half of the field. Eight giant strides and a beautifully measured punt ahead and the chase was on. He was clear and five metres from England's line; it only needed a reasonable bounce of the ball and a Campese try was certain. The gods decided otherwise. No score but we had been treated to one magic glimpse of this man's incomparable talent, the cherished juice of artistry. Just one moment later, Lynagh kicked a penalty goal and Australia were,deservedly, in the lead.

England re-started and Australia's 21-year-old centre Tim Horan took the ball. Brushing off three tackles he chose to run from inside his own 22 metre line. His burst took play to within a whisker of England's line. From the throw-in, Willie Ofahengaue, near the tail, made the perfect two-handed catch, turned and drove forward with the aid of his pack and prop forwards Daly and McKenzie touched down for a try. The name of Tony Daly will appear in the record book. Lynagh converted to put Australia nine points ahead. Before half-time Jon Webb missed two kicks at goal but neither was that easy, a little out of his range.

The only scores of the second half were two penalties from Webb and another for Michael Lynagh. The all too easy assumption is that 40 minutes with only three penalties would be dull. On the contrary it was prodigious stuff. The second half opened like a fire-cracker when Willie Ofahengaue collected an England kick-off and beat man after

man in a run that was all power and swerve and side-step and hand-off. Creativity is truly individual and this flank forward gave notice in this match that he is near the best in the world. So too the other loose forward, Simon Poidevin, whose tackling and covering were a feature. It had to be for England's forwards were rampant early in the second half – the back row in particular – and with Richard Hill sending out his usual express passes England's threequarters should have been able to breach any defence.

First Rob Andrew tried a shot at a drop goal but the danger to Australia was over as Farr-Jones gathered and cleared time after time. He has the persistence and sagacity of a Corgi dog and the most astute tactical brain. To see him orchestrating and pointing his forwards to the best spot in the mauls is to study a master at work.

His partner, Michael Lynagh, was cool and in command. So often in this game he put pressure on England by using his educated boot. He did make one almost fatal error in conjuction with Campese, when Guscott took advantage of a loose ball but failed to punish the error.

More thrilling England pressure, a Jon Webb penalty to which Lynagh responded and then the Campese deliberate knock-on which cost his team more points. The Australian drawbridge went up.

Derek Bevan blew the final whistle – and he had been exemplary in everything he did – and Australia had won the match. More than anything else it was the most brilliantly organised defence by them that turned the game their way. Never have I seen such tackling by centres and Jason Little and Tim Horan were heroes. What a future Horan has for he has all the gifts. When the videos are studied it will be seen that one two-handed catch at a line-out by 21-year-old John Eales was a crucial one and this young man was also mighty in broken play. It was a crunching tackle of his on Rob Andrew that saved a certain try. Eales is another man of the future. And rugby imposes on us a constant reference to the future of the game. There have been a few who have been maliciously derisive in their criticisms of tournament organisation, the commercial programme – everything really. They are lacking in true understanding and sympathy. Whatever else, the players must be the first priority and their well being, in every sense, must be taken into account. Wasn't it the flickering genius of David Campese that lifted our spirits during the Rugby World Cup 1991?

WHAT THEY SAID:

NICK FARR-JONES
(Australia captain)

It is a great feeling but England's attacking approach made it a very difficult task. I had to lie in the bath exhausted for half an hour after the match. It is a great thing for Australian rugby.

WILL CARLING
(England's captain)

Obviously, there is tremendous disappointment. We have come so far with this team and it will be the last time the team is together. We have had fantastic support from the coaching staff, the medical men and the guys on the bench and ultimately, we did England proud. We made some mistakes and it cost us dear.

BOB DWYER
(Australia coach)

England gave us a tremendous match and I would like to congratulate them but I would also like to congratulate Australia. I felt that we coped with the pressure and defended extremely well. I am delighted for the players.

ROB ANDREW
(England fly-half)

We felt that our approach was the correct one to use against Australia. Kicking into the strong wind in the second half was difficult but given the possession we secured we should have won. Having won so much ball merely intensifies the disappointment.

It was an outstanding effort by our forwards to have won so much ball and to dominate the Australians as they did. That is rare at the top level. We wanted to move the Australian pack around and we finished strongly, a testimony to our extraordinary levels of fitness. Yet it is over and our chances are gone. I expect to take a good while to get over this sense of complete letdown.

BOB FORDHAM
(Australian RU chief executive)

This is one of the greatest sporting triumphs in Australian history and it will do wonders for the game in Australia. We cannot afford to sit back and enjoy it. We now want to follow up the possibility of a five nations championship in the southern hemisphere and the return of South Africa will do wonders for that prospect. We want to give the public the very best of representative rugby.

This Campese tackle was typical of the fantastic Australian defence.

MIXED FEELINGS OF THE MAESTRO WING

David Campese *looks back*

Winning the World Cup was an outstanding achievement for Australian rugby but I wasn't really that happy because we didn't play to our potential against England in the final at Twickenham; we could have played a lot better, as we showed when we beat New Zealand in the semi-final in Dublin. Normally we were a very positive team but this time I have to say we stood back and waited for England to attack. It meant that, to my great disappointment, we didn't win the trophy in quite the style I had hoped for.

England won a lot of ball and our defence was absolutely fantastic but, standing there watching them trying to get the ball moving as they had not done previously, it was almost as if they were going through the motions, because they could have made a lot more of the opportunities they had. Peter Winterbottom kept popping up in the line, there was a lot of running across the field by the backs and Rory Underwood did not have the best of days. After England's previous games, when they hadn't moved the ball around, he probably had it too much and didn't know what to do with it. Jeremy Guscott twice had an overlap outside him but cut back inside. Will Carling took a few bad options as well.

If you want to play 15-man rugby you have to learn it. You can't just turn up on the day and play that type of game. Australia are used to it, so it's

different for us: we can play in any style that suits the occasion, and if we had had the opportunities England had I have no doubt we would have made much more of them. England have shown in the past that they have a lot of good players but I don't feel they make anything like the best use of their talent and, although they tried very hard in the World Cup final, our defence was such that they hardly got over the advantage line once.

I have to confess that my feelings after we won were mixed, with none of the elation you are supposed to feel on these occasions. In a way it was particularly hard for me because I'm not a very emotional person about anything, even something as obviously important as winning the World Cup. I was very happy for the team and happy for myself

Tony Daly scores the only try of the final.

after all the years we have spent building up to this, and it was my 100th game for the Wallabies, which made it even more special. But it's always very, very hard for me to get excited; great though it was to win, it has quickly become history and, to be honest, I felt a bit flat afterwards.

In fact, I had felt a lot better the previous week when we beat New Zealand than when we beat England. At Twickenham there was a great mental exertion and when I came off the field I felt drained of energy after concentrating so hard for 80 minutes. I didn't think I played badly but at the same time I didn't really contribute to the game. I didn't go looking for the ball as much as I like to, and England's defence were always looking for me, which I suppose cramped my style even more. It was just that I didn't do very much. OK, we're world champions and we've won the ultimate prize but my part in the final, in the game that won it, was far less than I would have wanted.

By the end of the tournament the pool games seemed an awfully long time ago but when we started out in Wales they went well for us. In a way they were what won us the World Cup because our confidence built up as we went from game to game, and each one of them was very different from the one before. Argentina weren't scared of us, ran after the ball and gave us a very hard, competitive game at Llanelli, though even when they got to within a few points of us during the second half I had no worries that we were about to lose. In fact when it mattered we went down to their end and scored almost immediately. We had what it took when the chips were down.

Western Samoa at Pontypool was one of those games when nothing much really happens. It was played in dreadful conditions, which helped them more than us. They didn't have an accurate enough goal-kicker and although we didn't play particularly well and didn't score a try, it was an adequate performance for our purposes. Even though we scored a handsome victory over Wales, the game at Cardiff Arms Park was probably the hardest, for psychological reasons as much as anything. We put ourselves under a lot of pressure by beating them by 60 points in the summer and it took a while to get into our stride but once we got on a roll the game was won comfortable enough. It was a really satisfying occasion because we started to fulfil a bit of potential and achieve a bit of form.

Our quarter-final against Ireland in Dublin was probably the hardest game because we went into it without any idea what to expect. We hadn't played the Irish for a long time – since the 1987 World Cup quarter-final in fact – and the one thing we did know was that they would never give up. This was exactly how it turned out; every time we thought we might be about to get away from them, they kept coming back, and when they scored their try time was obviously getting short. But even then, once I asked the touch judge and he had told me there were still six minutes to go, I was confident. The way we picked up was magnificent; it was as if we finally told each other 'Let's go and score' – and, as if to order, we did.

The semi-final against New Zealand was fantastic. For me, that was really the final. We missed each other in the 1987 World Cup and in this final too, which was a great shame because I firmly believe the Wallabies and All Blacks are the two finest sides in world rugby. We gave everything to beat New Zealand and we knew that if we beat them we would win the World Cup. They were the best, the previous champions, and the feeling of achievement we had when we had done it reflected how significant the game was for us all. I would dearly love to have faced – and beaten – them in the actual final but in any case to beat them when there was no second chance will remain one of my greatest rugby memories.

One of the things I disliked about the World Cup was the way the players of the teams that had been knocked out were sent home almost as soon as they had been beaten. In my view they should have been kept together right through to the final and so had the opportunity to see the later games between the best in the world. Not only for their own interest but as a means of increasing their enthusiasm for when they take the rugby message back to their own countries. It would, for instance, have been a splendid gesture if the Western Samoans and Canadians, after doing so well in the pool games and making a big impact right through to the quarter-finals, had been able to see the World Cup through. It was a chance sadly missed. It's not as if there's any shortage of money: this would have been one excellent, worthwhile use for the huge amounts the tournament generated.

The interest back in Australia was incredible. Thousands of faxes arrived at our hotel in Weybridge; we were being contacted by radio stations in Melbourne where they had never shown any interest in rugby – probably hardly knew of its existence – before. Mind you, some of the stories about me in some of the media were ridiculous. The only Lotus I've ever seen was a Matchbox car. I just wonder whether the interest at home will continue. Naturally I desperately hope so, but I can't help feeling that it will soon have disappeared again as people get on with their ordinary lives. Winter in England is summer in Australia, definitely not the rugby season, and most people will probably concentrate on going to the beach and having a good time as Aussie people tend to do.

For the rugby people it has obviously been fantastic but the Australian Rugby Union cannot afford to sit back and wait for things to happen. From here on into next season the authorities have got to promote the game as they never have before, use these guys who've just won the World Cup as vehicles for their campaign and make sure they are properly looked after for doing so. That's the only way they'll keep the people interested.

This year I set three goals: to win the Italian

championship with Milan, the Australian championship with Randwick and the World Cup with Australia. I've done all three and now that I've done so I think I'd find it very hard to go back home and play rugby, to cop the flak that I seem to get when I'm playing in Australia. This is why I so much prefer playing in Europe. In the World Cup, everywhere Australia went everyone was interested in what you could do and not in what you couldn't do, whereas in Australia there are an awful lot of people who seem to expect you to be doing something brilliant all the time. We all know it doesn't work like that and I just got sick of it after a while. In Britain, journalists don't 'bag' you all the time; they look after you and let you know if they think you are a good player.

As of the end of the World Cup I retired from international rugby and intend to enjoy the rest of my playing days in Italy, where my father was born. But there again, our coach Bob Dwyer has been working very hard trying to get me to carry on, and in six months' time who knows how I'm going to feel? This was my 10th season for Australia and frankly after all that time I needed a rest. Maybe I'll keep my options open after all...

Right: Rob Andrew leads an England raid.

Below: The final whistle — mission accomplished.

ANALYSING THE DAY OF PROFOUND DISAPPOINTMENT

Rob Andrew *on the build up, the pain and the glory.*

It has been very difficult to come to terms with England's defeat in the World Cup final against Australia. The overriding emotion remains profound disappointment and it will take a long time to get over it. It will be analysed: Why did we lose? Did we do it wrong? Were our tactics misconceived? Should we have kicked it in the air? Should we have run it as we did? Well there could have been a bit more kicking perhaps in certain situations but I suppose it would have been a lot worse if it had gone wrong in the quarter- or semi-final.

At the same time, I am aware of what we have been involved in. The tournament is part of world rugby now. The whole thing is absolutely fantastic. It's very pressured, of course, but if you don't like it you don't have to take part. The last World Cup was desperately important just to get the whole thing off the ground when the northern hemisphere wasn't very keen, and then the northern hemisphere quickly realised it wanted to be part of it and brought the circus to town. Everyone knew 18 months ago, when the build-up started, what a wonderful tournament it would be here because of the grounds, the history and the crowds. We all feel very privileged and have worked very hard to get where we've got.

I still believe England did it the right way all the way through the tournament. I still believe that if we'd tried to be really boring in the final Australia would probably have held us quite comfortably in the forwards, and I think that if we started a kicking game we would have ended up losing the battle as well. We had comprehensively lost the kicking game when we played them in the summer with Lynagh and Campese and we lost the forward battle too. Our forwards played especially well this time, particularly in the second half. We didn't actually play that well in the first half and that gave us a mountain to climb in the second half.

Against the second half wind, we could have gone under but because we kept the ball in the hand that allowed the forwards to start driving in support at the breakdown. That was why the statistics looked so comprehensive in our favour; they stacked up in the second half. We did have the better of the second half but we were 9–0 and 12–3

down, which made life very difficult. The New Zealanders got caught with that against Australia in the semi-final the week before and it showed how important it was to get points on the board early.

It was a huge improvement on our showing against the Wallabies in the summer, but then that was never going to be easy. After winning the Grand Slam playing a very limited game, and having dominated the Five Nations for a couple of years, we could have sat back, stayed at home and told ourselves not to worry about going away so that we could just carry our Five Nations momentum through to the World Cup. I still disagree with that. We had to go and find out what this new Australian side were like. We hadn't played them before; they'd been good enough to beat New Zealand the year before. It would have been a cop-out not to go. Of course the timing was wrong; it couldn't possibly have been right. Because it was out of season, we were not fully fit, not match-sharp, not mentally sharp either. It gave us a face-to-face look at the Australians and when we came back it made everyone work that much harder than they would have done if they had stayed at home. If we had never gone, people would have sat back a bit and rested in their Grand Slam laurels.

Our build-up matches during September were important to get ourselves sorted out. We had to play warm-up games, we had to have rugby, get the ball in our hands and kick it. We had to start somewhere. It was like the beginning of the domestic season really. September is always a rusty month and a bit frantic. In the circumstances the matches against the Soviet Union, Gloucester and England Students were about as good as we could get and served a useful purpose in getting people playing. We knew we weren't peaking in September but then we didn't want to.

Obviously, we wanted the first peak to come against New Zealand in our first match. The hype surrounding this game was a big problem for us. We had hyped it up ourselves. We'd all looked forward to the New Zealanders at Twickenham and wondered whether we could take the champions in the opening game. The media built the game up too much as well. It was only the first game of the World Cup, defeat didn't mean you couldn't win the tournament. It would have been great to beat them but there was always the knowledge that it wouldn't have been the end of the road. We pressurised ourselves a bit and we didn't play very well. We were very nervous and played nowhere near as well as in the final.

When I look back at the pool games that followed against Italy and the United States, I think we performed reasonably well in very difficult circumstances. We were criticised because we were expected to put 70 points on these two sides, everyone thinking back to the 1987 World Cup. But that doesn't happen very often these days; those sorts of thrashings have gone. I felt our performance against Italy was very good when we put it into context with the New Zealand performance against Italy. We cleaned them out in the first half and then they killed the game in the second.

England made a lot of changes for the game against the US but the half-backs remained the same and I didn't mind playing. We can get away with it but the forwards can't; it's hard for the boys to go through physical punishment every two or three days. We did sufficient to win but it was a bit scrappy. The teamwork which we had built up with the first-choice team was a bit missing, people were fighting for places and very keen to do well. We did sufficient without really turning it on.

After that the management dropped Dean Richards from the quarter-final in France, which came as a bombshell to everyone else but there had been a feeling within the squad that it was coming. The summer tour had not gone particularly well, not only for Dean but for everyone. The pack had not functioned particularly well. It became obvious in the warm-up games that everyone else had done an enormous amount of fitness work and was looking sharp, eager and hungry – but perhaps Dean had not done the work that was required and I think he would be the first to admit that. His rugby season is generally a slow build-up through the autumn to Christmas to be fit for the Five Nations Championship.

On the other hand Mick Skinner, Mike Teague

and Peter Winterbottom really put the work in. It was a difficult decision for the management to have made. It could have backfired. The fact that we were playing France may have influenced the decision because the Skinner/Teague/Winterbottom back row had played in Paris when we beat France in 1990. We have always identified against France that you must take the game to them in a big way. If you stand off, they just come at you. With those three, it's very much an aggressive back row to meet the opposition head-on.

This was really where the competition started for us. We were expected to qualify, which is perhaps why the edge wasn't there against the States in the sense that we more or less knew we would win. Once we got to France, after our weekend in Jersey, the mood changed. It was unfortunate that the game against France was rather ugly but you can't go faint-hearted to Paris, which is why England have done better against them than any other home-union team – we have the physical presence to stand up to them. Our forwards are big and physical and unfortunately the French temperament means that if things aren't going well it sometimes turns out that way. We talked about this a lot before the game, that we mustn't stand off and we must take it to them. At that point we would know we were winning. They came at us for a long period in the second half but in the end it was a great win.

By the time of the semi-final, in Scotland, we were really into it. There is no bigger fixture in the British rugby calendar at the moment than Scotland-England because they are the two best sides. We were faced with the situation that it could be revenge for our defeat at Murrayfield in 1990, when they outfoxed us. It seems impossible but it was much more than a World Cup semi-final because there was so much hingeing on the game. We were somewhat inhibited; we felt we had forward power and that we could win the game by keeping the pressure on. The Scots were trying to keep the game loose because they had to; they didn't have the forward power. We didn't want to take the risk that if we opened it up we would be playing into their hands – which is what happened 18 months earlier. It was another great win, playing to our strengths against a Scotland team who are very, very good at Murrayfield.

After all that the final was a desperate experience but I know full well what a magnificent occasion it was and how much rugby impinged on everyone's consciousness. England were the laughing-stock for most of the Eighties but we worked incredibly hard

Above: Nick Farr-Jones (left) and David Campese share the glory.

Right: English coach Roger Uttley discovers that the Queen enjoyed the final.

– in our own time – to put England back into a place of respectability in world rugby. If we played Australia tomorrow, perhaps we could beat them. The Wallabies are a wonderful side but we aren't that far, if at all, behind them. To be able to say that about an English rugby team means something. The players have earned profound respect.

155

SCHHH…YOU·KNOW·WHO GOT ONE IN.

CAMPESE, THE DIAMOND: PLAYER OF THE TOURNAMENT

BARRY JOHN

It is a rare privilege to declare David Campese as my player of the tournament for World Cup 1991. I confess that this is not such a sensational or difficult declaration, for, in truth, had a poll been undertaken amongst commentators, journalists, players, spectators and any Tom, Dick or Harry, Campese would have emerged the winner by a landslide, claiming that overwhelming majority that all politicians dream about. His impact on the 1991 World Cup was as profound as was that of Pele in the soccer World Cup of 1962.

Like Pele, Campese is associated with the very best and historic moments in sport; he has special genius which shows that an individual can still paint his own portrait and leave an indelible mark for all to treasure. The ingredients are the same: stature, presence, personality, style and an immense belief in the God-given talents.

Campese, like Pele and other sporting maestros, could deliver when it mattered and in a game which has been going for well over a century, the focus of attention has never been so great as in this tournament. Thankful, Campese never faltered from the script that had been given to him. Campese, above all, to my eyes, gave that extra special cutting edge to the World Cup. He was a diamond.

I would have liked to have seen Serge Blanco and Philippe Sella challenge Campo's dream, seeking the ultimate. Sadly, it all fell flat for the flamboyant French. Sella, though 'carrying a leg', displayed quite extraordinary skills against Fiji; Blanco did not really respond, and in his last appearance at Parc des Princes, his punch on Heslop is only forgotten thanks to coach Daniel Dubroca's attempted mugging of referee David Bishop, as he wandered off for a quiet coffee.

Other players, like Gavin Hastings, Jeremy Guscott, Steve Bachop (WS), Gary Armstrong, John Kirwan, Tim Horan, Jason Little, John Eales, Simon Poidevin and the rest were a fantastic supporting cast.

However, at the final analysis, Campo stands head and shoulders above the rest. He was the man that made heads swivel, whether it be on or off the field. He was full of expression and was the darling of the press corps, who thrive on his no-nonsense approach and forthright stance to any question, whether it be about his own game or any particular individual. You would not be surprised that an Irish and Italian blood cocktail would leave him with a fiery and volatile temperament. He is a total contradiction. He can be mellow and kind, aware but always in command and a step ahead, but, above all, knowing what is important in life. Self-belief is paramount to him, as is the case with All Black Michael Jones.

On the field, Campese wears number 11 and plays on the right wing; he prefers to run out last but come off first. Smiling and communicating comes so easy to him that you'd think he was carrying an Equity card.

For example, Campese did not join the other 14 Wallabies who stood full frontal as the All Blacks performed the haka in Dublin. I suppose he could have joined the All Blacks themselves for that matter, for after 23 appearances against them, he must know the haka as well as any of them! No – it was not for him. Instead, 50 yards away and messing around with the ball as though it was a training session, in a quiet moment to organise his thoughts, he was like an explosion waiting to happen.

Typically, within half-an-hour, he had taken the game by the scruff of the neck and Australia were Twickenham-bound. A try of exquisite quality followed by a mesmeric run, and the pass of the tournament – a reverse flip which sent Horan over – will not be forgotten.

Rumour has it that Campo is vulnerable in defence – I find that quite astonishing. Yes, his eccentricity has caused a few problems – notably leading to Ieuan Evans' try, which allowed the Lions to win the series in '89, but, as it was, his defensive qualities played a more effective part in that monumental final than anything else – particularly in the tackle. Just ask Rory Underwood!

157

Campese, the player of the tournament, on his way to scoring the Heinz Golden Try.

Finally, for me, it is the free spirit that he has brought to the game which will linger long in the memory, and more particularly, with all those youngsters who were fortunate to see him in action. If he does go through with his threat to retire from the international stage, I will fully understand, but on behalf of the whole world of rugby David, thank you.

AUSTRALIA: THE BEST AND THE FASTEST

Bill Beaumont *on the unquestioned team of the tournament.*

It is pretty obvious which is the World Cup team of the tournament but the reason I have chosen Australia is not simply because they won it. It was the manner of their win that was so impressive and that tipped the scales for me over my closest alternatives, Western Samoa and England.

England did more than was expected of them. To lift themselves up from the defeat by New Zealand in the first match of the tournament was a great achievement in itself. They knew they didn't do themselves justice in that game and would have to get through via Parc des Princes and Murrayfield which was an incredibly daunting prospect. But they produced two performances of great character and determination, and there was no lack of skill either.

I was a bit annoyed at all the harping and carping about England. At the end of the day this country was suddenly obsessed with rugby because England were in the final. The All Blacks have never been known for flashy play and they never had to take the kind of criticism England did. We all like romance but not everyone can achieve it. England

The England squad before the World Cup final.

The Australian line-up at Twickenham after being presented to the Queen.

felt comfortable with their tactics and were well justified in playing that way.

In actual fact, if they had played that type of rugby against the Australians in the final who knows what would have happened? I thought the Wallabies looked slightly weaker round the forward fringes than they did around the outside – but this isn't to criticise England, who did tremendously well to get there. Every credit to Will Carling, Geoff Cooke, Roger Uttley and all the boys. Apart from the forward performance against New Zealand their performance throughout the rest of the tournament was exceptional.

Western Samoa gave the World Cup its buzz in the first few weeks. Everyone was talking about Samoa. All right, it's a credit to the great strength of New Zealand provincial rugby rather than Samoa itself; when you think that these guys can't even get into the top 40 or 50 players in New Zealand. They

played with a breath of fresh air. They still had the flamboyance of the Samoans but also the steel of the New Zealanders, a formidable combination. They didn't beat Wales and Argentina by throwing the ball around willy-nilly. They did it by basic New Zealand play in the opposition half of the field, putting them under pressure and picking up the pieces. I thought that Steve Bachop was a super player at outside-half, Frank Bunce a good centre and the no. 8 Pat Lam another threat. Those guys could have slotted into any team in the world.

But having said all that, it has to be Australia for me. They came as favourites and when they reached injury time against Ireland at Lansdowne Road in the quarter-final three points down not many sides would have come back from that trusting themselves with the ball in hand. Ireland deserved great credit for the way they played against the Australians. It was a game that showed how vital Nick Farr-Jones is to them: he points everyone in the right direction, organises them all and has great vision, not just for himself but for everyone else in his team as well. They have a formidable pack of forwards who can look after themselves, and can cover and tackle well but it is the all-round ball ability of everyone in the

angle of running and the ball is put into space for him to run on to it.

The centres, Jason Little and Tim Horan, were good with the ball in their hands and were willing to play saftey-first rugby by moving the ball, which not many sides do. They run on a flat line, with flat balls being moved across to men running on. It's totally different from our back play: we tend to stand back a bit more with a lot of miss-moves without running onto it properly. The half-backs are the key to any side and in Michael Lynagh and Nick Farr-Jones Australia had world-class performers who consistently made the right decisions. It was largely through them that the forwards kept going forwards, that the backs were able to run their flat lines and put the ball through for Campese.

The Wallaby front row were thoroughly dependable, with the hooker, Phil Kearns, the vital man and a fine player. The props, Tony Daly and Ewen McKenzie, were honest journeymen who knew their roles and got on with it without much fuss. It's ironic that they scored the try in the final. Apart from the Irish match, when they struggled a bit, they were seldom under any great pressure in the scrums. What a player the lock John Eales is at 21. He was outmanoeuvred by Wade Dooley in the line-out in the final but he is a stunningly good prospect with a great pair of hands for a second row. At 6′ 8″ he is better suited there than at no. 8, where he is a bit too tall. Rod McCall, like the two props, was an honest, solid grafter which every side needs. He wins the balls for the fancy dans.

Willie Ofahengaue was an awesome player at blind-side flanker, where he was obviously more comfortable than at no. 8. I'll bet the Australians were glad he didn't have a visa to go back to New Zealand when he decided to settle in Australia. He came into his own in the final; every time he picked up the ball he seemed to make 30 or 40 yards. I felt Troy Coker was a rather makeshift no. 8 but he came through well in the semi-final against New Zealand. The amount of graft Simon Poidevin, the old campaigner, did on the floor was extraordinary, more in a blind side than an out-and-out open-side type of way.

These Wallabies, worthy World Cup winners, have been fine ambassadors not just for their country but for rugby as a whole. But let's take our hats off to England too, for pushing them all the way. Both of the finalists were exactly what the tournament needed.

side that caught my eye. They all know when to give and take a pass.

But despite their great attacking skill, the Australian team is based on solid defence more than anything else. England never really got to the gain-line; Australia were prepared to let England move the ball in the confidence that they would make the tackles to stop them. They played a percentage game, making the opposition come from deep. Above all they had pace and in defence even more than attack this is a precious asset. Australia had it all over, forwards who could run around the park all day and backs who put in some crunching tackling.

Running through the team, I wouldn't say Marty Roebuck was anything special at full-back but his angles of running were good and he was reliable under the high ball. I didn't think he had a particularly good final with his kicking but he was always prepared to run at the opposition. The much-maligned Rob Egerton on one wing in fact did everything right, no one got round him and he had a very good pair of hands. The way the Australians play the game allows the brilliant David Campese to float about doing his own thing; he picks up the

MY TOP FIFTEEN

Fergus Slattery, *the celebrated former Irish captain, selects his 'team of the tournament'.*

Even armed with all the video evidence and having keenly followed what was an outstanding tournament, it is still a difficult task to come up with the best player in each position. Players tend to stand out more in successful teams when perhaps, individuals who have not been given the chance to shine because of team deficiency merit closer consideration. Some players were easy to select, others took a good deal of heart-searching (and late alterations!).

FULL-BACK:
GAVIN HASTINGS
(SCOTLAND)
This position did not take much time because I felt that Gavin was head and shoulders above everyone else (almost literally, too!). If he is remembered for the penalty miss, which would have taken Scotland into the lead in the closing stages of the semi-final against England, then it would be unfair.

He simply played to his potential in the tournament. He is so physically strong, he has a turn of pace for a big man. He is an outstanding defender and he was always involved in the action.

RIGHT WING:
DAVID CAMPESE
(AUSTRALIA)
We saw David at his best in Dublin, because among many outstanding performances he was particularly brilliant in the quarter-final against Ireland and a week later, in the semi-final against New Zealand. These were two great games and Campese's role was so memorable.

Perhaps his chief contribution to the tournament was in the effect he had, not so much on the regular followers of the game, but on the non-rugby followers. For so many people coming into rugby for the first time he typified the appeal of the tournament. A great player and entertainer.

CENTRE:
TIM HORAN
(AUSTRALIA)
Again, Horan was a player of whom we saw a lot in Dublin. For a rather squat figure he is a lovely player. He had everything but perhaps the attribute which impressed me the most was his tackling and defending in general.

It was not just the way he tackled, although he was outstanding in that department throughout. It was the way he and his colleagues co-ordinated their defensive plans. There was a telepathic unison between the Australians out on the field.

CENTRE:
JEREMY GUSCOTT
(ENGLAND)
Some people may be a little surprised that I choose Guscott because England were criticised during the tournament for not making more use of him and of the other England backs and although it is too easy to criticise it is regrettable that all the talents of a team cannot be used. Yet I feel that he was the most stylish player in the tournament. I particularly remember the elegant try he scored at Twickenham against Italy. A wonderful talent.

LEFT WING:
RORY UNDERWOOD
(ENGLAND)
Rory Underwood was another player who might have expected more employment during the World Cup but here is a tremendous athlete. Another great stylist and above all, a try-scorer. Just as you cannot argue with a soccer striker with a hat-full of goals to his credit, you cannot overstate the significance of Underwood's try-scoring record at all levels.

FLY-HALF:
MICHAEL LYNAGH
(AUSTRALIA)
For me, the most impressive thing about Lynagh's World Cup was the way he took responsibility as

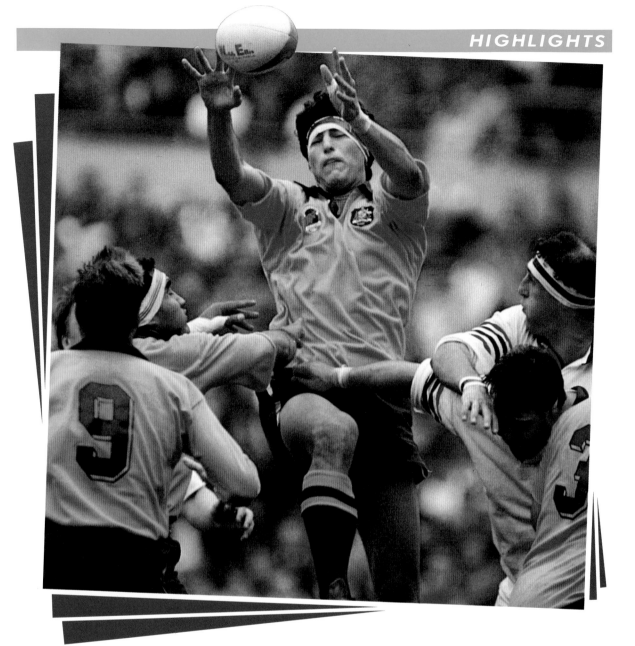

John Eales rules the middle of the line-out.

the senior player when Nick Farr-Jones was experiencing injury problems – Farr-Jones had to leave the field against Western Samoa and against Ireland and he missed the Wales match altogether. But Lynagh stepped in.

He was a little inconsistent in his play and his kicking earlier in the tournament but when the pace stepped up later he produced the goods, especially in the final.

GARY ARMSTRONG
(SCOTLAND)

I thought long and hard about this position. It as almost sacriligious to leave out Nick Farr-Jones, especially because of his outstanding leadership qualities, not to mention his general play.

But I am going for Armstrong. He had a superb tournament in his typically strong and bustling style. Against Ireland at Murrayfield, he kept Scotland in the game in the first half; then he kept Ireland out of the game in the second half.

Against England and against Western Samoa, he was excellent again even though Scotland did not have it their own way, by any means.

163

PROP:
STEVE McDOWELL
(NEW ZEALAND)

I have very few New Zealanders in my team even though when the tournament began, you might have expected five or six or even more to make it. In general, they were disappointing and will have to re-build. McDowell was one of the few to maintain true form. He is a solid dependable scrummager and in the loose, he always retains possession.

I would also put in a word for the Irish here, because I thought that Nick Popplewell of Ireland was one of the best young forwards around in the tournament.

HOOKER:
PHIL KEARNS
(AUSTRALIA)

He was very big, very fit and extremely good. He could do the essential chores of hooking the ball in the scrum and throwing in to the line-out so well. He has the physique and the instincts to play like a world-class tight forward but he also showed the ability to play like a loose forward too. Part of a powerful front row.

PROP:
RICHARD LOE
(NEW ZEALAND)

Like McDowell, he managed to retain his form when some of his team appeared to be on the decline. A fierce forward, a good scrummager and effective in the line-out and loose play. He was the cornerstone of the New Zealand effort and typically for the southern hemisphere forward, he was always fit enough to be up with the action.

LOCK:
PAUL ACKFORD
(ENGLAND)

It is difficult to separate Ackford and the other outstanding English lock, Wade Dooley. Both were remarkably effective in the tournament. Ackford is so good at the front of the line and such a powerful scrummager. He seems to have such a good attitude to the game and it was very rare in the last few years that anyone had the better of him. A world-class forward and he had a great tournament, especially in the final.

LOCK:
JOHN EALES
(AUSTRALIA)

This is a major talent. In the line-out, he had the ability to win the ball standing at no. 4 and also towards the tail of the line-out. He was so good at holding off the opposition to get a hand to the ball and he seemed to have the temperament of a top international forward.

Then there were his other attributes. In the final ha brought off two magnificent tackles, one of which could be said to have saved the game. Eales is obviously a key man for the Australian sides of the next few years.

FLANKER:
WILLIE OFAHENGAUE
(AUSTRALIA)

This is a difficult choice because there were so many good tight flankers around. Willie gets my vote for his power. He is a very physical player and a difficult proposition for the tackler. Yet he also had the capacity to play No. 8 and even the pace to play at openside.

He gave Australia another dimension as well as fulfilling all the normal supporting duties of a good flanker. He will obviously be a major target for rugby league but Australia will be praying that he resists the temptation.

NO. 8:
GLEN ENNIS
(CANADA)

He would be my 'springer', or surprise choice. However, anyone who saw Canada play in the World Cup would not be surprised. Ennis was just one of the very fine Canadian pack. He was consistent, he was physical and hard.

I closely considered Western Samoa's Pat Lam and also England's Mike Teague, even though I do not consider them as true No. 8s. Teague had an outstanding tournament and was so good in the final.

FLANKER:
LAURENT CABANNES
(FRANCE)

Perhaps people may be surprised that I did not go for Michael Jones of New Zealand but he did not play a significant part in the tournament. I thought that Cabannes was extraordinary. France did not have a happy tournament and they depended on Cabannes so much. He has a blistering pace and played superbly against England.

DUBROCA'S MOMENT OF MADNESS

Andy Irvine *recalls the few but vivid controversial moments.*

At the end of 32 matches, in just four weeks, between 16 very competitive and ambitious countries, I think it is to the great credit of the game that there were only three major controversial incidents of any real consequence in the World Cup, and, in a curious way, the high reputation of rugby emerged intact after each incident and the reaction to it. By far the worst example was the physical attack on referee David Bishop by the French coach, Daniel Dubroca, in the tunnel immediately after England had beaten France in the quarter-finals at Parc des Princes.

To'o Vaega is awarded the try but Robert Jones clearly made the touchdown.

An eye-witness account of this dreadful scene claimed that Dubroca grabbed David Bishop by his jersey, pushed him against a wall and shouted in English several times the word 'cheat', prefaced by the most appalling profanities. It was an unbelievable and totally inexcusable outburst. There was a sense of moral indignation when Dubroca denied everything, claiming he had simply hugged the referee afterwards because they were old friends and had thanked him for refereeing the match.

The French authorities played the incident down and the following day after the New Zealand match against Canada at Lille, it was announced at a specially convened press conference by Rugby World Cup that after discussions with all the relevant people who were involved, no action would be taken and the matter was closed.

David Bishop had problems with France on and off the field.

The initial reaction of the authorities, encouraged by the French, had been to lift the carpet up to the sky and sweep everything underneath it with one hand whilst using the other hand to do a whitewash job. Fortunately, there was an outcry from the British media, the French media and the public which demanded action. For over one hundred years, rugby had proudly boasted of a moral code of honour and an ethos steeped in integrity which accepted the referee's decision was always final and never questioned. If a famous international coach was allowed to physically assault and verbally abuse a referee in the tunnel after a match and find his action condoned, not condemned, by the game's ruling body and allowed to go unpunished, then rugby was hurtling headlong towards anarchy.

If Dubroca escaped censure then every coach or player would have carte blanche to assault and abuse referees whenever they wanted in the future without fear or punishment because a precedent had been set. Such a situation would be unthinkable and intolerable. The outcry by the media helped to save rugby's good name and reputation as the following sequence of events shows.

On Saturday, the Dubroca incident took place. On Sunday, it was announced there would be no action taken against Dubroca. The media demanded justice on Monday and on Tuesday the referee submitted his report which shocked Russ Thomas, the highly-respected chairman of Rugby World Cup. He knew at once that firm action had to be taken and justice had to be seen to be done to safeguard the future of rugby. He conveyed his feelings to the French Federation in strong terms and by Friday morning Dubroca had resigned. Rugby was able to hold its head high once again. Players and coaches knew what they had always known – the referee's word is final and must never be questioned.

That was the most controversial incident off the field of play and, ironically, it was indirectly related to the most controversial incident on the field of play. That occurred during the Wales match against Western Samoa when the Samoan centre Vaega and the Welsh scrum-half Robert Jones were involved in a furious chase to reach the ball which had been kicked over the Welsh line. Both players, in desperation, threw themselves at the ball. It seemed clear at the time, and the television replays confirmed afterwards, that Jones definitely won the touchdown.

Incredibly, the French referee, Patrick Robin, awarded the try. The try was converted to compound the felony and Wales never recovered. They lost 16–13 in the full knowledge that six of the Samoan points should never have been awarded. The defeat meant Wales failed to qualify for the quarter-finals and yet to their eternal credit, not one player disputed the decision at the time, no-one spoke to or harrassed the referee, all fifteen guys

accepted the injustice without any dissent because that is the code of discipline which is instilled into every rugby player. Rugby simply mirrors life and you have to learn to take the rough with the smooth. The Welsh players did; Daniel Dubroca did not.

My own reaction to that Western Samoan try is probably a fairly contentious and controversial one. I would like the referee to have guidance on any decision of doubt in a crucial situation such as that Western Samoan try. In similar circumstances in American Football a second opinion would be sought. After a referee has made a decision, it can be referred to the 'replay officials booth'. Here, very experienced officials with at least 20 years' background as judges can instantly watch the replay and let the referee know if he was right. I believe that such high tech equipment could be installed for use at all major internationals. For rugby such 'replay officials' should be recently-retired international referees and they would have been able to inform Patrick Robin he was wrong and the 'try' could have been disallowed.

I also happen to feel that if Scottish referee Jim Fleming had asked for a second opinion when he sent off one Western Samoan, Keenan, and one Argentine, Sporleder, for throwing a flurry of punches at each other in their final pool game at Pontypridd, he might have changed his mind. It seemed a little harsh when compared to the double attack by Eric Champ and Serge Blanco on Nigel Heslop.

Having said that, I believe rugby's image emerged with flying colours at the end of 2,560 minutes of intense competition; only two players sent off and just a handful of other outbursts to spoil a very good record on discipline. No violence can be condoned but I was delighted at the tremendous spirit of good sportsmanship which prevailed right through the four weeks of the tournament, particularly when you consider the enormous pressure the players were under and the very high stakes.

The whole competition was a wonderful cross-fertilisation of different styles and cultures, a glorious mixture of great players, great tries and great moments which will live on long after the odd moment of controversy has been forgotten. That is how it should be and my abiding memory will be of the great rugby Australia played over four exciting weeks to win the World Cup. Their triumph was highlighted by their courage at the end of the Irish match when they trailed by three points and they

167

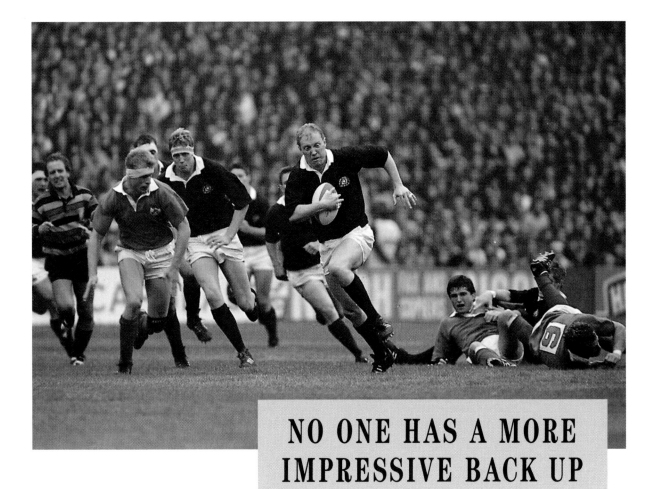

NO ONE HAS A MORE IMPRESSIVE BACK UP

Pensions &
Mortgages

Scottish Life

THE LIFE TO LEAD

RUGBY UNION'S PATH TO AUSSIE ASCENDANCY

Bob Dwyer, *the winning coach, on the backdrop to the greatest triumph*

After a triumph like Australia's in the World Cup, this may sound ridiculous but the feeling I had then and still do was of a quiet satisfaction rather than any great whooping it up for joy. It's been a big job which has shown everyone that you do not win World Cups without an enormous amount of effort. You only have to look back to the 1987 World Cup to realise that at that stage New Zealand were the only team which who understood just what was required, but now there are quite a lot of countries who do and next time round there will be many more again.

I shouldn't want to give the impression that we didn't enjoy it because there were plenty of good times, but it was an incredibly intense experience and we had to focus our minds very clearly on the tournament; we couldn't afford to lose sight of what we were about and the way we had to prepare if we were to make a success of it. And because of that, once it was all over there was a feeling almost of let-down and anti-climax. You might suppose we would be jumping over the moon, yelling out yahoo and whoopee but in those days after we had won the final against England it was more a case that every time Nick Farr-Jones and I caught each other's eye we couldn't get the smile off our faces. I think we were asking ourselves whether this could really be true.

Back in Australia, though, there was an unbelievable euphoria. The build-up in interest was something that astonished all of us. We ended up receiving something over 5,000 and possibly as

Bob Dwyer

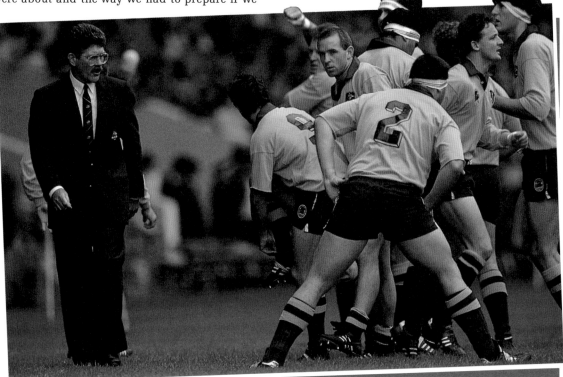

many as 7,000 faxes at our local hotel before the final; the most we had ever received in my previous experience with the Wallaby team was about 30. Hotels in Australia applied successfully to have their licensing hours extended so that they could show the games during the night-time and they erected a massive video screen in the Rocks area of Sydney for an all-night party with the World Cup final at its centre. Those scenes were even more surprising than when Australia sailed off with the Americas Cup.

In fact the World Cup has made me believe more than ever that because rugby union is such a global game and because it's so much better a game, it's only a logical extension that one day it would overtake rugby league. This isn't the moment when it happened; however, it's 10 steps forwards and if we only go five backwards that's a giant improvement. And as we progress commercially things will also improve for the players, keeping them in our game and protecting them from the temptation that comes with the big money league can offer. Even though the laws have changed, there's been virtually no opportunity in Australia for guys to capitalise, but I hope this will open up now because nationally the players have become famous, far better known than they were before the World Cup.

Our performances in the pool matches were below what we were looking for but, although I tend to be pretty critical, there were some good things to draw on. Scoring five tries against Argentina, who don't often give many away, was a big plus; against Western Samoa we were subjected to a very difficult situation by the torrential rain and had the composure and strength of our convictions to win through. Against Wales we started to play quite well in the second half but I wasn't necessarily struck with our performance and it got to the stage where I was really hammering the team for improvement.

We were very disappointed with our forwards' performance against Ireland in the quarter-final, although it did give them the shake-up they needed. When we sat and watched the game on video I told them that if they felt this game was a measure of their ability we were in a bit of trouble – and they responded. I hadn't been happy with the work of the

backs leading up to the game and I had to have a few harsh words with them as well to buck up their ideas.

Our semi-final against New Zealand was very gratifying but I didn't actually feel it was much different from our performance against England at home in July and maybe our first Test against the All Blacks in August, although perhaps the intensity of the first 20 minutes was in excess of what we did in those two earlier matches. We were a little disappointed with our performance against England in the final but I felt it was the immensity of the occasion that produced the errors and so we ought to excuse them – we did win the Cup after all. It was as if sheer fear had gripped them and all reason had gone out of the window. But our resolve and character never once disappeared and in some ways our other problems really brought out the best in the team. They are a tremendous bunch and I'm very keen to carry on as coach; the only trouble was I forgot to give my application to Bob Fordham, the ARU executive director, when he was in London.

It was certainly a momentous month. Quite apart from our success in it, the 1991 World Cup was an outstanding success. It was quite clear to me a couple of years ago that it was going to be an unbelievably successful event. I could feel the increase in interest in the tournament and I'd said for 12 months in Australia that the major sporting event in the world in '91 would be Rugby World Cup. I'm not sure if people believed me but this is exactly what came to pass. The staging of the games by and large was excellent, the coverage in the press and TV was very well done. The spectator interest was astounding. The games were of varying standard, as one would expect in any competition of this nature, though one of the things that has emerged is the improvement in the lesser-known rugby nations – and that will increase. It's given them a focus and perhaps given their governments an interest as well.

I was a spectator at the 1987 World Cup and I thought that as the tournament progressed it became more and more exciting. Just to be at the final was a fantastic experience. But all that was magnified this time, and not only because we were directly involved. We didn't experience the excitement so much as the tension but even in a city the size of London I could feel the massive interest. The feeling in the stadium at Twickenham on final day was electric, as if the world had stood still and nothing else mattered.

Nick Farr-Jones was an inspirational Australian captain.

171

AUSTRALIA: THE DREAM MACHINE

Ian McGeechan *of Scotland with a coach's review of the champions.*

I had set Scotland a target of reaching at least the semi-finals in the knowledge that if we made it that far, we would have a chance of winning the tournament. To that extent, I was satisfied with our World Cup campaign, although it was obviously very disappointing to lose to England at Murrayfield in the semi-finals and then in the 3rd place play-off match in Cardiff to fail in our attempt to beat the New Zealand All Blacks for the first time in history.

On both occasions, we defended and tackled really well but we were outscrummaged by two tremendous packs and that took the initiative away from us. We did a lot of things really well and only conceded one try in two matches – and that was in injury time in the second game – but it is very difficult for a side to conjure up a victory when the other pack is bigger, stronger and heavier and they are able to dominate set-piece possession.

The simple truth is that New Zealand, England and Australia had the best three sets of tight

Below: Ian McGeechan

Right: Zimbabwe lost all their matches but won the Heinz Fair Play Award.

forwards in the competition. They each had a really big, strong, mobile front row and at least two outstanding line-out jumpers. It must be a wonderful luxury to have a 6′ 8″ athletic lock like John Eales of Australia, Ian Jones of New Zealand or Wade Dooley of England to build your line-out around. The English pack deserve the highest praise for their fantastic performance against France, Scotland and Australia in the space of 14 days. Roger Uttley did an excellent job as coach bringing the very best out of his forwards.

The All Blacks also had a pretty good tournament but they were outplayed by Australia in Dublin and there is no doubt in my mind the Wallabies were the best rugby team in 1991. They played the best rugby and had the best record. They won nine of their ten internationals spread over five months and it is a huge tribute to their coach Bob Dwyer, that he was able to help his side peak in July when they overwhelmed Wales (63–6) and England (40–15), in August when they beat New Zealand (21–12) and again in October and November when they won six Tests out of six in the World Cup. That is a remarkable record for any coach. The only defeat was by New Zealand (6–3) on a day when Lynagh missed six penalty kicks at goal for Australia.

Bob Dwyer should be congratulated, not just on guiding and masterminding the Wallabies' World Cup win but also on the style of their victory. They had a very positive approach and played exciting 15-man open rugby right through 1991 culminating in the World Cup. They were incredibly slick and sharp against Wales in the summer and they managed to maintain that momentum right through the next few months. That is the hallmark of a great side and there is no doubt that this was a great Australian side.

In trying to analyse what made them the best in the world, it seems to me they were outstanding individually and collectively and had just about everything a rugby team could wish for except perhaps a specialist no. 8. Even there, with Tim Gavin injured, Troy Coker did very well, winning a lot of line-out possession and working well with two tremendous flankers. In many ways it was their collective skills which were so impressive. The loose forward combination worked a treat with Poidevin playing the best rugby of his career and Ofahengaue a dynamic strike player who led all sorts of attacks which allowed Poidevin and Coker to feed off his explosive bursts.

The locks, McCall and Eales, dominated almost every match at the line-out as a pair, with the third giraffe, Coker, giving them more options than any other side in the competition. All their front row players are experts in their own position and as a trio there was no better unit than Daly, Kearns and McKenzie.

This was by any standards an exceptionally well-balanced pack. The forwards were able to win the highest quality set-piece possession. They could drive, ruck, maul, run and support the ball and cover and tackle with equal facility. They were a strike force in their own right which took the pressure off the backs. The work-rate of the players was fantastic, notably, the new young lock, John Eales, who had a couple of covering tackles in the final which were nothing short of sensational.

Behind that pack, Australia had the best half-backs in the world in Farr-Jones and Lynagh, just about the best all-round partnership in the centre where Horan and Little were equally lethal in attack and defence and the best wing, arguably the best player, in the World Cup – David Campese. I was particularly struck by the performance of Farr-Jones, who was a major influence both as captain and as scrum-half despite having some problems with a knee injury.

He was an inspirational figure as tactician and organiser and as a scrum-half his service was terrific, his kicking first-class and his occasional breaks varied play skilfully to divert attention from the back row and the midfield trio. He did all that and found time to put in one priceless tackle on Guscott in the final which almost certainly saved a try. Always aware of what was going on around him even in the heat of battle, he did all the little things which, when added together, decide World Cups.

I thought Tim Horan was the top centre in the competition, producing some of the best bone-shuddering tackling especially against the All Blacks and England, but also showing amazing insight and imagination as well as power and pace in attack. The most telling examples of his brilliant running off the ball came against Argentina, when he read perfectly a couple of meandering, elusive runs by Campese, to pop up right beside him when he needed support and this resulted in two tries. Similarly, in the semi-final against New Zealand he anticipated Lynagh's chip ahead and Campese's reaction and manoeuvred himself effortlessly in to the right position to take the scoring pass.

Campese was outstanding in virtually everything he did for the Wallabies in 1991 and he deserved to win the Heinz Golden Try Award and to be chosen the Player of the Tournament. His tries against Ireland and New Zealand were breathtaking. Egerton ran hard and tackled well on the wing and at full-back, Roebuck was very tidy in defence and very good in attack.

Whichever way you look at it, Australia looked the best team in the tournament and they deserved to win the World Cup. Of the sides which failed to reach the semi-finals, I would like to pay tribute to Western Samoa and Canada because in the pool matches they blasted their way past seeded sides to make the quarter-finals and played some very good rugby in the process. The Samoans ran the ball whenever possible, often counter-attacking quite dramatically and their crash-tackling produced some of the most memorable moments of the whole competition. The Canadians played particularly well to beat Fiji and Romania and they gave the All Blacks a hard contest in the quarter-finals.

Italy also played superbly against the All Blacks and one of the best and most entertaining victories in the pool games came at the very end when Japan had a spectacular win over Zimbabwe. And if Zimbabwe were upset at losing all the three matches, at least they did win the Heinz Fair Play Award for conceding the fewest number of penalties. There was something for everyone in the 1991 World Cup but the biggest prize went, quite rightly, to Australia.

Tim Horan was lethal in attack and defence.

DIRECTIVES TOO STRONG FOR RELAXED REFEREES

Clive Norling, *the leading referee turned TV panellist, discusses the problems of World Cup officials.*

Eventually, people forgot about referees during the World Cup but to start with, they were a subject on most people's lips. They had been given a particular job because just before the World Cup the organisers came out with their announcement about laws 18 and 19 – players going to ground – and whereas the southern-hemisphere referees had been refereeing it religiously over the last few years, the northern-hemisphere referees had been rather lax about it.

To come out just before the World Cup with this announcement meant that the referees were going to get very strict, and it had a dramatic effect on the early pool matches – on players and referees alike. It was like most law changes. Referees are human. When they are told they are to concentrate on a certain thing, they sometimes overconcentrate on it so that the benefit of the doubt disappears completely, and in the World Cup we sometimes saw players accidently being knocked over and being penalised for it.

Also, referees concentrated so much on that area that perhaps they did not concentrate on other aspects such as the line-out, and that was especially the case during the pool matches. There was no doubt about that, and I also felt the advantage law seemed to go out of the window for infringements on the ground. They were always blown up, as if to say 'we've been told this so we're going to do it to the letter'. That attitude culminated in the England-Italy match when all those penalties were awarded.

What surprised me is that they would have sent out this directive at the time they did. There was an International Board meeting last March which would have been a better time to do it, so that all the players could have familiarised themselves with what was required. I've been told that the managers were warned this might take place but it did not appear to have got across to the teams. The point was that the referees were under instruction. It's like the directors of an organisation making a statement – and the poor old managers having to carry it out.

The other problem was that the referees were initially appointed only for the pool games and it would have been at the back of several referees' minds that, if they were seen not to adhere to instructions, when the final 12 were being selected it would have some influence. The occasional failure to use advantage was perhaps a case of referees being aware that the final-stage referees had not been selected and out of the original 24 only 12 would be going through. It was a classic case of assessors in the stand affecting referees on the field.

Once the pools were over, I would say the pressure was off. The last 12 referees could relax to an extent, and they were helped by the fact that by this stage the players were aware of how the refs were refereeing and realised that once the knock-out stage was reached the giving-away of penalties meant certain defeat. Old habits may die hard but there were fewer penalties for on-the-ground offences once the message to stay on your feet had been driven home.

But was it the right thing to do to make such a big thing of this? As I tell my business students in Swansea, the option facing people is short-term profit against long-term growth. In this instance, the long-term growth will come from referees all over the world penalising people on the ground, provided they referee accurately. It will change the game in a highly beneficial way. It has brought it to players' more than referees' attention; I just wish that once the ball had come out advantage could have been played more generously to keep the game, especially those early stop-start games, moving. At one stage it went to an extreme in this World Cup in that no advantage was applied just for the sake of making a point.

With the referees, at the end of the day the cream came to the top. There was no doubt that the senior referees applied common sense in the closing stages and we had some fine games. I don't think we can say there was one really bad game from the last eight onwards, and credit must go to the referees. Derek Bevan had a very good game in the final between Australia and England – which made me realise what I was missing. I would have given my right arm to be there. That was where I wanted to be, far more than on the television. I was very disappointed and upset that I wasn't chosen to be at the World Cup as a referee but I'm only 41 and my aim now is to get there in 1995.

The World Cup was a wonderful spectacle. I suppose the disappointment was the teams who didn't play to their strengths, but Australia went in with the only style they knew – 15-man rugby – and the fact that that was entertaining was a bonus. The most disappointing side for me was France; if they had played the ball through the backs instead of taking it back to their forwards England might have gone under in the quarter-final. Fiji never played to their potential, maybe because of the weather, Wales were obviously a big disappointment to me but in a way that was expected.

We have some solid young players at under-19 and under-21 level and at both levels we've beaten New Zealand recently, so I'm quite confident that we will be back with a new young team within a couple of years – provided, of course, we don't lose our resources and we do get our administration right off the field.

England played to their strength for the quarter- and semi-finals and broke into a 15-man game in the final. They weren't accustomed to it and suffered accordingly. It was a disappointment that we did not see the flowing skills of Guscott, Carling and Underwood. On the other hand, the positive aspect is that we have seen the emerging nations emerge. Canada have long threatened. Everyone expected Western Samoa to be the most difficult of this group and they, like the Canadians, played some very good rugby.

I'd like to finish with the Dubroca affair in Paris, the incident in which the French coach was involved with David Bishop. Refereeing is a thankless job. The referee is the one person on the field who never wins and to manhandle a referee is a cardinal sin. I certainly hope that Daniel Dubroca's resignation will act as a deterrent. I have always considered him a cool man and nice guy, which only goes to show the pressure that coaches and players were under during the World Cup.

Clive Norling

RUGBY'S MARVELLOUS MONTH

Russell Thomas, *chairman of Rugby World Cup,*
looks back on the tournament of a lifetime

It has been a long, hard road. An event like the Rugby World Cup takes years of hard work, not only by the RWC directors and by playing squads and coaches, but also by the army of volunteer helpers. There can surely be very few who are disappointed by the fantastic success of the event. It was the biggest festival of rugby ever held, it put the sport firmly on the world map. I am delighted to report that the tournament exceeded even our highest expectations.

Russ Thomas

We expected public interest to go through the roof. It did! We were confident that Rugby World Cup would be a showcase for the long-term benefit of the game as a whole. That happened too.

The financial indications are very good. As the tournament grew in scope and stature then so, obviously, did our costs, which were high. Yet although it will take a long time to fully assess income and expenditure, we are well on course to fulfil one of the most fervent wishes, that money should be made available to assist the development of the game worldwide. A special body, The International Settlement Trust, will decide how best the surplus will be distributed.

We owe a duty to the rugby public to produce an account of the income and expenditure and final figures will be reported at our March 1992 meeting.

There are so many indications of the widespread success of this tournament. More than 1 million spectators attended the 32 matches. The receipts for the final at Twickenham reached £1m for the first time in the history of the game and remarkably, a crowd of 50,000 watched the play-off at Cardiff Arms Park, when Wales were not even involved.

The TV and media coverage was staggering. There were at least 150,000 cuttings from the media in the host countries from September until the end of the tournament. At least 40 countries broadcast the final live, while over 70 countries took TV coverage in some form. ITV estimated that the final had an audience in the British Isles alone of 13m, easily a record for rugby. Altogether, it is estimated that more than 2 billion people watched some part of the tournament around the world. Even viewers in China were able to switch on. The country received 17 one-hour programmes. Some people, meanwhile, preferred to watch the action in person. Gullivers Travel, who did so well as the official travel operator for the tournament, sold more than 20,000 travel packages to visitors to the tournament from overseas.

Not surprisingly, other countries want to come into the family. Even before the tournament ended, five more countries applied to join the International Rugby Board, to become part of the international rugby scene. Remarkably, a small delegation from Latvia, consisting of two men and their interpreter, came over just before the final to ask how they might join the family of the game. We just managed to find them some tickets for the final and they enjoyed themselves.

Importantly, sponsors report excellent reaction and one of the large number of highly-valued sponsors, Steinlager, reported an increase of 100% in UK distribution of their product thanks to the effect of the sponsorship and the tournament. In addition, merchandising sales were enormous and were expected to continue until well after Christmas.

On the playing side, obviously the new holders of the Webb Ellis Cup, Australia, deserve the highest praise although one of the most gratifying aspects to the event was the performance of the so-called emerging nations. Their skill and fitness obviously shocked the more established teams and this gave even greater impact to the tournament.

Obviously, the focus will quickly shift to discussion of the venue for the next World Cup. I would hope that it would not be the case that we simply go to venues where the sponsorship and commercial prospects are high. We would not want sponsorship and finance to be the sole criteria. It is also difficult to imagine that we could increase the number of participating teams in the finals from the current number of 16. Already, the tournament imposes a great deal of pressure on the players and to impose even more games would not be correct. No decision has yet been made as to what form the qualifying will take for the 1995 tournament.

At the moment, that is in the future. Now, I prefer to reflect on the many wonderful memories of Rugby World Cup 1991, an unforgettable event which showed the world what a marvellous sport rugby can be, which held millions of people spellbound and which, in general, produced the highest standards of sportsmanship and of friendship on and off the field.

For me as chairman, it meant thousands upon thousands of miles of travelling and like all the players, we the organisers are particularly grateful to wives and families, who were often neglected. There are so many people to thank, from the army of volunteers forming the backbone, to the directors of Rugby World Cup, Marcel Martin and Sir Ewart Bell; Ray Williams, tournament director and Keith Rowlands, secretary of the IRB; the host unions, the commercial partners and sponsors and the other firms involved; the players, of course, for their magnificent efforts on the field.

The tournament is now established. Like the game of rugby union as a whole, it can only go from strength to strength.

Finally, congratulations to Australia, worthy winners of the 1991 World Cup.

The
PERFECT ENDING...

BELL'S
Old Scotch Whisky

True Spirit · Genuine Character

A RETROSPECTIVE

AUSTRALIA ADVANCED AS THE WORLD STOOD STILL

STEPHEN JONES

Everyone had certain expectations for the Rugby World Cup. There was no way it was going to be a failure, of course. The commercial operation was not without the odd hitch but came through strongly to guarantee the financial success and hopefully, a decent share-out for the impecunious lesser rugby countries.

And when the tournament was handed to the players with that secure background, then success was assured. The international rugby-playing community had prepared for the event with such selfless dedication, pride and sacrifice and they were never going to let anyone down. Sure enough, they did everyone proud.

Certainly, the matches themselves served up enormous portions of drama and brilliance, colour and pathos; and also, only infrequently, more lurid dishes. The World Cup was, in general, a vast playing success.

Yet there was nothing that prepared even the eternal optimists for the sheer impact of the event. The World Cup caught fire, it raged through the world, burning through the 70 countries where it was seen on TV; in Britain and Ireland, even though the tournament was scattered around the place, the impact was nothing less than phenomenal. I must confess that I am still staggered by it all.

There was the fact that the major league soccer clubs had to change their kick-off times; other sports, large and small, switched their times too. Reports came in that the fortunates up in the myriad hospitality booths in the soccer grounds were eagerly clustered round the TV sets with the soccer game going on outside their booths and behind their backs, almost unnoticed.

Every radio DJ seemed to be discussing it (if you regard that as a bonus). All your friends and family who had never before even acknowledged the existence of the game were talking about Carling or Campese; or Western Samoa or Canada. They were exhuming those hoary old jokes making fun of Wales, or humming the theme music to ITV's excellent coverage.

The media spotlight was overwhelming. It is entirely possible, in my opinion, that in Britain there were as many column inches and hours of airtime devoted to the Rugby World Cup as there were to the recent soccer event and even to the Gulf War, infinitely more significant though that latter subject was.

Other sports reported diminishing interest and participation as the youngsters flocked to the TV set or the rugby grounds. The Royal Family and politicians descended on the games in droves – no wonder there was a ticket shortage. It seemed that Buckingham Palace and the Houses of Parliament had snapped up half of them.

And the crowds? In 1987, and understandably because both Australia and New Zealand have relatively small populations scattered around widely dispersed cities and towns, some of the games had low attendances. This time, perhaps only one match, in Toulouse, attracted a disappointing attendance. Apart from that, the grounds used were simply teeming, wave upon wave of people wanting to share in the event, to say in later years that they were there.

Some of the statistics are remarkable. Twickenham was filled to capacity not only for the opening match, against New Zealand; not only for the final, but also for the match against the United States of America on a Friday afternoon, a working day match against one of the lesser (though fervent) teams of the tournament.

Down in Wales, where the playing impact was muted by the lack of Welsh success, the gates were superb. Llanelli, Pontypridd and Pontypool drew massive attendances and even though Wales played at Cardiff three times inside seven days, with one game on a Sunday – an unpopular day for the Welsh sporting public – there were three large crowds and then, incredibly, a crowd approaching 50,000 at the Arms Park for a game not involving Wales and having no major bearing on the tournament – the third-place play-off between New Zealand and Scotland.

181

The Scotland/Ireland pool drew large crowds, with the lone pool match in Belfast, when Japan cut Zimbabwe to pieces in dazzling style, saw Ulstermen turn out in droves. In France, where the French were able to show off the incredible number of incredible stadia they possess, the interest was also at an all-time high.

All in all, this blew away for ever the notion that rugby is somehow a narrow-based sport of the small section of the middle classes. The sheer numbers illustrated that rugby is egalitarian, vastly popular and, most amazing of all, still growing and dragging in new followers every day. That process started before the World Cup but what a rate of acceleration the marvellous tournament brought.

It is a waste of time to say that rugby will never be the same again. Of course it will not. It was not so much a tournament, more a cataclysm. I firmly believe that even dyed-in-the-wool rugby men were amazed just how big and popular the old game has become.

Now, it is vital, absolutely vital, that the game's authorities give clear, precise and wise direction; that they control and fan the flames of rugby in the next year, five years and 10 years. If they do their job well, then there is simply no limit to the spread and appeal of the game. Incidentally, if they fail, if they remain hidebound and harking back, if they remain unaccountable, then they will be drastically negligent.

One of the great misapprehensions which most people held regarding the actual playing of the tournament was that it would be held in two distinct phases – that there would be a colourful and energetic first phase as the smaller rugby-playing countries had their place in the sun, suffered some heavy defeats with stoicism and perhaps even the odd penalty goal or try in reply, before waving fond farewells; then the mighty second phase, when the big boys got down to business.

The highly-significant truth of Rugby World Cup 1991 was that it was a seamless tournament. There was no real split between old giants and new blood. The gap between what was supposed to be the old hierarchy and the others simply disappeared, and gloriously so.

Richard Hill launches the England back-line.

How could anyone patronise them? Western Samoa and Canada thundered into the quarter-finals and perhaps remarkable to relate, they figured strongly in the pre-match prognostications of those quarter-finals because there was no way that Scotland, who played the Samoans, or New Zealand, who played Canada, could afford to underestimate the opposition, or to contemplate the semi-final before the final whistle. So it proved.

Both teams played marvellously and even though the Samoans, with their ferocious tackling and organisation and their fervent, almost theatrical approach, were at first regarded as the team which

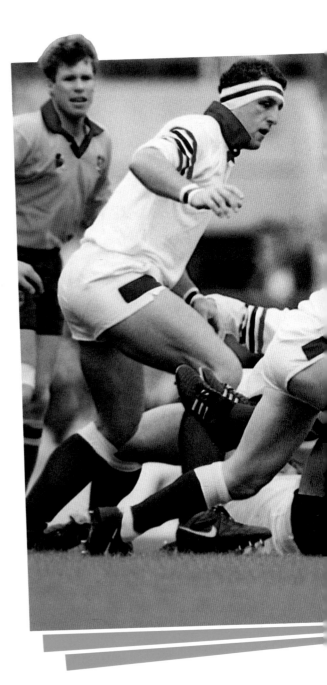

had improved the most, had caused the big boys most grief, it is conceivable that Canada's achievement was as great. Canada lost hardly anything by comparison with the All Blacks or with France and gave the event some wonderful forwards in all three rows of the scrum – Norman Hadley at lock, Dan Jackart at prop and Gord MacKinnon on the flank to name just three.

Elsewhere, there were very few runaway victories, none of the 70-point processions which characterised the group matches in 1987. The effort of the countries outside the supposed elite reached a

height at Leicester, where Italy played with genuine international class in forwards and backs alike, stayed with New Zealand for long periods of a vivid afternoon and eventually went down by a margin of only 10 points, and that only if what looked like a valid case for a penalty try had gone against them in the first half. In 1987, they had conceded 70 points to the All Blacks.

This was the perfect measure of the way in which the other countries have closed the gap and they will surely continue to do so. This time, there was no single country which did not contribute

something of real and lasting value and class. Possibly, only Zimbabwe were really out of their class. Every country, certainly, had valid contenders for any 'team of the tournament'.

The weekend of the quarter-finals, when the knock-out stages started, was probably the most vivid weekend in the long history of the sport. In strict chronological order, we had the remarkable match at Murrayfield when the magnificent Samoans drew from Scotland a performance which, in the opinion of the experienced flanker, John Jeffrey, was the best he had ever been associated with in a long career. After a brilliant match, the Samoans came back on to the pitch with a lap of honour which was loudly received; then they followed up with a final and furious rendition of their war-dance.

There was war in Paris too, for the action switched across the Channel to an occasion of real and possibly lasting bitterness. The France-England match boiled over early when Nigel Heslop, who tackled Serge Blanco late, was punched to the ground by Blanco and Eric Champ. It was a harsh match with a particularly lurid conclusion when Daniel Dubroca, as he was to admit after initial denials, manhandled and abused the match referee, David Bishop, in the tunnel leading to the dressing room.

The affair was not well-handled by the Rugby World Cup authorities. It partly overshadowed the final departure from Test rugby of the brilliant Blanco in the most inappropriate finale for him that it is possible to imagine. It also partly distracted from a fine, driving English effort.

Next day, the pace even increased. A glowing, teeming, electric Lansdowne Road saw one of the all-time great matches, an afternoon of pure theatre. The ground exploded as Gordon Hamilton's stirring run put Ireland ahead inside the dying minutes; then everyone sighed, first with bitter frustration, then with admiration as the Australians came back to score and win. Hours after, Australian knees were still knocking.

The marvellous and fervent stadium in Lille was full to bursting despite appalling weather later that afternoon for the final quarter-final, when the All Blacks, though never going to lose, were shaken up in an initial Canadian assault and later, by a Canadian pack which established something very close to control over the All Black pack.

Canada pushed New Zealand all the way, scored two fine tries and departed to another thunderous reaction from the crowd as they made a lap of honour. It was great stuff and Canada had achieved their objective – no-one can deny their status in the elite of world rugby. It was a colossal achievement.

The story of the rest of the tournament is well-known. The narrow, passionate English victory at Murrayfield; the glorious semi-final in Dublin and the unbelievable media barrage and build-up to the final; and lastly, the way in which the final beautifully topped off the whole thing, how it was, for all but the thwarted English, the perfect, fitting climax.

So give or take a few days of fierce festivities, give or take the pain of defeat, and the wondrous satisfactions of success, that was that. Suddenly, perhaps, the four years till the next event seemed too long an interval, too long to wait for the wide world of rugby to gather and to thrill us all.

Unquestionably, it was a triumph. The organisers made mistakes. Some of these were admitted, some were not. But the army of volunteer helpers did a magnificent job and rugby will always be in their debt. The refereeing was not of world-class standard but it got by; some of the play was criticised for lack of passing and running yet a good deal (not all) of those making this argument simply expected cheap thrills of some form of extended sevens. This expectation was totally unrealistic, especially in the final stages. On the other hand, rugby must retain the new converts, and can do so, in part, by presenting the more attractive side.

The biggest debt is to those on active service. The coaches and back-up men and especially, the players. It is sad and a cause for immediate investigation that so many apparently felt that their contribution was undervalued in some areas. Yet the dedication and courage of the players was outstanding. So was their fitness – there were remarkably few injuries, a tribute to the new scientific fitness regimes. There was also a remarkable absence of foul play, given what was at stake. And all this on the part of a group which was still, bar a few pounds here and there, amateur. They gave up their work and family life to prepare and to play. The world says thanks. As Bob Dwyer, the winning coach, said: 'It was a great tournament. While it was on, the interest was remarkable. The world stood still.'

The experience of Michael Lynagh proved important to Australia.

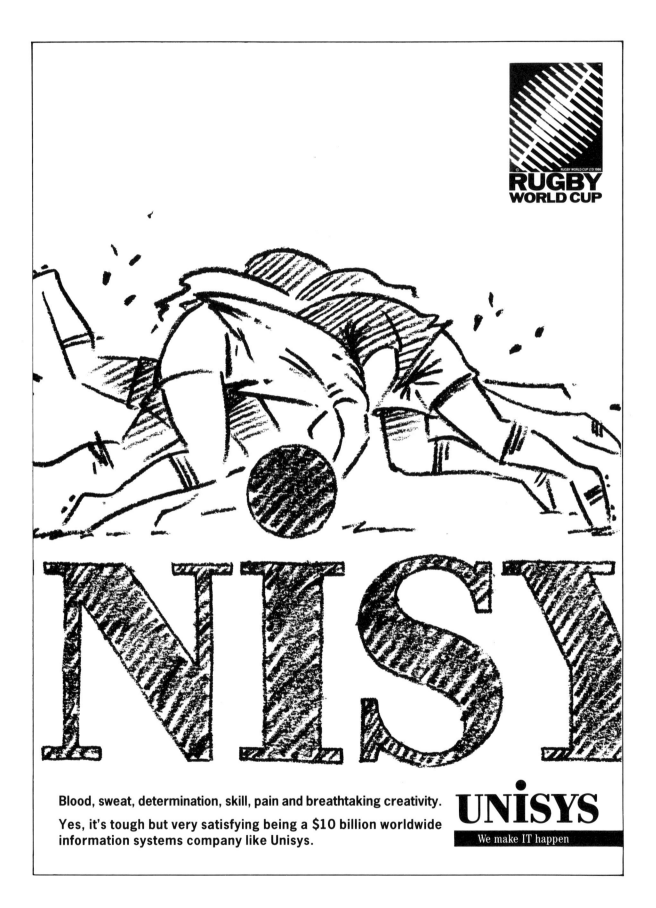

STATISTICS

POOL 1

October 3 1991; Twickenham
ENGLAND 12 (3**PG** 1**DG**)
NEW ZEALAND 18 (1**G** 4**PG**)
England: Webb; Underwood, Carling (capt), Guscott, Oti; Andrew, Hill; Leonard, Moore, Probyn; Ackford, Dooley; Teague, Winterbottom, Richards
PG: Webb (1m, 14m, 29m) **DG**: Andrew (40m)
New Zealand: Wright; Kirwan, Innes, McCahill, Timu; Fox, Bachop; McDowell, Fitzpatrick, Loe, I Jones, G Whetton (capt); A Whetton, M Jones, Brooke
Replacement: Earl for Brooke (69m)
T: M Jones (50m) **C**: Fox (50m) **PG**: Fox (3m, 8m, 24m, 53m)
Attendance: 57,000
Referee: J M Fleming (Scotland)
Notes: New Zealand hauled back an England 12–9 half-time lead with a fine try by Michael Jones, created by Bachop, Innes and Kirwan with a loop. First defeat at Twickenham for England since Wales won 11–3 in 1988. Michael Jones also scored first try of 1987 World Cup. New Zealand won line-outs 22–17, and scrums 16–2, and England only fed the ball into the scrums on five occasions in the whole match.

October 5 1991; Cross Green, Otley
ITALY 30 (4**G** 2**PG**)
USA 9 (1**G** 1**PG**)
Italy: Troiani; Vaccari, Gaetaniello, Barba, Marcello Cuttitta; Dominguez, Francescato; Massimo Cuttitta, Pivetta, Properzi Curti; Favaro, Croci; Saetti, Checchinato, Zanon (capt)
T: Barba (3m), Francescato (43m), Vaccari (64m), Gaetaniello (75m) **C**: Dominguez (3m, 43m 64m 75m) **PG**: Dominguez (38m, 80m)
USA: Nelson; Hein, Williams, Higgins, Whitaker; Dejong, Daily; Lippert, Flay, Paoli; Swords, Leversee; Vizard (capt), Farley, Ridnell
Replacement: Lipman for Vizard (58m)
T: Swords (68m) **C**: Williams (68m) **PG**:

Wiliams (30m)
Referee: O E Doyle (Ireland)
Attendance: 7,500
Notes: A win for the Italians thanks to a marvellous individual try by Francescato. USA lost Vizard, their captain, with a dislocated elbow, which put him out of the tournament.

October 8 1991; Kingsholm, Gloucester
NEW ZEALAND 46 (4**G** 2**PG** 4**T**)
USA 6 (2**PG**)
New Zealand: Wright; Timu, Innes, McCahill, Tuigamala; Preston, Bachop; McDowell, Fitzpatrick, Purvis; I Jones, G Whetton (capt); A Whetton, M Jones, Earl
T: Earl (22m), Wright (25m 29m 80m), Purvis (45m), Timu (53m), Tuigamala (73m), Innes (78m) **C**: Preston (29m, 45m, 78m, 80m) **PG**: Preston (15m, 39m)
USA: Sheehy; Hein, Williams, Burke, Whitaker; O'Brien, Pidcock; Lippert, Johnson, Mottram; Swords (capt), Tunnacliffe; Sawicki, Lipman, Ridnell
Replacement: Manga for Lippert (50m)
PG: Williams (35m, 56m)
Referee: E Sklar (Argentina)
Attendance: 12,000
Notes: Not an entirely convincing win for the All Blacks, who fielded three new caps in Preston, Tuigamala and Purvis. Lippert's injury put him out of the Cup, his replacement was Graham Downes (OMBAC, San Diego). The USA had lost the two previous encounters against New Zealand by over 50 points and have yet to score a try against them.

October 8 1991; Twickenham
ENGLAND 36 (4**G** 4**PG**)
ITALY 6 (1**G**)
England: Webb; Oti, Carling (capt), Guscott, Underwood; Andrew, Hill; Leonard, Moore, Probyn; Ackford, Redman; Teague, Winterbottom, Richards
Replacement: Rendall for Probyn (58m)
T: Underwood (11m), Guscott (40m, 49m), Webb (61m) **C**: Webb (11m, 40m, 49m, 61m)
PG: Webb (2m, 8m, 15m, 24m)

Italy: Troiani; Vaccari, Barba, Gaetaniello, Marcello Cuttitta; Dominguez, Francescato; Massimo Cuttitta, Pivetta, Properzi Curti; Favaro, Croci; Saetti, Giovanelli, Zanon (capt)
Replacement: Bonomi for Troiani (46m)
T: Marcello Cuttitta (58m) **C**: Dominguez (58m)
Referee: J B Anderson (Scotland)
Attendance: 30,000
Notes: Jon Webb broke the English record of 23 points (held by Simon Hodgkinson v Argentina in 1990) with 24. Guscott scored two fine tries, the second being a superb solo effort but it was a penalty-ridden match.

October 11 1991; Twickenham
ENGLAND 37 (3**G** 3**PG** 2**T**)
USA 9 (1**G** 1**PG**)
England: Hodgkinson; Heslop, Carling (capt), Halliday, Underwood; Andrew, Hill; Leonard, Olver, Pearce; Redman, Dooley; Skinner, Rees, Richards
T: Underwood (8m, 80m), Carling (32m), Skinner (62m), Heslop (68m) **C**: Hodgkinson (8m, 32m, 62m, 68m) **PG**: Hodgkinson (5m, 12m, 25m)
USA: Nelson; Hein, Williams, Higgins, Sheehy; O'Brien, Pidcock; Manga, Flay, Mottram; Swords (capt), Tunnacliffe; Lipman, Farley, Ridnell
Replacements: Dejong for Higgins (40), Wilkinson for Farley (75m)
T: Nelson (47m) **C**: Williams (47m) **PG**: Williams (20m)
Referee: L J Peard (Wales)
Attendance: 45,000
Notes: Hodgkinson reached 200 international points in an English record of 14 Tests. Only Grant Fox (13) has been quicker and only Dusty Hare (240) is ahead of him in the England points charts. Underwood's tries took him to 31, third on all-time international lists. Gary Pearce became England's longest serving international with 12 years 250 days since his first cap. Will Carling broke Bill Beaumont's record of 21 matches as

England's captain – he now had 16 wins in 22 international.

October 13 1991; Welford Road, Leicester
NEW ZEALAND 31 (3**G** 3**PG** 1**T**)
ITALY 21 (2**G** 3**PG**)
New Zealand: Wright; Kirwan, Innes, Little, Tuigamala; Fox, Hewett; McDowell, Fitzpatrick, Loe; I Jones, G Whetton (capt); A Whetton, Carter, Brooke
Replacement: Philpott for Wright (73m)
T: Brooke (1m), Innes (26m), Tuigamala (43m), Hewett (65m) **C**: Fox (1m), 43m, 65m)
PG: Fox (6m, 15m, 53m)
Italy: Vaccari; Venturi, Gaetaniello, Dominguez, Marcello Cuttitta; Bonomi, Francescato; Massimo Cuttitta, Pivetta (capt), Properzi Curti; Favaro, Croci; Bottacchiari, Giovanelli, Checchinato
Replacement: Grespan for Properzi Curti (44m)
T: Marcello Cuttitta (57m), Bonomi (76m)
C: Dominguez (57m, 76m) **PG**: Dominguez (23m, 52m, 70m)
Referee: K V J Fitzgerald (Australia)
Attendance: 16,200
Notes: This match in the 1987 World Cup produced a score of 70–6; in 1991 Italy left the field to a standing ovation. Gary Whetton equalled Colin Meads' NZ record of 55 caps. There were first caps for Hewett and Philpott. Dominguez kicked 12 out of 13 in the pool for the best record of the tournament.

POOL 2

October 5 1991; Murrayfield
SCOTLAND 47 (5**G** 3**PG** 2**T**)
JAPAN 9 (1**G** 1**DG**)
Scotland: G Hastings; Stanger, S Hastings, Lineen, Tukalo; Chalmers, Armstrong; Sole (capt), Allan, Burnell; Gray, Weir; Jeffrey, Calder, White
Replacements: Wyllie for Chalmers (68m), D Milne for Sole (72m)
T: S Hastings (12m), Stanger (30m), Chalmers (35m), Penalty try (43m) White (64m), Tukalo (67m), G Hastings (69m) **C**: G Hastings (35m, 43m, 64m, 67m, 69m) **PG**: Chalmers (18m) G Hastings (48m, 55m)
Japan: Hosokawa; Masuho, Kutsuki, Hirao (capt), Yoshida; Matsuo, Murata; Ohta, Kunda, Takura; Hayashi, Tifaga; Kajihara, Nakashima, Latu
T: Hosokawa (39m) **C**: Hosokawa (39m)
PG: Hosokawa (20m)

Referee: E Morrison (England)
Attendance: 60,000
Notes: There were 20 pts for Gavin Hastings. David Milne joined brothers Iain and Kenny as Scotland internationals. They have yet to appear for Scotland all together.

October 6 1991; Lansdowne Road, Dublin
IRELAND 55 (4**G** 5**PG** 4**T**)
ZIMBABWE 11 (1**PG** 2**T**)
Ireland: Staples; Geoghegan, Cunningham, Curtis, Crossan; Keyes, Saunders; Popplewell, Smith, D Fitzgerald; Lenihan, Francis; Matthews (capt), Hamilton, Robinson
T: Robinson (8m, 37m, 62m, 70m), Geoghegan (39m), Popplewell (57m, 79m), Curtis (74m) **C**: Keyes (8m, 37m, 39m, 57m)
PG: Keyes (3m, 12m, 16m, 20m 33m)
Zimbabwe: Currin (capt); Brown, Tsimba, Letcher, Walters; Kuhn, Ferreira; Hunter, Beattie, Garvey; Demblon, Martin; Botha, Dawson, Catterall
Replacement: Schultz for Kuhn (30m)
T: Dawson (64m), Schultz (80m) **PG**: Ferreira (52m)
Referee: K H Lawrence (New Zealand)
Attendance: 40,000
Notes: Brian Robinson equalled Greg Cornelsen's world record for a forward of four tries in an international. Ralph Keyes broke Ollie Campbell's Irish record with 23 points. Kuhn's injury put him out of the Cup. Dawson's brilliant try for Zimbabwe was one of the highlights.

October 9 1991; Lansdowne Road, Dublin
IRELAND 32 (2**G** 4**PG** 2**T**)
JAPAN 16 (2**G** 1**T**)
Ireland: Staples; Clarke, Mullin, Curtis, Crossan; Keyes, Saunders; J Fitzgerald, Kingston (capt), Halpin; Galwey, Francis; O'Hara, Hamilton, Mannion
Replacement: Cunningham for Crossan (63m)
T: O'Hara (13m), Mannion (28m, 66m), Staples (40m) **C**: Keyes (28m, 40m) **PG**: Keyes (9m, 46m, 48m 53m)
Japan: Hosokawa; Masuho, Kutsuki, Hirao (capt), Yoshida; Matsuo, Horikoshi; Ohta, Fujita, Takura; Hayashi, Oyagi; Tifaga, Kajihara, Latu
Replacements: Kunda for Fujita (52m), Miyamoto for Tifaga (75m)
T: Hayashi (35m), Masuho (61m), Yoshida (79m) **C**: Hosokawa (35m, 79m)

Referee: L Colati (Fiji)
Attendance: 30,000
Notes: Japan conjured some brilliant movements but 16 points for Keyes (39 pts in first two games) took Ireland through.

October 9 1991; Murrayfield
SCOTLAND 51 (5**G** 2**PG** 1**DG** 3**T**)
ZIMBABWE 12 (2**G**)
Scotland : Dods (capt); Stanger, S Hastings, Lineen, Tukalo; Wyllie, Oliver; Watt, K Milne, Burnell; Cronin, Weir; Turnbull, Marshall, Wyllie
Replacement: Chalmers for Stanger (78m)
T: Tukalo (3m, 62m, 70m), Turnbull (30m), Stanger (41m), Weir (79m), White (80m) **C**: Dods (3m, 30m, 37m, 62m, 70m) **PG**: Dods (24m, 52m) **DG**: Wyllie (46m)
Zimbabwe: Currin (capt); Schultz, Tsimba, Letcher, Walters; Brown, MacMillan; Nicholls, Beattie, Garvey; Martin, Nguruve; Muirhead, Dawson, Catterall
Replacements: Hunter for Garvey (45m), Chimbima for Walters (56m), Roberts for Hunter (78m)
T: Garvey (2m, 33m) **C**: Currin (2m, 33m)
Referee: D Reordan (USA)
Attendance: 35,000
Notes: Tukalo became the second highest Scotland scorer behind Ian Smith. Peter Dods passed 200 points in international rugby and Zimbabwe contributed two fine tries.

October 12 1991; Murrayfield
SCOTLAND 24 (2**G** 3**PG** 1**DG**)
IRELAND 15 (4**PG** 1**DG**)
Scotland: G Hastings; Stanger, S Hastings, Lineen, Tukalo; Chalmers, Armstrong; Sole (capt), Allan, Burnell; Gray, Weir; Jeffrey, Calder, White
Replacement: Shiel for Chalmers (47m)
T: Shiel (55m), Armstrong (75m) **C**: G Hastings (55m, 75m) **PG**: G Hastings (14m, 28m, 63m) **DG**: Chalmers (24m)
Ireland: Staples; Geoghegan, Mullin, Curtis, Crossan; Keyes, Saunders; Popplewell, Smith, D Fitzgerald; Lenihan, Francis; Matthews (capt), Hamilton, Robinson
PG: Keyes (4m, 19m, 32m, 45m) **DG**: Keyes (37m)
Referee: F A Howard (England)
Attendance: 60,000
Notes: Ralph Keyes became the first player to pass 50 points in the 1991 World Cup. Donal Lenihan became the seventh

Irishman to reach 50 caps in this fierce pool-decider.

October 14 1991; Ravenhill, Belfast
JAPAN 52 (5G 2PG 4T)
ZIMBABWE 8 (2T)
Japan: Hosokawa; Masuho, Kutsuki, Hirao (capt), Yoshida; Matsuo, Horikoshi; Ohta, Kunda, Takura; Hayashi, Oyagi; Tifaga, Kajihara, Latu
T: Horikoshi (22m), Yoshida (30m, 58m), Masuho (52m, 64m), Kutsuki (70m, 78m), Tifaga (72m), Matsuo (80m) **C**: Hosokawa (30m, 52m, 58m, 70m, 80m) **PG**: Hosokawa (4m, 37m)
Zimbabwe: Currin (capt); Schultz, Tsimba, Letcher, Walters; Brown, MacMillan; Nicholls, Beattie, Garvey; Martin, Botha; Nguruve, Dawson, Catterall
Replacement: Roberts for Garvey (68m)
Referee: R Hourquet (France)
Attendance: 9,500
Notes: Zimbabwe conceded 50 points in all three pool matches – and have conceded over 50 points in five of their six matches at the finlas. This was Japan's first victory at the World Cup finals, and their biggest win in a major international; their nine tries was a record thus far at the 1991 World Cup and it was a superb display.

POOL 3

October 4 1991; Stradey Park, Llanelli
AUSTRALIA 32 (3G 2PG 2T)
ARGENTINA 19 (1G 1PG 2DG 1T)
Australia: Roebuck; Campese, Little, Horan, Egerton; Lynagh, Farr-Jones (capt); Daly, Kearns, McKenzie; McCall, Coker; Poidevin, Ofahegaue, Eales
Replacement: Nucifora for Kearns (49m)
T: Campese (7m, 69m), Horan (30m, 76m), Kearns (41m) **C**: Lynagh (30m, 69m, 76m) **PG**: Lynagh (15m, 17m)
Argentina: del Castillo; Teran, Laborde, Garcia Simon, Cuesta Silva; Arbizu, Camardon; Medez, Le Fort, Cash; Sporleder, Llanes; Garreton (capt), Santamarina, Carreras
Replacement: Bosch for Le Fort (41m)
T: Teran (32m, 65m) **C**: del Castillo (65m) **PG**: del Castillo (59m) **DG**: Arbizu (19m, 74m)
Referee: D J Bishop (New Zealand)
Attendance: 11,000
Notes: Quality tries from Australia

including Campese's 41st and 42nd in internationals. Teran's two tries were also fine efforts. Arbizu dropped his fourth goal in his last two internationals.

October 6 1991; Cardiff Arms Park
WALES 13 (1G 1PG 1T)
WESTERN SAMOA 16 (1G 2PG 1T)
Wales: Clement; I Evans (capt), Gibbs, Hall; Emyr; Ring, R Jones; Griffiths, Waters, Delaney; May, Moseley; Lewis, Collins, P Davies
Replacements: Morris for May (30m), Rayer for Clement (47m), Jenkins for Collins (51m)
T: Emyr (62m), I Evans (80m), **C**: Ring (62m) **PG**: Ring (23m)
Western Samoa: Aiolupo; Lima, Vaega, Bunce, Tagaloa; Bachop, Vaea; Fatialofa (capt), Toomalatai, Alalatoa; Birtwhistle, Keenan; Vaifale, Perelini, Lam
T: Vaega (42m), Vaifale (51m) **C**: Vaea (42m) **PG**: Vaea (19m, 77m)
Referee: P Robin (France)
Attendance: 45,000
Notes: This was an amazing win for the Samoans, but all 15 of their side had played club or provincial rugby in New Zealand in 1991. Welsh injuries to May and Collins helped to end their interest in the World Cup.

October 9 1991; Pontypool Park, Pontypool
AUSTRALIA 9 (3PG)
WESTERN SAMOA 3 (1PG)
Australia: Roebuck; Campese, Herbert, Horan, Flett; Lynagh, Farr-Jones (capt); Lillicrap, Kearns, Crowley; Coker, Cutler; Miller, Nasser, Eales
Replacement: Slattery for Farr-Jones (11m)
PG: Lynagh (3m, 38m, 73m)
Western Samoa: Aiolupo; Lima, Vaega, Bunce, Fa'amasino; Bachop, Vaea; Fatialofa (capt), Toomalatai, Alalatoa; Birtwhistle, Keenan; Paramore, Kaleopa, Perelini
Replacement: Tagaloa for Lima (50m)
PG: Vaea (65m)
Referee: E Morrison (England)
Attendance: 15,000
Notes: Australians won 3–1 on penalties, in pouring rain. Farr-Jones won his 50th cap but injured knee ligaments. The first defeat for Western Samoa since Oct 1989, when they were beaten 32–24 by Romania at Bucharest

October 9 1991; Cardiff Arms Park
WALES 16 (4PG 1T)
ARGENTINA 7 (1PG 1T)
Wales: Rayer; I Evans (capt), Gibbs, Hall Emyr; Ring, Jones; Griffiths, Jenkins, Delaney; Arnold, Moseley; Lewis, Webster, P Davies
T: Arnold (73m) **PG**: Ring (8m, 21m, 37m) Rayer (73m)
Argentina: del Castillo; Teran, Laborde, Garcia Simon, Cuesta Silva; Arbizu, Camardon; Mendez, Le Fort, Molina; Sporleder. Llanes; Garreton (capt), Santamarina, Carreras
T: Garcia Simon (75m) **PG**: del Castillo (65m)
Referee: R Hourquet (France)
Attendance: 35,000
Notes: Wales' first win in eight games at Cardiff, and first win since Namibian tour in 1990. Argentina missed six penalties and a conversion while Wales missed three penalties.

October 12 1991; Cardiff Arms Park
WALES 3 (1PG)
AUSTRALIA 38 (4G 2PG 2T)
Wales: Clement; I Evans (capt), Gibbs, Hall, Emyr; Ring, Jones; Griffiths, Jenkins, Delaney; Arnold, Moseley; Lewis, Webster, P Davies
Replacements: D Evans for Emyr (77m), Rayer for Gibbs (79m)
Australia: Roebuck; Campese, Little, Horan, Egerton; Lynagh (capt), Slattery; Daly, Kearns, McKenzie; McCall, Eales; Poidevin, Miller, Ofahengaue
T: Roebuck (35m, 79m), Slattery (46m), Campese (49m), Horan (76m), Lynagh (78m) **C**: Lynagh (46m, 49m, 76m, 79m) **PG**: Lynagh (9m, 29m)
Referee: K H Lawrence (New Zealand)
Attendance: 54,000
Notes: Wales' worst-ever home defeat erasing the 9–34 result v New Zealand in 1989. Michael Lynagh became the first player to 650 points in international rugby, despite missing 12 kicks in the pool matches. The line-out figures were astonishing – 24–2 to Australia.

POOL 4

October 4 1991; Stade de la Mediterranée, Béziers
FRANCE 30 (1G 4PG 3T)
ROMANIA 3 (1PG)
France: Blanco (capt); Saint André,

Lacroix, Mesnel, Lagisquet; Camberabero, Gaithié; Lacubé, Marocco, Ondarts; Cadieu, Roumat; Champ, Cabannes, Benazzi

Replacement: Lafond for Lagisqet (48m)

T: Penalty try (60m), Saint André (63m), Roumat (69m), Lafond (76m), **C**: Camberabero (60m) **PG**: Camberabero (25m, 34m, 45m, 52m)

Romania: Dumitru; Sasu, Lungu, Sava, Racean; Nichitean, Neaga; Leonte, Ion, Stan; Ciorascu, Cojocariu; Dinu, Guranescu, Dumitras (capt)

PG: Nichitean (54m)

Referee: L J Peard (Wales)

Attendance: 22,000

Notes: Lagisquet was injured again after recently returning from second knee operation. Camberabero missed five kicks and Nichitean four.

October 5 1991; Parc Municipal Saint-Leon, Bayonne
CANADA 13 (3**PG** 1**T**)
FIJI 3 (1**DG**)

Canada: S Stewart; Palmer, C Stewart, Lecky, Gray; Rees, Tynan; Evans, Spiers, Jackart; Robertsen, Hadley; Charron, MacKinnon, Ennis (capt)

T: S Stewart (20m) **PG**: Rees (35m, 67m, 72m)

Fiji: Koroduadua; Seru, Aria, Nadruku, Lovo; Serevi, Tabulutu; Taga (capt), Naivilawasa, Naituivau; Savai, Domoni; Kato, Dere, Tawake

Replacement: Baleiwai for Naivilawasa (75m)

DG: Serevi (13m)

Referee: K V J Fitzgerald (Australia)

Attendance: 5,000

Notes: This was a shock win for Canada, despite the withdrawal of Wyatt, the captain and world record holder with eight penalties in an international. Canada's pack average was 231 lbs a man and included 14 from British Columbia, plus Charron (Ontario).

October 8 1991; Stade Lesdiguières, Grenoble
FRANCE 33 (3**G** 1**PG** 3**T**)
FIJI 9 (1**G** 1**PG**)

France: Blanco (capt); Lafond, Sella, Mesnel, Saint André; Camberabero, Galthié; Lascubé, Marocco, Ondarts; Cadieu, Roumat; Champ, Cabannes, Benazzi

T: Sella (12m, 71m) Lafond (33m, 40m, 68m), Camberabero (59m) **C**: Camberabero (12m, 40m, 71m) **PG**: Camberabero (18m)

Fiji: Koroduadua; Seru, Aria, Naisoro, Lovo; Serevi, Vosanibole; Taga (capt), Balewai, Vuli; Savai, Domoni; Naruma, Dere, Tawake

Replacements: Volavola for Taga (10m), Tabulutu for Vosanibole (40m)

T: Naruma (74m) **C**: Koroduadua (74m) **PG**: Koraduadua (1m)

Referee: W D Bevan (Wales)

Attendance: 17,500

Notes: Sella reached 25 international tries. For Fiji, both Taga and Domoni were injured and out of the World Cup. Fiji continued to under-achieve.

October 9 1991; Stade Municipal, Toulouse
CANADA 19 (1**G** 2**PG** 1**DG** 1**T**)
ROMANIA 11 (1**PG** 2**T**)

Canada: Wyatt (capt); Palmer, S Stewart, Lecky, C Stewart; Rees, Tynan; Evans, Svoboda, Jackart; Van den Brink, Hadley; Breen, MacKinnon, Ennis

T: MacKinnon (43m), Ennis (48m) **C**: Wyatt (48m) **PG**: Wyatt (8m, 55m) **DG**: Rees (71m)

Romania: Dumitru; Sasu, Lungu, Fulina, Racean; Nichitean, Neaga; Leonte, Ion, Stan; Ciorascu, Cojocariu; Dinu, Doja, Dumitras (capt)

Replacements: Brinza for Doja (20m), Sava for Dumitru (37m), Vlad for Leonte (70m)

T: Lungu (68m), Sasu (80m) **PG**: Nichitean (40m)

Referee: A McNeill (Australia)

Attendance: 10,000

Notes: Canada reached the quarter-finals for the first time with this victory, against the best Romanian effort of the tournament.

October 13 1991; Stade Armandie, Agen
FRANCE 19 (1**G** 3**PG** 1**T**)
CANADA 13 (2**PG** 1**DG** 1**T**)

France: Blanco (capt); Lafond, Sella, Mesnel, Saint André; Camberabero, Galthié; Lascubé, Marocco, Ondarts; Cadieu, Roumat; Champ, Cabannes, Benazzi

Replacements: Lacroix for Camberabero (40m), Sadourny for Sella (47m)

T: Lafond (10m), Saint André (47m) **C**: Camberabero (10m) **PG**: Camberabero (4m), Lacroix (68m, 74m)

Canada: Wyatt (capt); Palmer, C Stewart,

Woods, Gray; Rees, Tynan; Evans, Svoboda, Jackart; Robertsen, Hadley; Charron, MacKinnon, Ennis

Replacements: Van den Brink for Robertsen (23m), S Stewart for Wyatt (46m)

T: Wyatt (40m) **PG**: Wyatt (26m), Rees (78m) **DG**: Rees (60m)

Referee: S R Hilditch (Ireland)

Attendance: 15,000

Notes: This was a match to determine quarter-final venues and group leadership. France were taken all the way by Canada's determination.

October 12 1991; Stade Municipal, Brive
ROMANIA 17 (1**G** 1**PG** 2**T**)
FIJI 15 (2**PG** 3**DG**)

Romania: Racean; Sasu, Lungu, Fulina, Colceriu; Nichitean, Neaga; Stan, Ion, Vlad; Cojocariu, Ciorascu; Dinu, Marin, Dumitras (capt)

Replacement: Ivanciuc for Nichitean (51m)

T: Ion (35m), Dumitras (51m), Sasu (55m) **C**: Racean (51m) **PG**: Racean (39m)

Fiji: Turuva; Seru, Nadruku, Naisoro, Vonolagi, Rabaka, Tabulutu; Vuli, Balewai, Volavola; Savai, Nadolo; Tawake, Dere (capt), Olsson

Replacements: Naituivau for Volavola (31m), Narumu for Olsson (41m)

PG: Turuva (8m, 70m) **DG**: Rabaka (27m, 42m) Turuva (48m)

Referee O E Doyle (Ireland)

Attendance: 8,500

Notes: Fiji, seeded fifth, lost all three matches. Turuva's drop goal was from 45 metres. Fiji used all 26 players during pool matches without finding true form.

QUARTER-FINALS

October 19 1991; Murrayfield
SCOTLAND 28 (2**G** 4**PG** 1**T**)
WESTERN SAMOA 6 (1**PG** 1**DG**)

Scotland: G Hastings; Stanger, S Hastings, Shiel, Tukalo; Chalmers, Armstrong; Sole (capt), Allan, Burnell; Gray, Weir; Jeffrey, Calder, White

T: Stanger (30m), Jeffrey (39m, 70m) **C**: G Hastings (39m, 70m) **PG**: G Hastings (17m, 56m, 63m, 70m)

Western Samoa : Aiolupo; Lima, Vaega, Bunce, Tagaloa; Bachop, Vaea; Fatialofa (capt), Toomalatai, Alalatoa, Birtwhistle, Ioane, Vaifale, Perelini, Lam

PG: Vaea (6m) **DG**: Bachop (58m)

Referee: W D Bevan (Wales)

Attendance: 60,000

Notes: Western Samoa left to a standing ovation after a marvellous game. Jeffrey took the Scottish forward try record back from White. He led 11–10 at the end. Gavin Hastings reached 350 pts for Scotland.

October 19 1991; Parc des Princes, Paris
FRANCE 10 (2**PG** 1**T**)
ENGLAND 19 (1**G** 3**PG** 1**T**)
France: Blanco (capt); Lafond, Sella, Mesnel, Saint André; Lacroix, Galthié; Ondarts, Marocco, Lascubé; Roumat, Cadieu; Champ, Cabannes, Cecillon
T:Lafond (51m) **PG**: Lacroix (16m, 22m)
England: Webb; Heslop, Carling (capt), Guscott, Underwood; Andrew, Hill; Leonard, Moore, Probyn; Ackford, Dooley; Skinner, Winterbottom, Teague
T:Underwood (19m), Carling (80m) **C**: Webb (80m) **PG**: Webb (6m, 9m, 75m)
Referee: D J Bishop (New Zealand)
Attendance: 48,500
Notes: Unsavoury scenes marred a splendid England win in which Skinner and Teague were immense. The incident involving referee David Bishop and French coach Dubroca had lasting consequences for the sport. It was a sad way for Blanco to bow out after a record 93 international caps.

October 20 1991; Lansdowne Road, Dublin
IRELAND 18 (1**G** 3**PG** 1**DG**)
AUSTRALIA 19 (2**G** 1**PG** 1**T**)
Ireland: Staples; Geoghegan, Mullin, Curtis, Clarke; Keyes, Saunders; Popplewell, Smith, D Fitzgerald; Lenihan, Francis; Matthews (capt), Hamilton, Robinson
T: Hamilton (75m) **C**: Keyes (75m) **PG**: Keyes (26m, 34m, 63m) **DG**: Keyes (51m)
Australia: Roebuck; Campese, Little, Horan, Egerton; Lynagh, Farr-Jones (capt); Daly, Kearns, McKenzie; McCall, Eales; Poidevin, Miller, Ofahengaue
Replacement: Slattery for Farr-Jones (18m)
T: Campese (17m, 53m), Lynagh (79m) **C**: Lynagh (17m, 53m) **PG**: Lynagh (45m)
Referee: J M Fleming (Scotland)
Attendance: 54,500
Notes: Ireland were beaten by two world record holders, Lynagh (reaching 673 pts) and Campese (reaching 45 tries).

October 20 1991; Stade du Nord, Lille
NEW ZEALAND 29 (3**G** 1**PG** 2**T**)
CANADA 13 (1**G** 1**PG** 1**T**)
New Zealand: Timu; Kirwan, Innes, McCahill, Tuigamala; Fox, Bachop; McDowell, Fitzpatrick, Loe; I Jones, G Whetton (capt); A Whetton, Henderson, Brooke
T: Timu (9m, 75m), McCahill (19m), Brooke (39m), Kirwan (55m) **C**: Fox (9m, 19m, 39m)
PG: Fox (27m)
Canada: Wyatt (capt); S Stewart, C Stewart, Woods, Gray; Rees, Tynan; Evans, Speirs, Szabo; Van Den Brink, Hadley; Charron, MacKinnon, Ennis
T:Tynan (60m), Charron (80m) **C**: Wyatt (80m) **PG**: Wyatt (33m)
Referee: F A Howard (England)
Attendance: 30,360
Notes: Canada, like the other unseeded quarter-finalists, Western Samoa, left to a standing ovation after scoring two tries against the All Blacks.

SEMI-FINALS

October 26 1991; Murrayfield
SCOTLAND 6 (2**PG**)
ENGLAND 9 (2**PG** 1**DG**)
Scotland: G Hastings; Stanger, S Hastings, Lineen, Tukalo; Chalmers, Armstrong; Sole (capt), Allan, Burnell; Gray, Weir; Jeffrey, Calder, White
PG: G Hastings (9m, 32m)
England: Webb; Halliday, Carling (capt), Guscott, Underwood; Andrew, Hill; Leonard, Moore, Probyn; Ackford, Dooley; Skinner, Winterbottom, Teague
PG: Webb (34m, 57m) **DG**: Andrew (75m)
Referee: K V J Fitzgerald (Australia)
Attendance: 60,000
Notes: Rob Andrew equalled the world record for drop goals with 15 (14 for England, one for the British Isles), now held along with Botha, Porta and Lescarboura in major internationals. Hill equalled Steve Smith's record of 28 caps as England's most capped scrum-half. Scotland went into the match with 13 consecutive wins (since 1988) at Murrayfield.

October 27 1991; Lansdowne Road, Dublin
AUSTRALIA 16 (1**G** 2**PG** 1**T**)
NEW ZEALAND 6 (2**PG**)
Australia: Roebuck; Campese, Little, Horan, Egerton; Lynagh, Farr-Jones (capt);

Daly, Kearns, McKenzie; McCall, Eales; Poidevin, Ofahengaue, Coker
T: Campese (6m), Horan (35m) **C**: Lynagh (35m) **PG**: Lynagh (13m, 61m)
New Zealand: Crowley; Kirwan, Innes, McCahill, Timu; Fox, Bachop; McDowell, Fitzpatrick, Loe; I Jones, G Whetton (capt); A Whetton, Carter, Brooke
PG: Fox (42m, 71m)
Referee: J M Fleming (Scotland)
Attendance: 54,500
Notes: Lynagh and Fox maintained records of scoring in each international that they have played.

THIRD PLACE MATCH

October 30 1991; Cardiff Arms Park
NEW ZEALAND 13 (3**PG** 1**T**)
SCOTLAND 6 (2**PG**)
New Zealand: Wright; Kirwan, Innes, Little, Tuigamala; Preston, Bachop; McDowell, Fitzpatrick, Loe; I Jones, G Whetton (capt); Earl, M Jones, Brooke
Replacement: Philpott for Tuigamala (40m)
T: Little (77m) **PG**: Preston (15m, 34m, 54m)
Scotland: G Hastings; Stanger, S Hastings, Lineen, Tukalo; Chalmers, Armstrong; Sole (capt), Allan, Burnell; Gray, Weir; Jeffrey, Calder, White
Replacement: Dods for Stanger (50m)
PG: G Hastings (4m, 74m)
Referee: S R Hilditch (Ireland)
Attendance: 47,000
Notes: Calder and Jeffrey announced their international retirements after this match.

1991 WORLD CUP FINAL

November 2 1991; Twickenham
ENGLAND 6 (2**PG**)
AUSTRALIA 12 (1**G** 2**PG**)
England: Webb; Halliday, Carling (capt), Guscott, Underwood; Andrew, Hill; Leonard, Moore, Probyn; Ackford, Dooley; Skinner, Winterbottom, Teague
PG: Webb (60m, 71m)
Australia: Roebuck; Campese, Little, Horan, Egerton; Lynagh, Farr-Jones (capt); Daly, Kearns, McKenzie; McCall, Eales; Poidevin, Ofahengaue, Coker
T: Daly (30m) **C**: Lynagh (30m) **PG**: Lynagh (27m, 65m)
Referee: W D Bevan (Wales)
Attendance: 56,208
Notes: The world records now stand with Campese (46 tries) and Lynagh (689 points).

Cathay Pacific. The Airline for a world where gentlemen occasionally forget their manners.